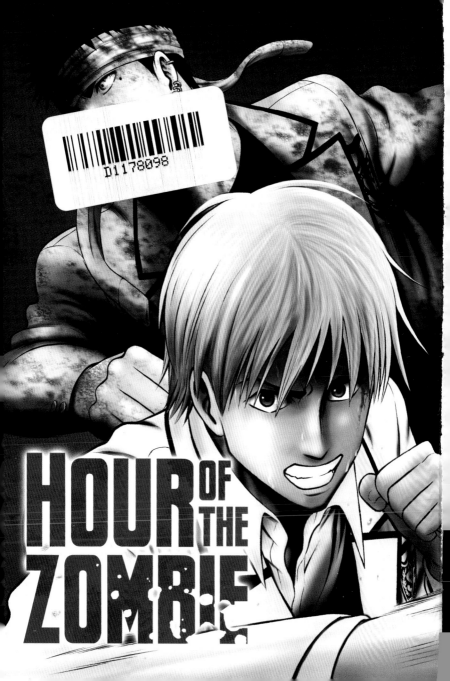

HOUR OF THE ZOMBIE

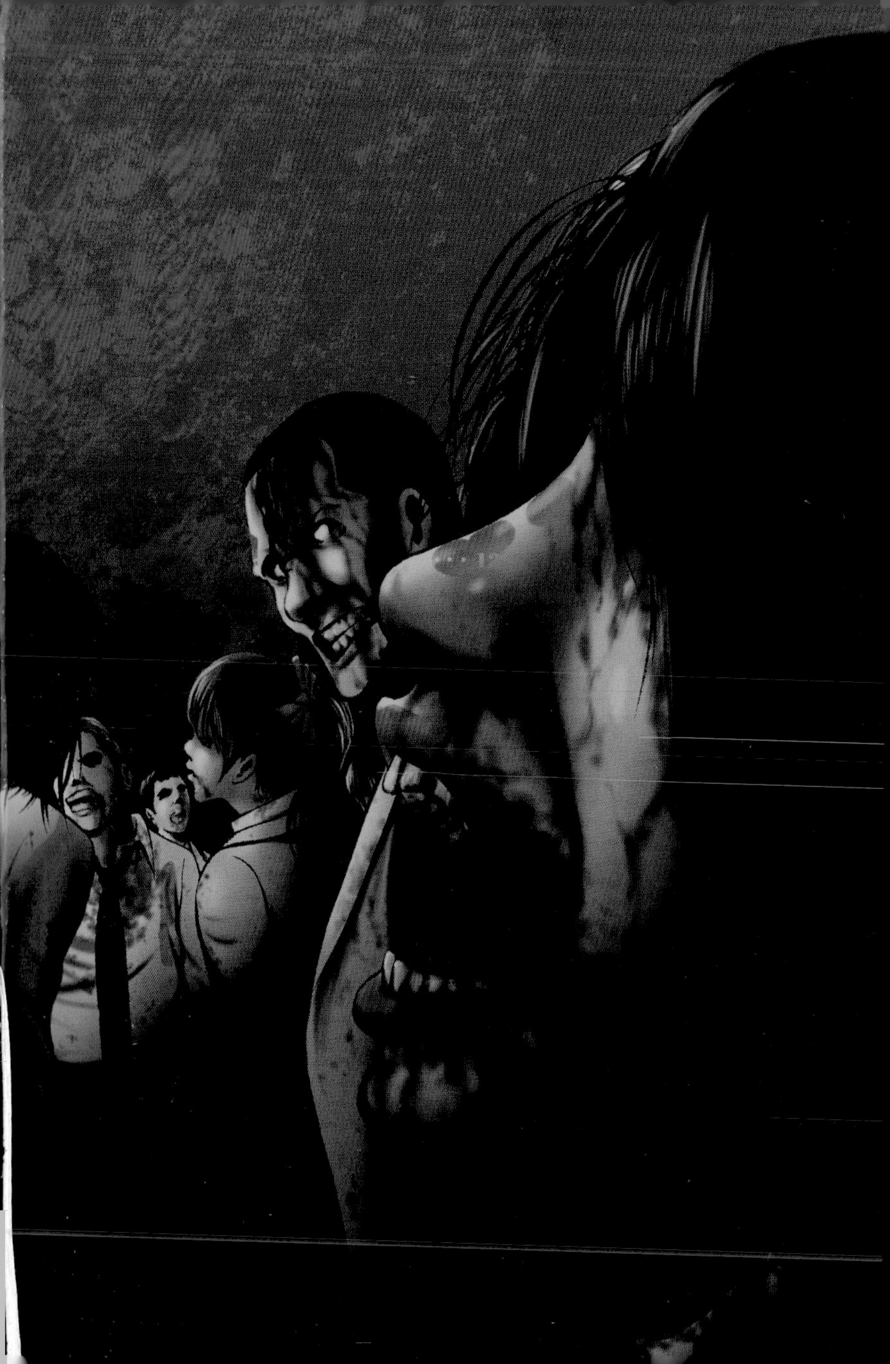

PHASE 11: After School

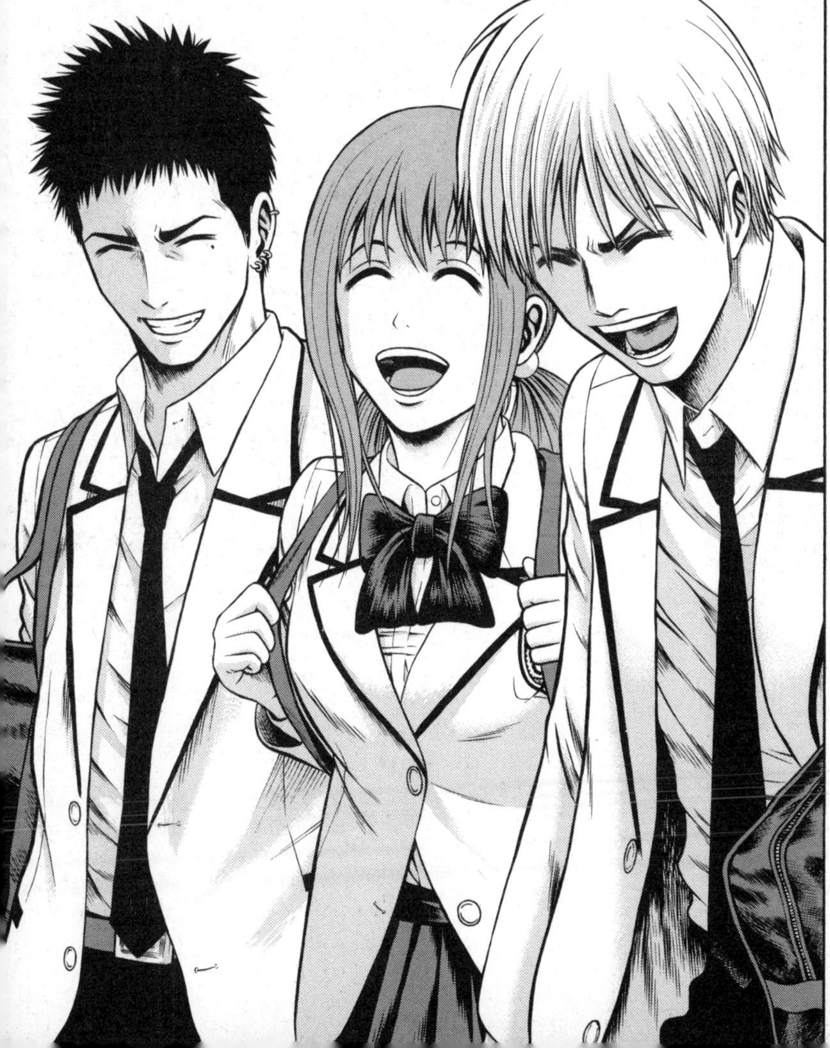

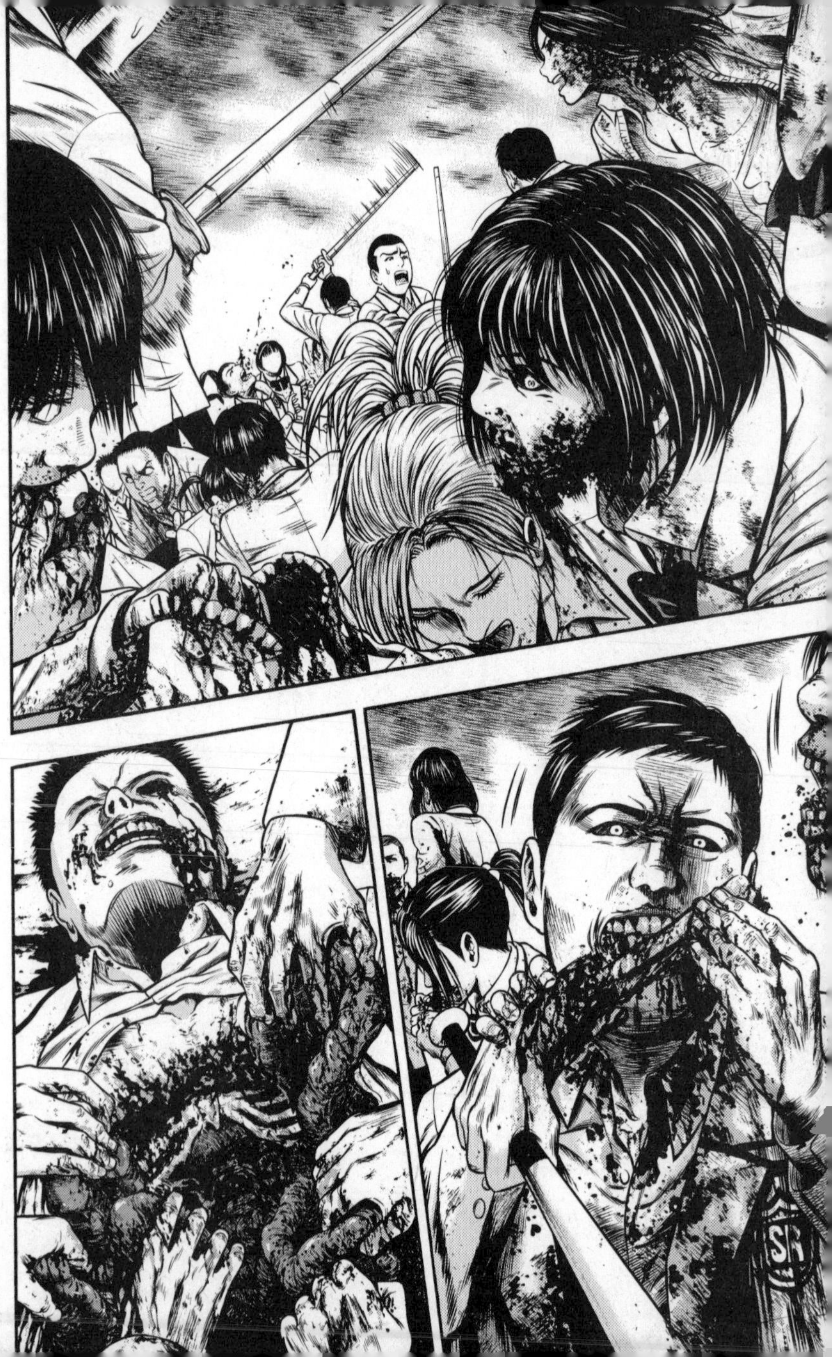

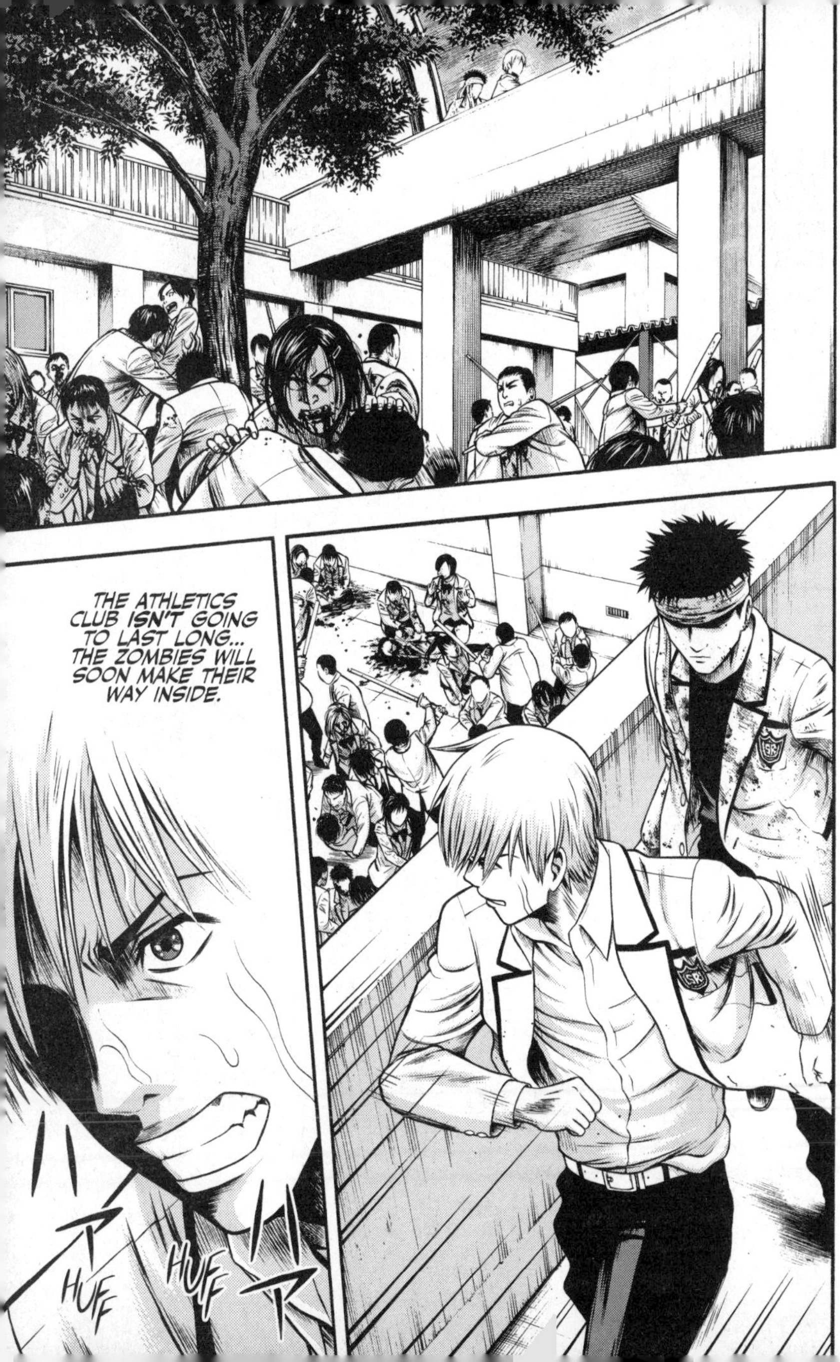
THE ATHLETICS CLUB ISN'T GOING TO LAST LONG... THE ZOMBIES WILL SOON MAKE THEIR WAY INSIDE.
HUFF
HUFF

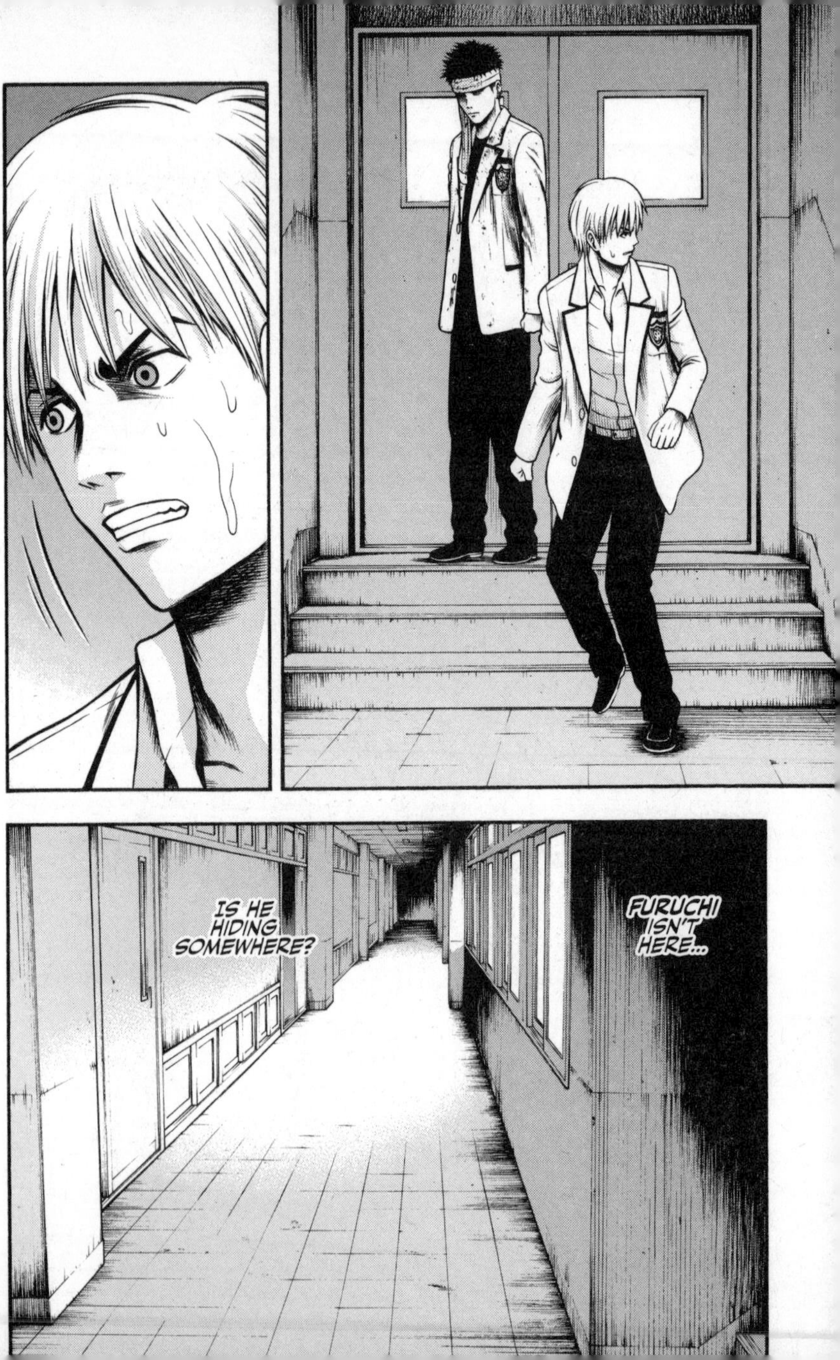
FURUCHI ISN'T HERE...
IS HE HIDING SOMEWHERE?

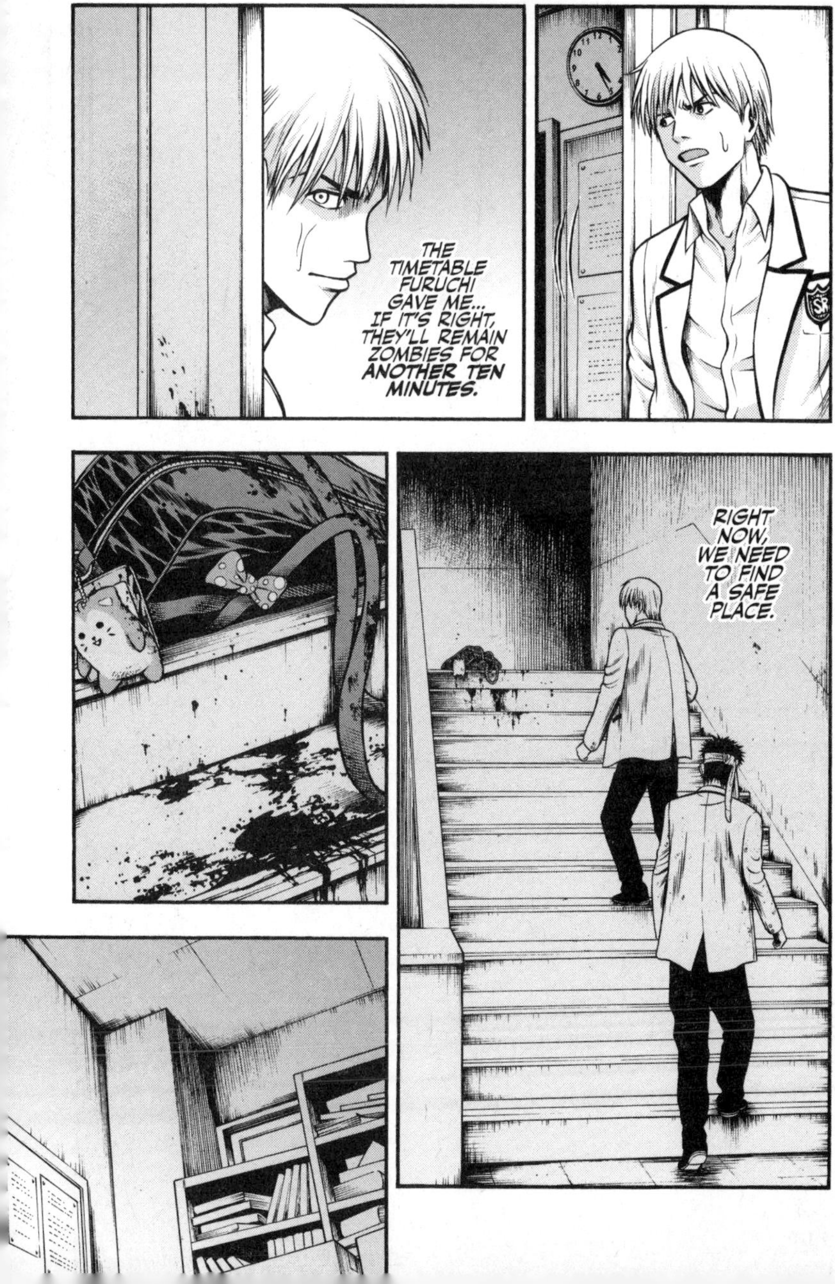
THE TIMETABLE FURUCHI GAVE ME... IF IT'S RIGHT, THEY'LL REMAIN ZOMBIES FOR ANOTHER TEN MINUTES.
RIGHT NOW, WE NEED TO FIND A SAFE PLACE.

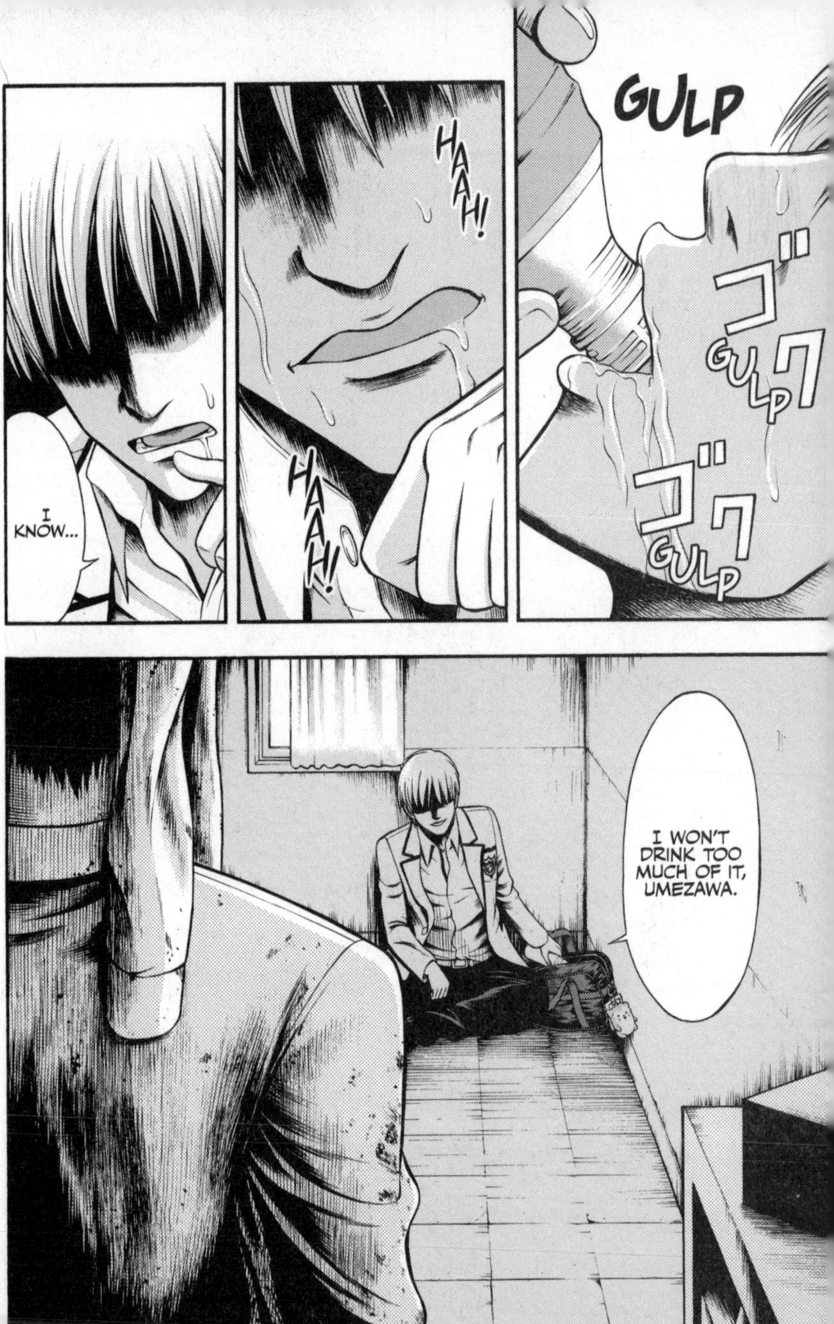
GULP
ゴク
GULP
ゴク
GULP
HAAAH!
HAAAH!
I KNOW...
I WON'T DRINK TOO MUCH OF IT, UMEZAWA.

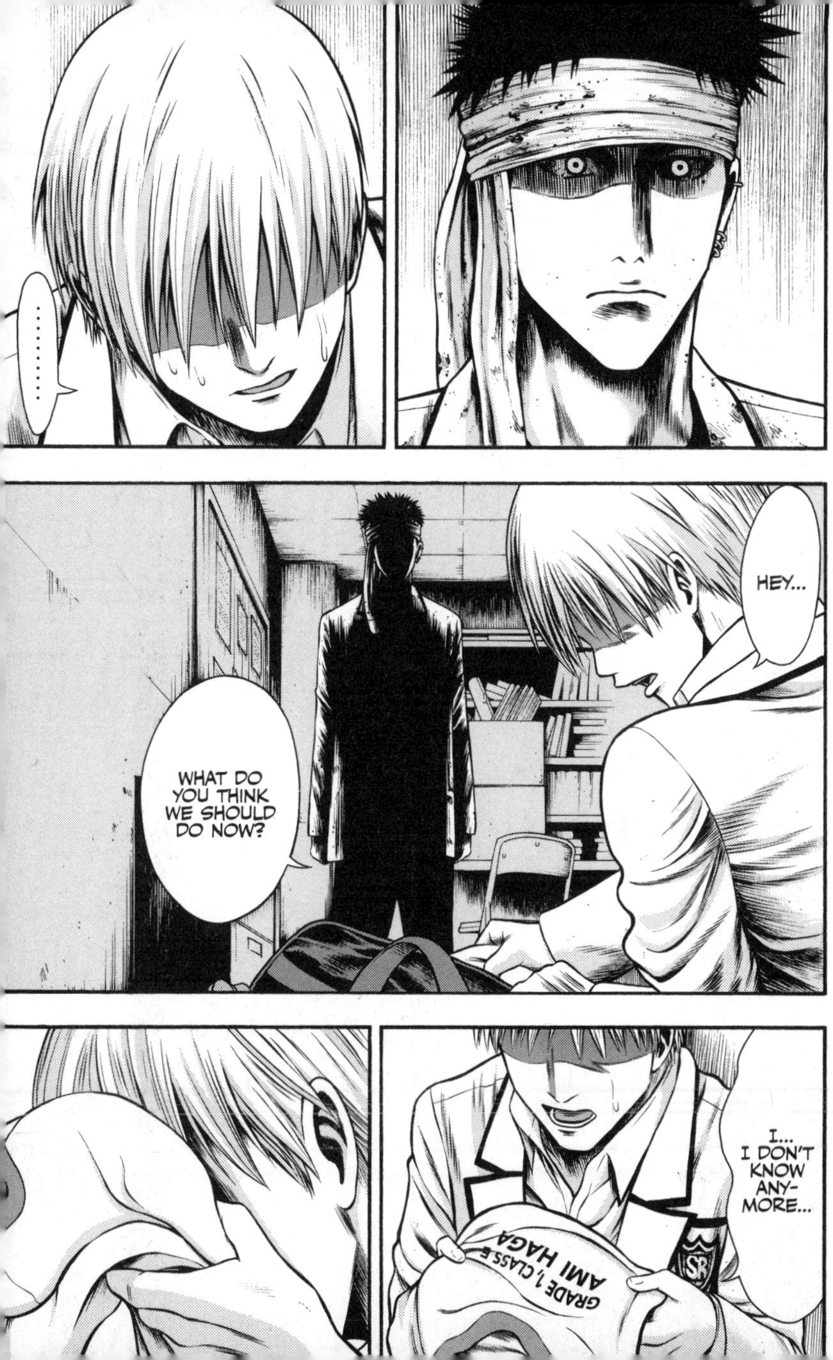
......
HEY...
WHAT DO YOU THINK WE SHOULD DO NOW?
I... I DON'T KNOW ANY-MORE...
GRADE 1, CLASS E
AMI HAGA

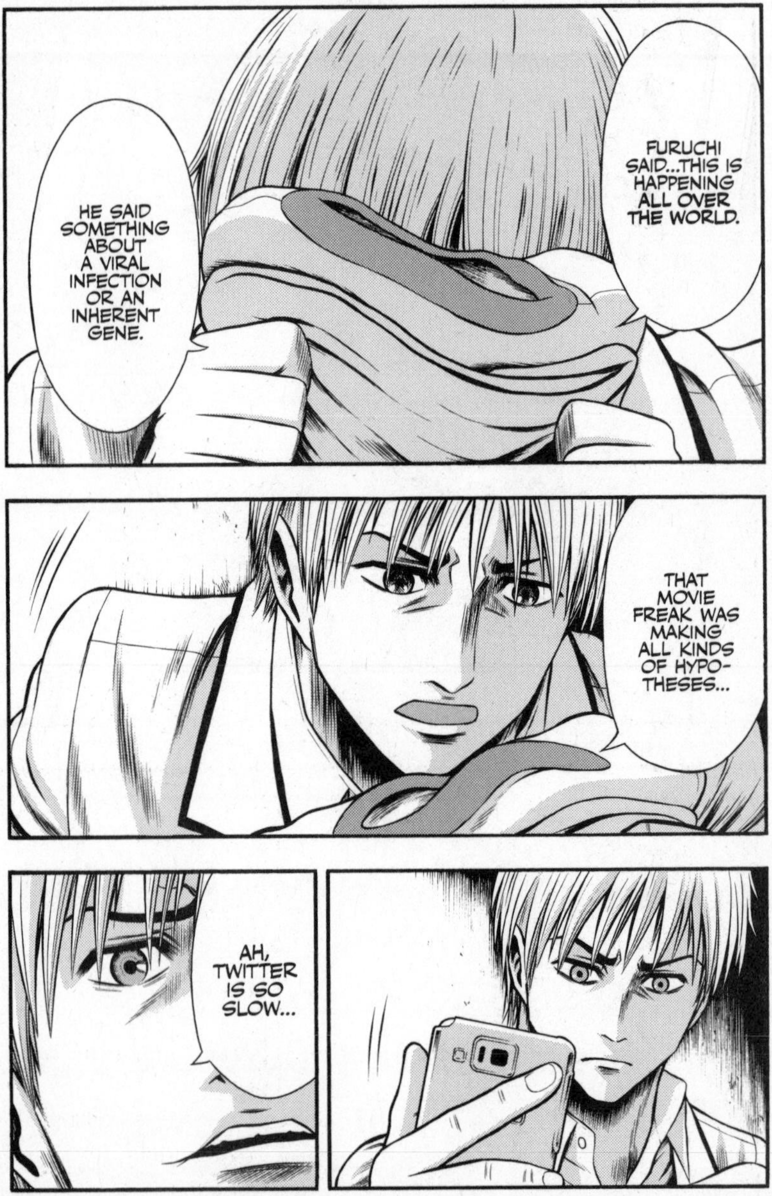
FURUCHI SAID...THIS IS HAPPENING ALL OVER THE WORLD.
HE SAID SOMETHING ABOUT A VIRAL INFECTION OR AN INHERENT GENE.
THAT MOVIE FREAK WAS MAKING ALL KINDS OF HYPO-THESES...
AH, TWITTER IS SO SLOW...

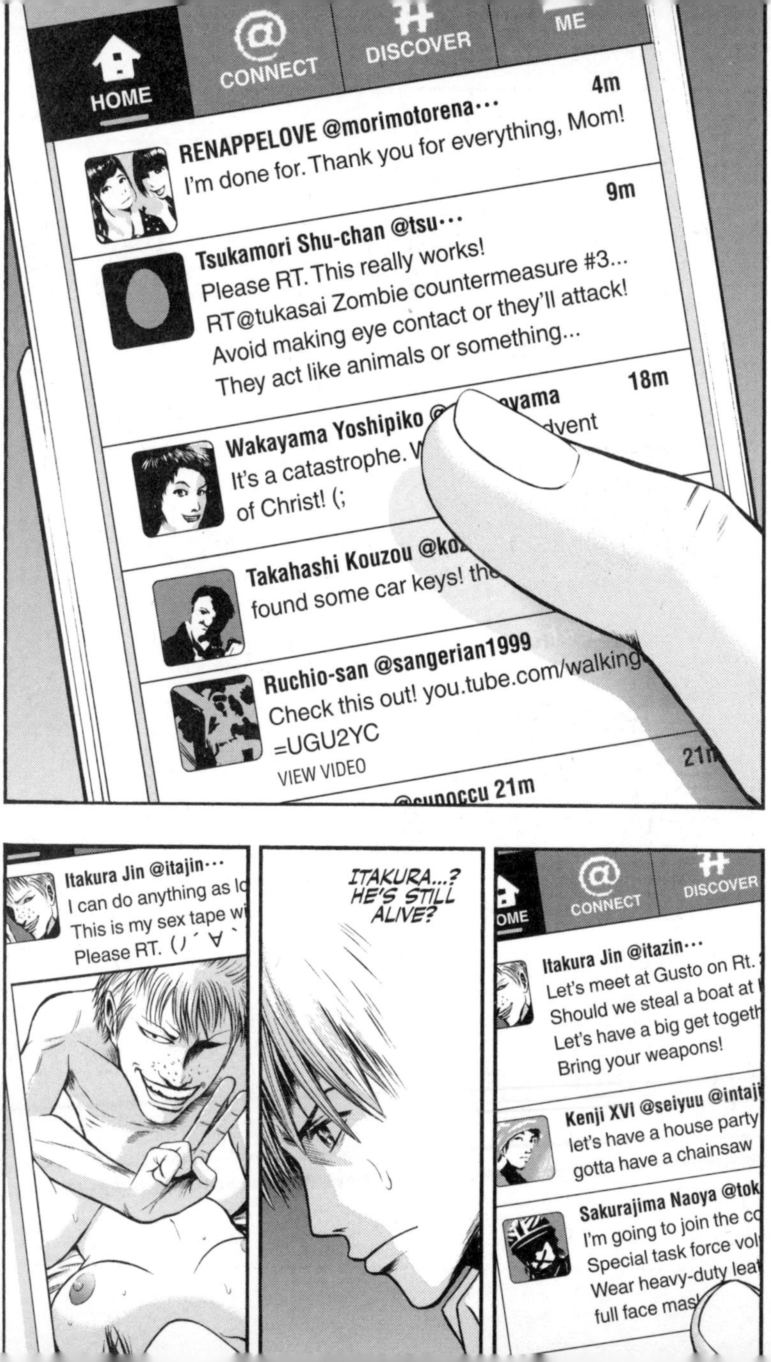
HOME
CONNECT
DISCOVER
ME
RENAPPELOVE @morimotorena··· 4m
I'm done for. Thank you for everything, Mom!
Tsukamori Shu-chan @tsu··· 9m
Please RT. This really works!
RT@tukasai Zombie countermeasure #3...
Avoid making eye contact or they'll attack!
They act like animals or something...
Wakayama Yoshipiko @ yama 18m
It's a catastrophe. W dvent
of Christ! (;
Takahashi Kouzou @ko
found some car keys! th
Ruchio-san @sangerian1999
Check this out! you.tube.com/walking
=UGU2YC
VIEW VIDEO
21m
@cunoccu 21m
HOME
CONNECT
DISCOVER
Itakura Jin @itazin···
Let's meet at Gusto on Rt.
Should we steal a boat at
Let's have a big get togeth
Bring your weapons!
Kenji XVI @seiyuu @intaj
let's have a house party
gotta have a chainsaw
Sakurajima Naoya @tok
I'm going to join the co
Special task force vol
Wear heavy-duty leat
full face mas
ITAKURA...? HE'S STILL ALIVE?
Itakura Jin @itajin···
I can do anything as lo
This is my sex tape wi
Please RT. (ﾉ´∀`

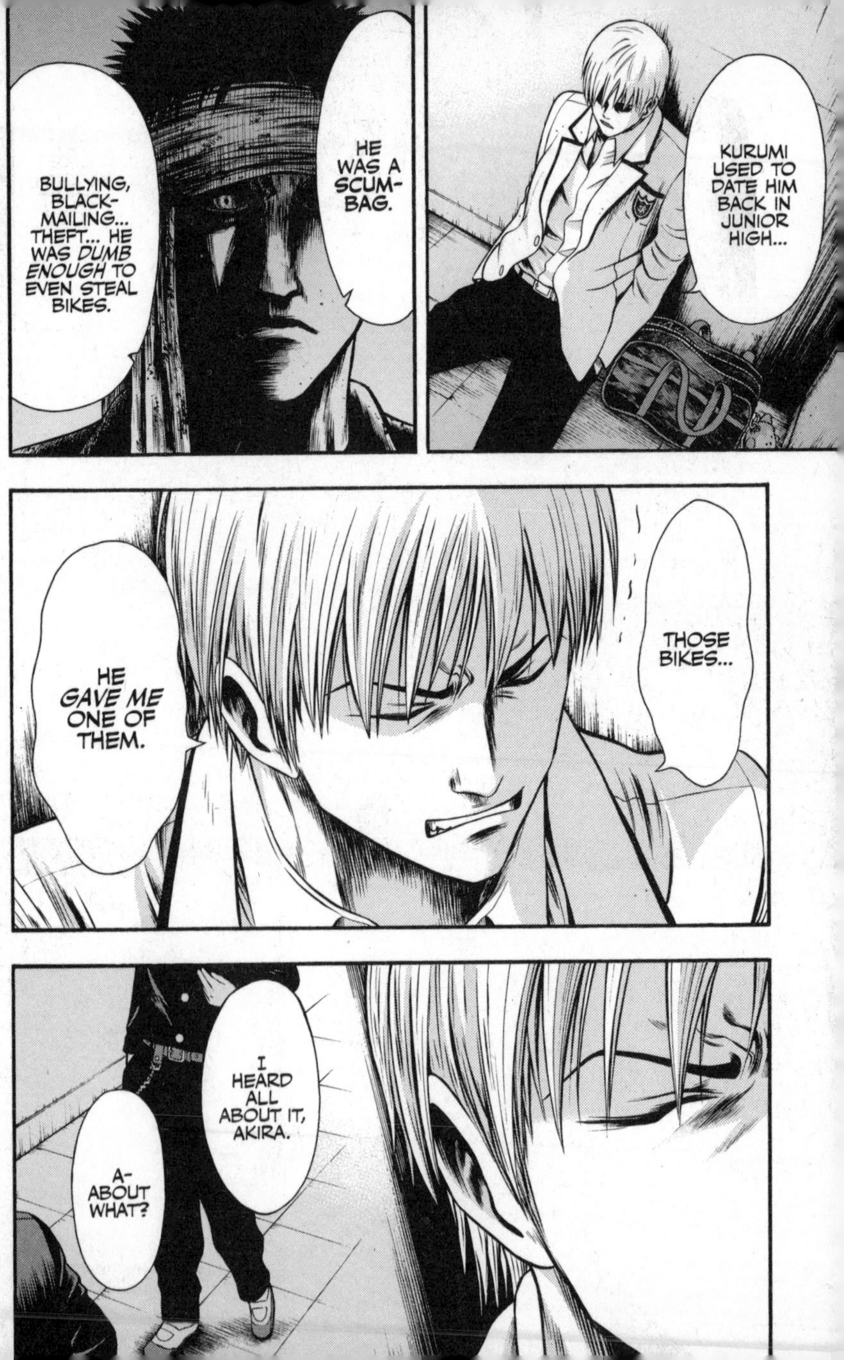
KURUMI USED TO DATE HIM BACK IN JUNIOR HIGH...
HE WAS A SCUM-BAG.
BULLYING, BLACK-MAILING... THEFT... HE WAS *DUMB ENOUGH* TO EVEN STEAL BIKES.
THOSE BIKES...
HE *GAVE ME* ONE OF THEM.
I HEARD ALL ABOUT IT, AKIRA.
A- ABOUT WHAT?

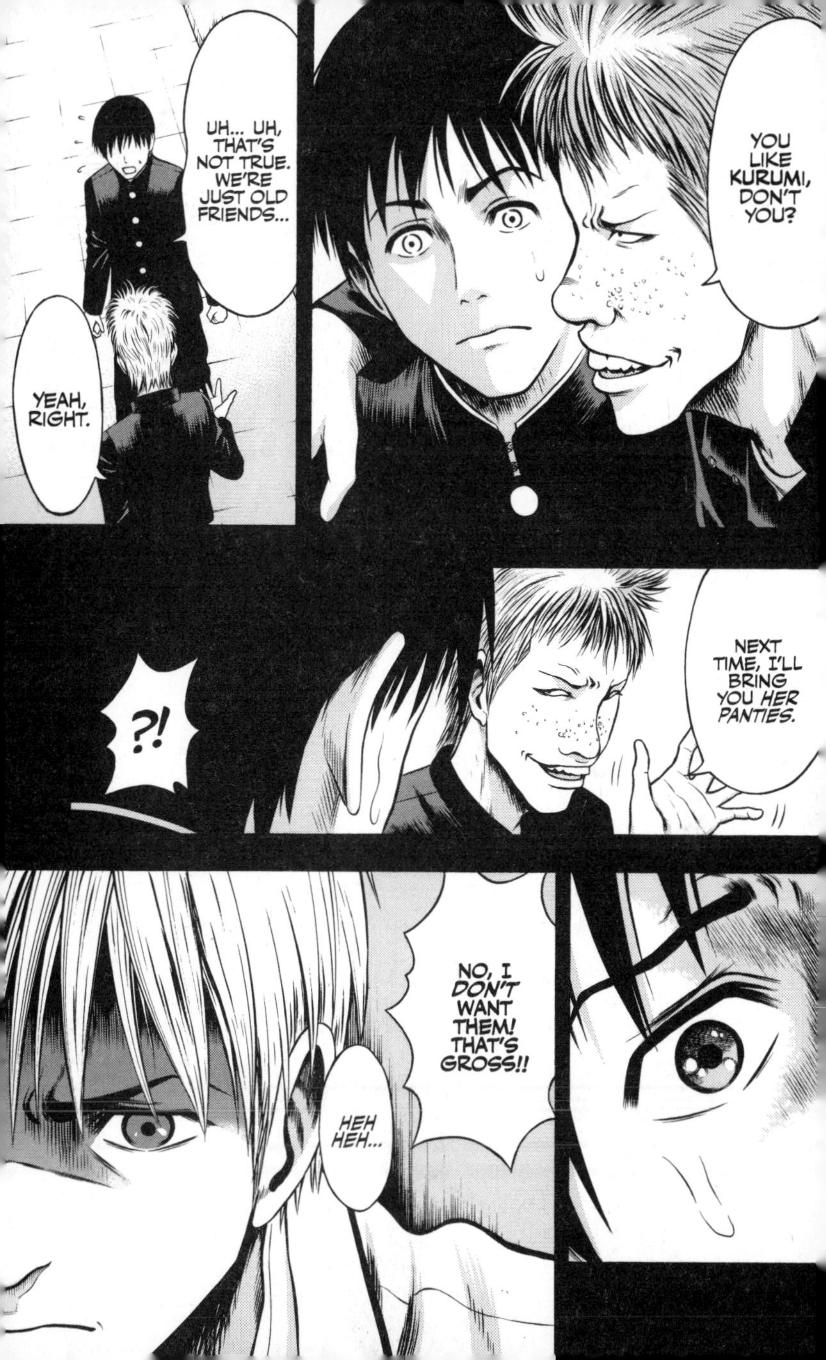
YOU LIKE KURUMI, DON'T YOU?
UH... UH, THAT'S NOT TRUE. WE'RE JUST OLD FRIENDS...
YEAH, RIGHT.
NEXT TIME, I'LL BRING YOU *HER* PANTIES.
?!
NO, I *DON'T* WANT THEM! THAT'S GROSS!!
HEH HEH...

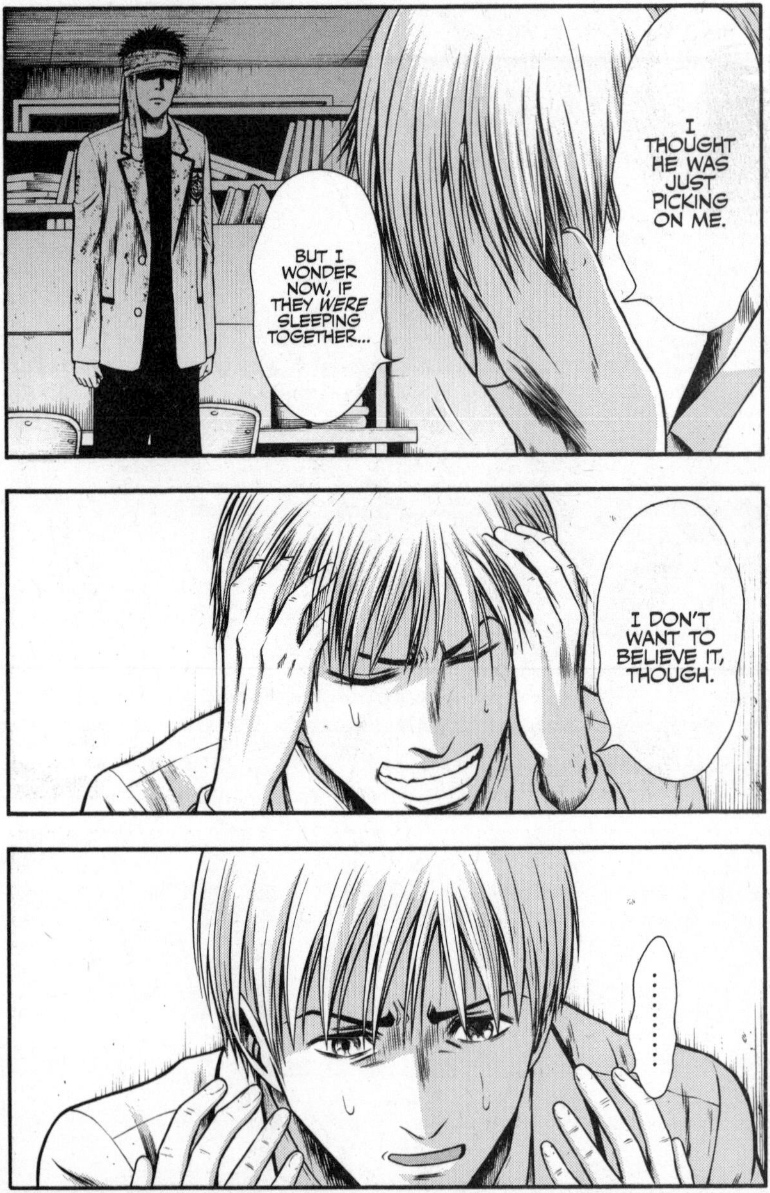
I THOUGHT HE WAS JUST PICKING ON ME.
BUT I WONDER NOW, IF THEY *WERE* SLEEPING TOGETHER...
I DON'T WANT TO BELIEVE IT, THOUGH.
....

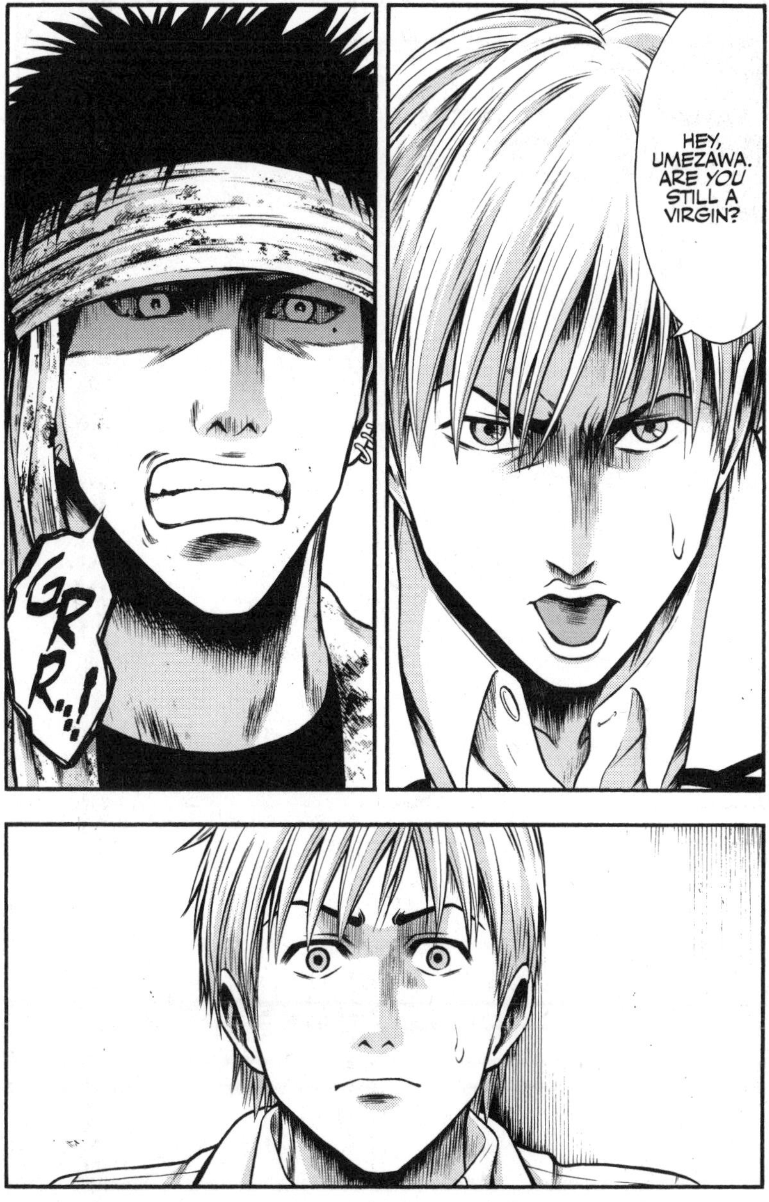
HEY, UMEZAWA. ARE *YOU* STILL A VIRGIN?
GRR...!

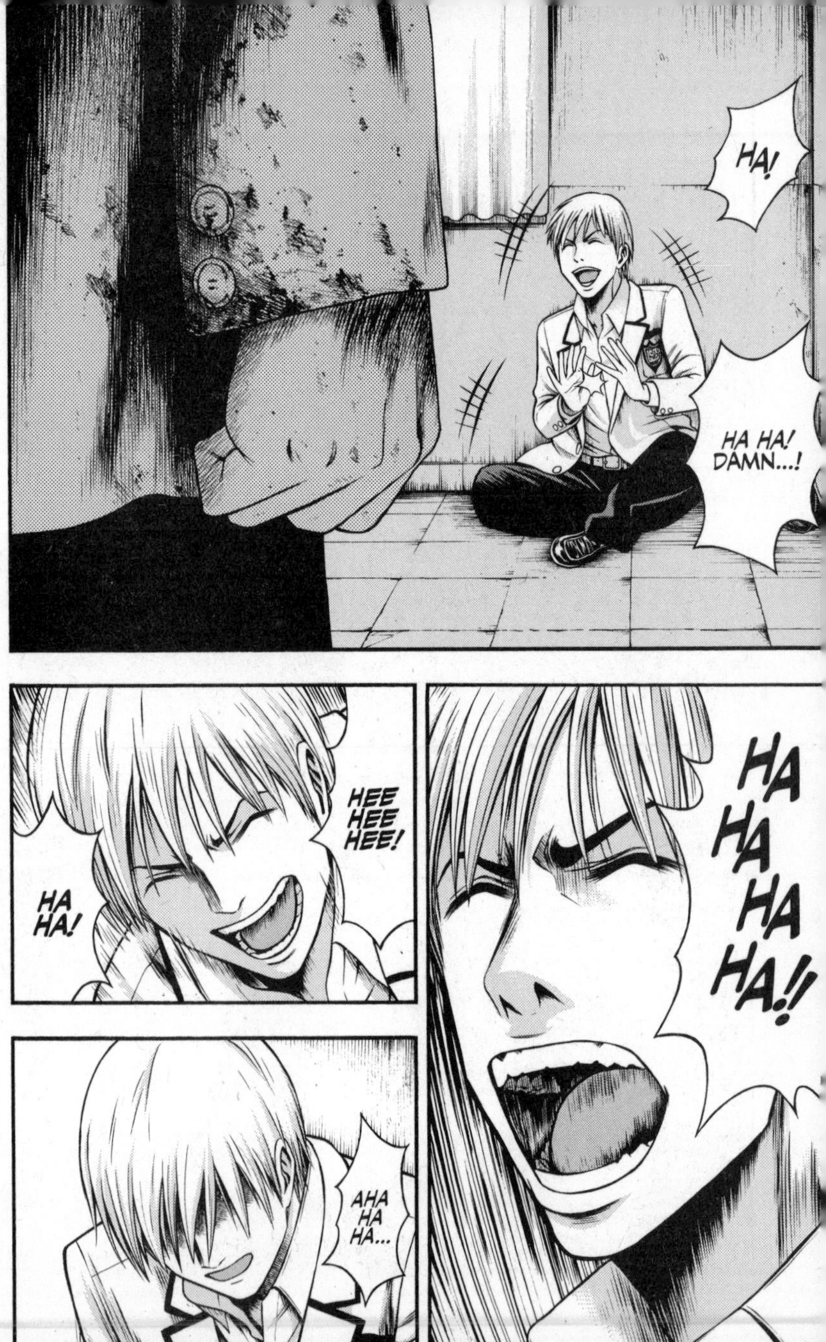
HA!
HA HA! DAMN...!
HA HA HA HA HA HA HA HA!!
HEE HEE HEE!
HA HA!
AHA HA HA...

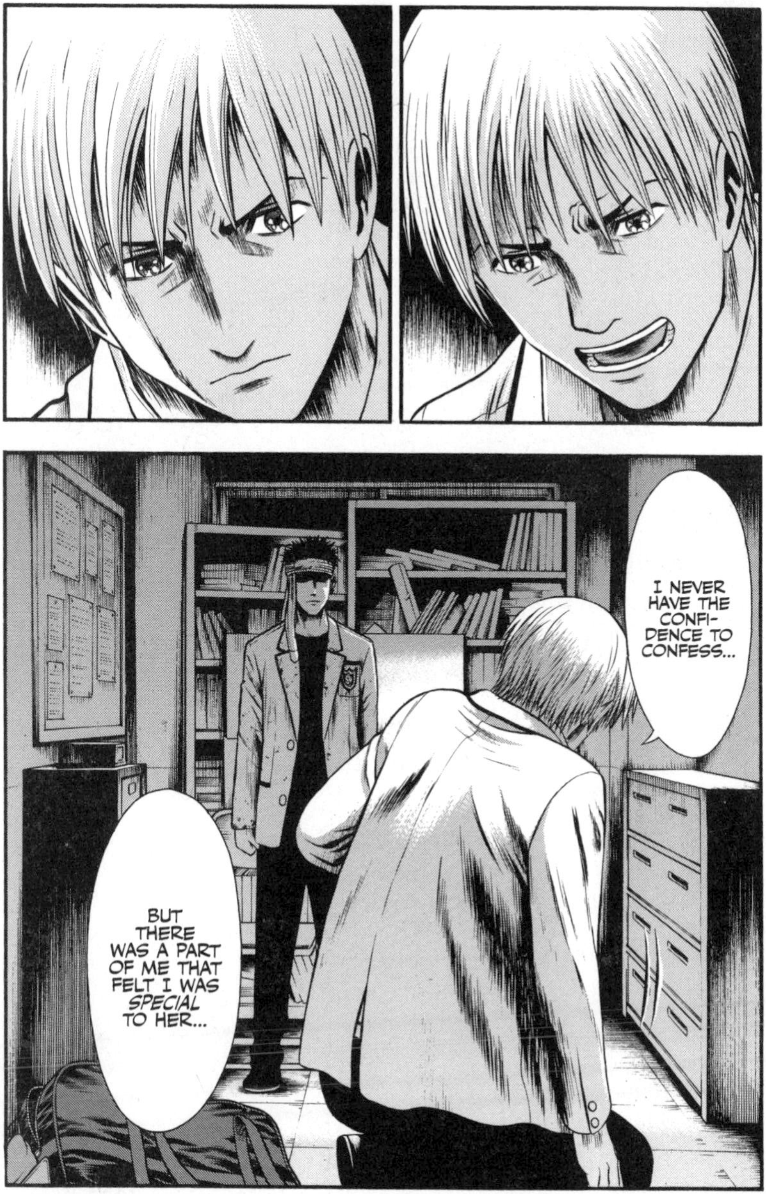
I NEVER HAVE THE CONFI-DENCE TO CONFESS...
BUT THERE WAS A PART OF ME THAT FELT I WAS *SPECIAL* TO HER...

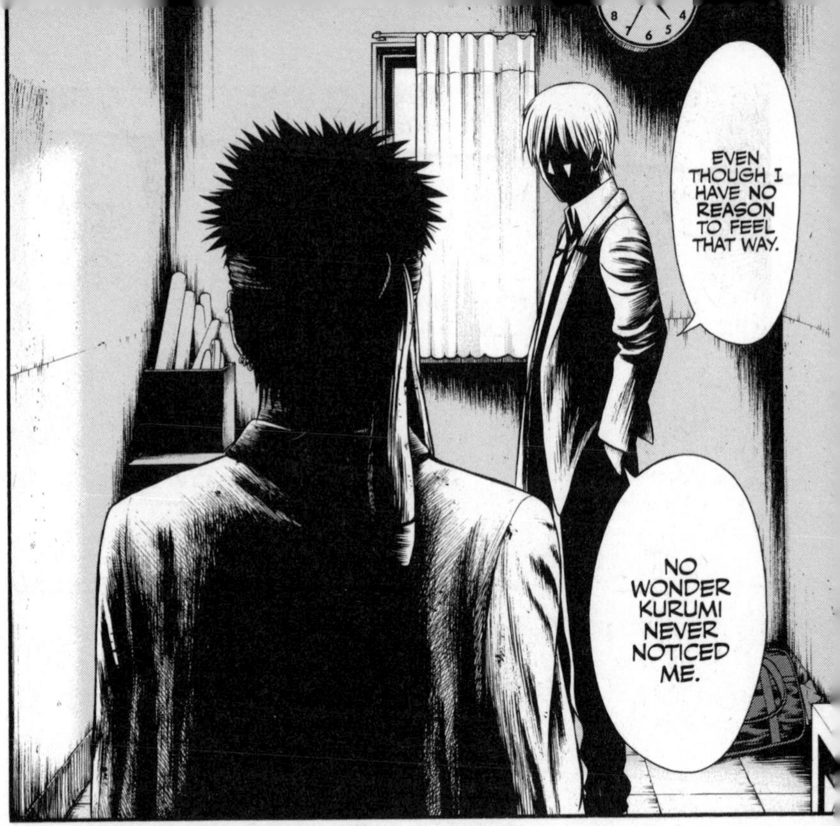
EVEN THOUGH I HAVE NO REASON TO FEEL THAT WAY.
NO WONDER KURUMI NEVER NOTICED ME.
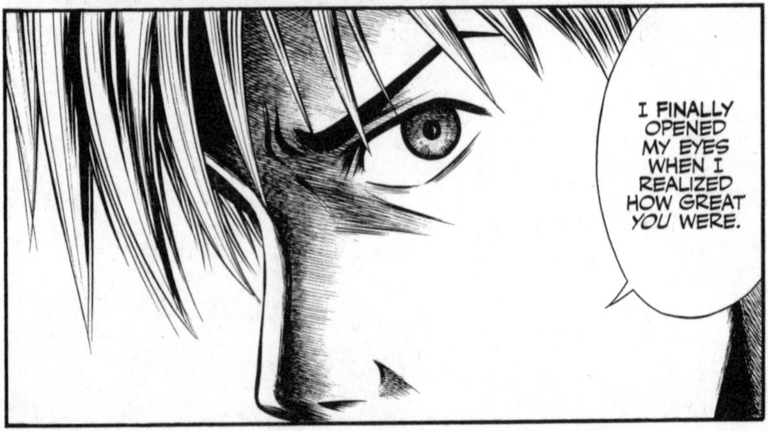
I FINALLY OPENED MY EYES WHEN I REALIZED HOW GREAT YOU WERE.

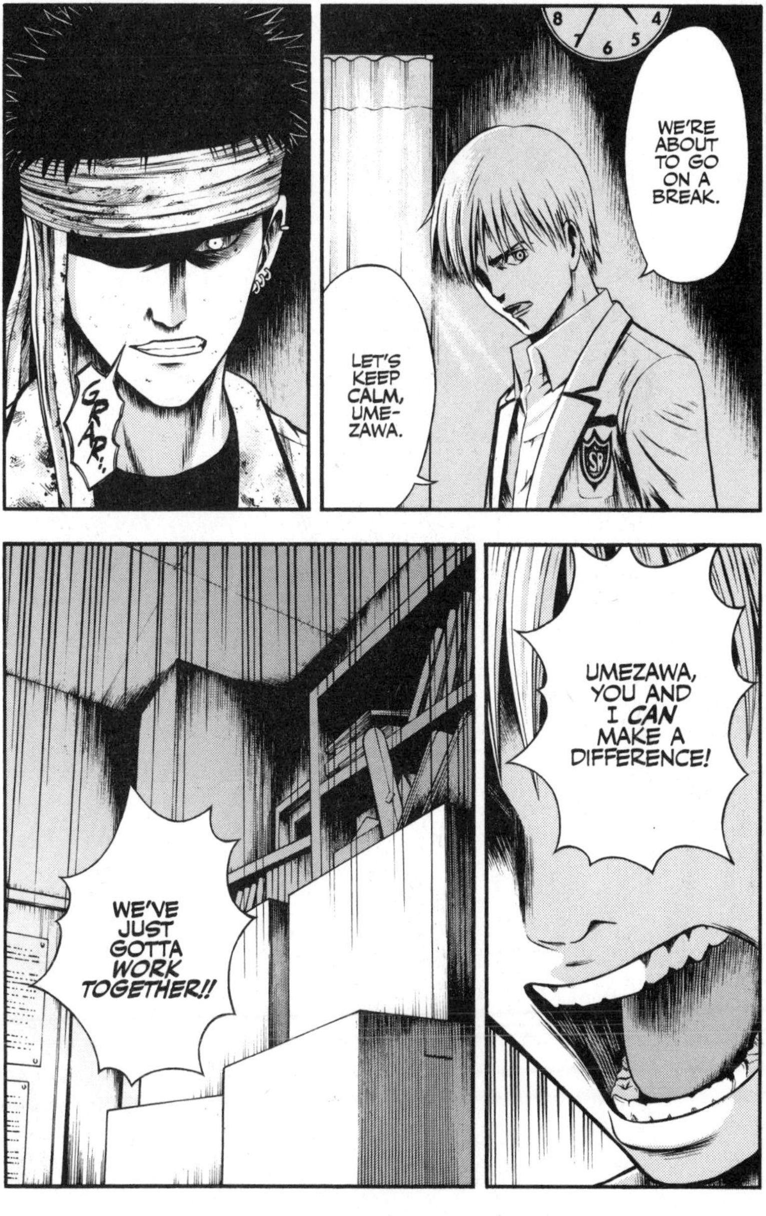
WE'RE ABOUT TO GO ON A BREAK.
LET'S KEEP CALM, UME-ZAWA.
GRAR!!
UMEZAWA, YOU AND I *CAN* MAKE A DIFFERENCE!
WE'VE JUST GOTTA *WORK TOGETHER!!*

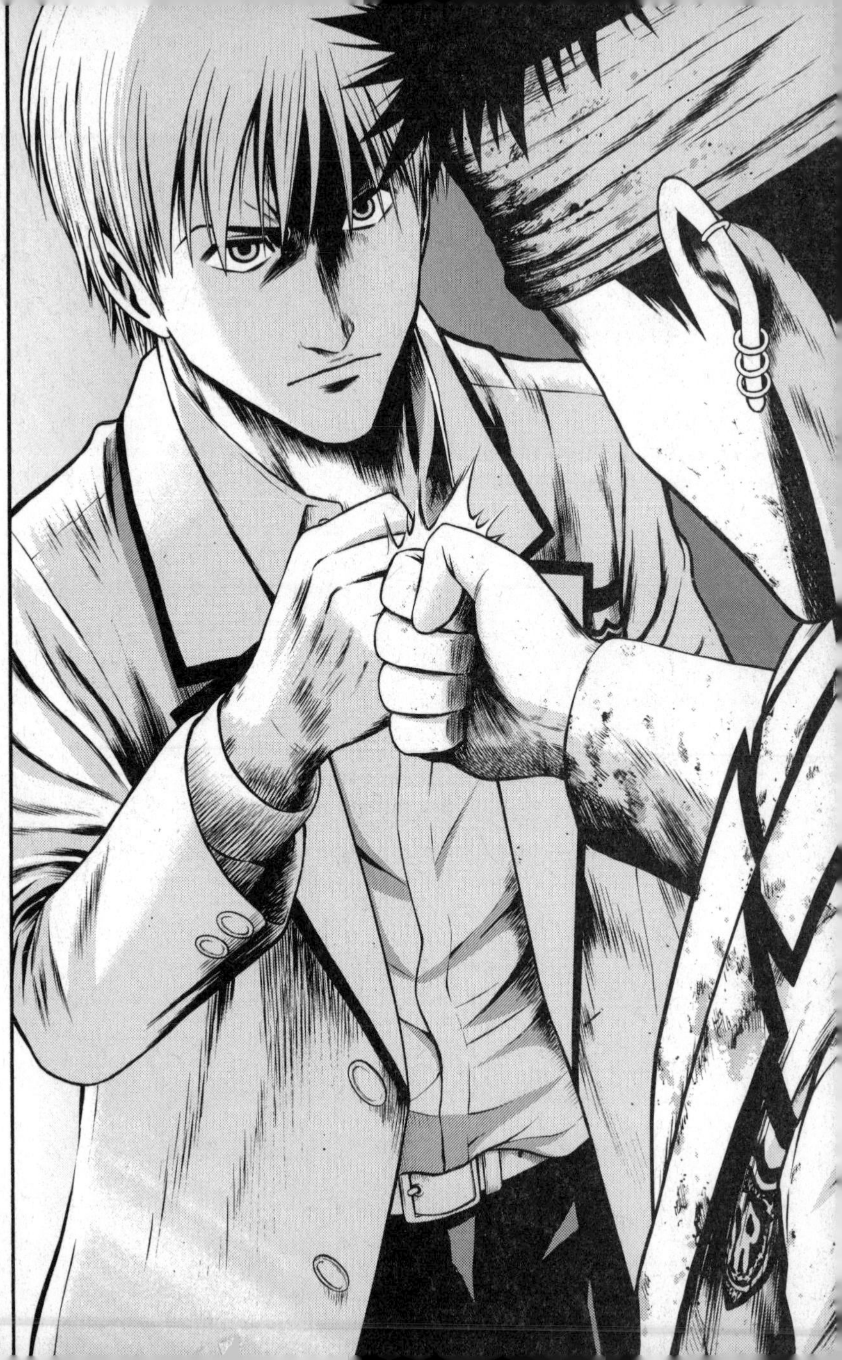

HOUR OF THE ZOMBIE

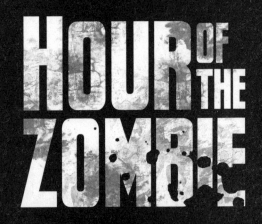

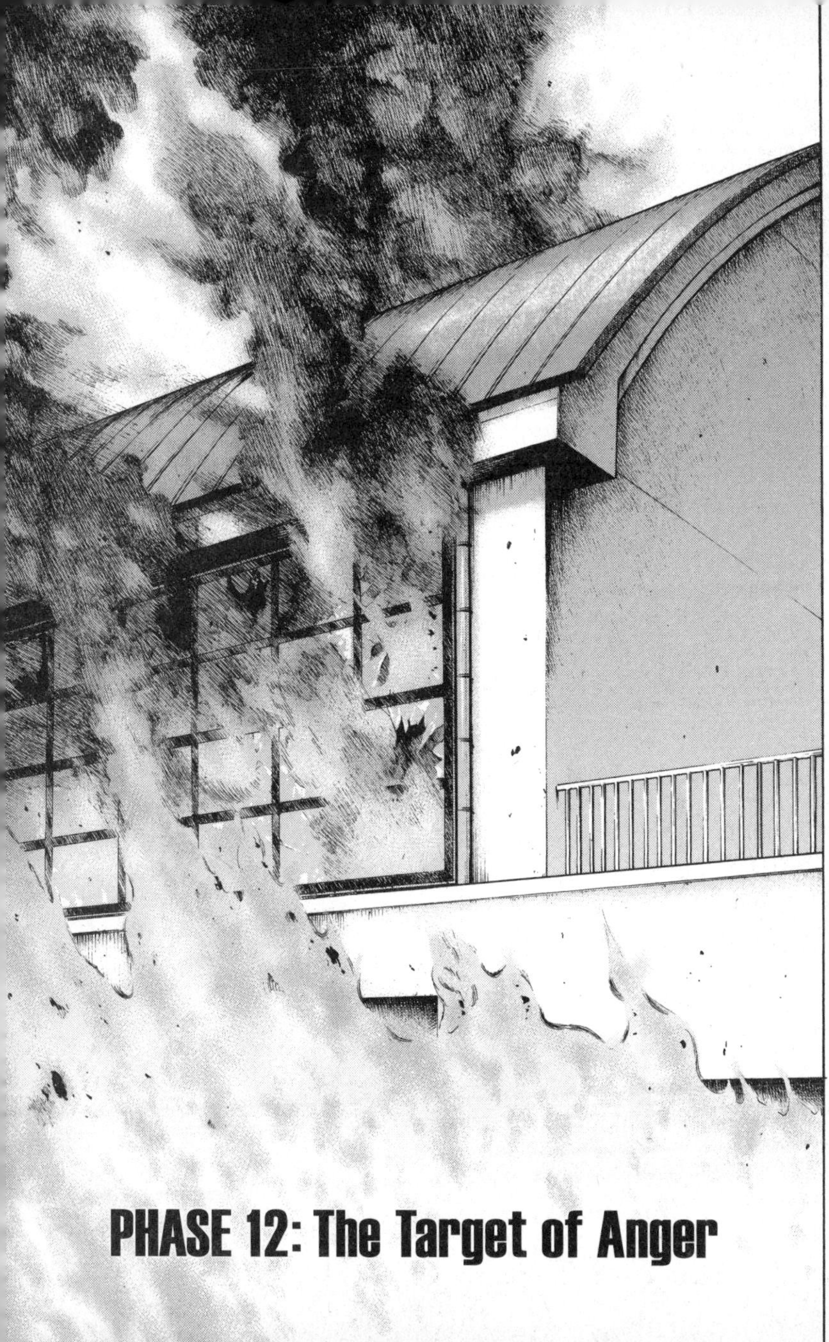

PHASE 12: The Target of Anger

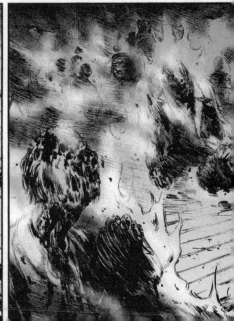

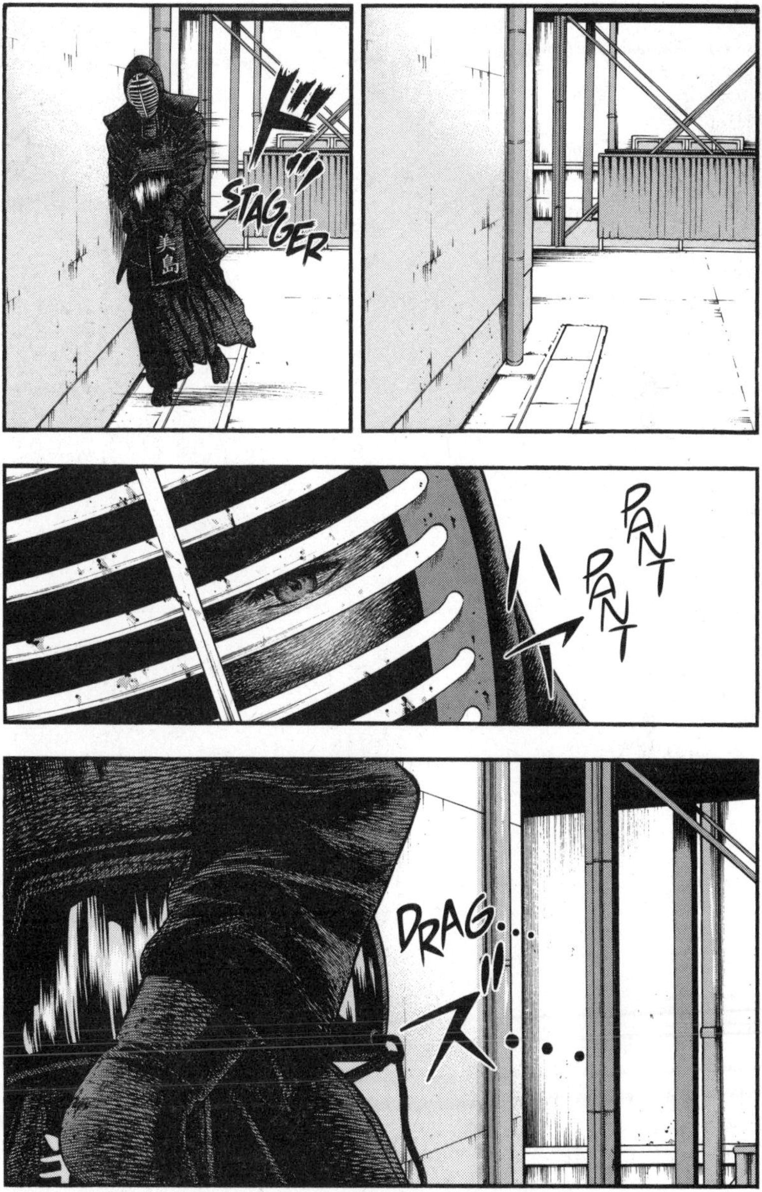
ドッ
STAGGER
美島
PANT PANT
ハァ
DRAG...
ズ...

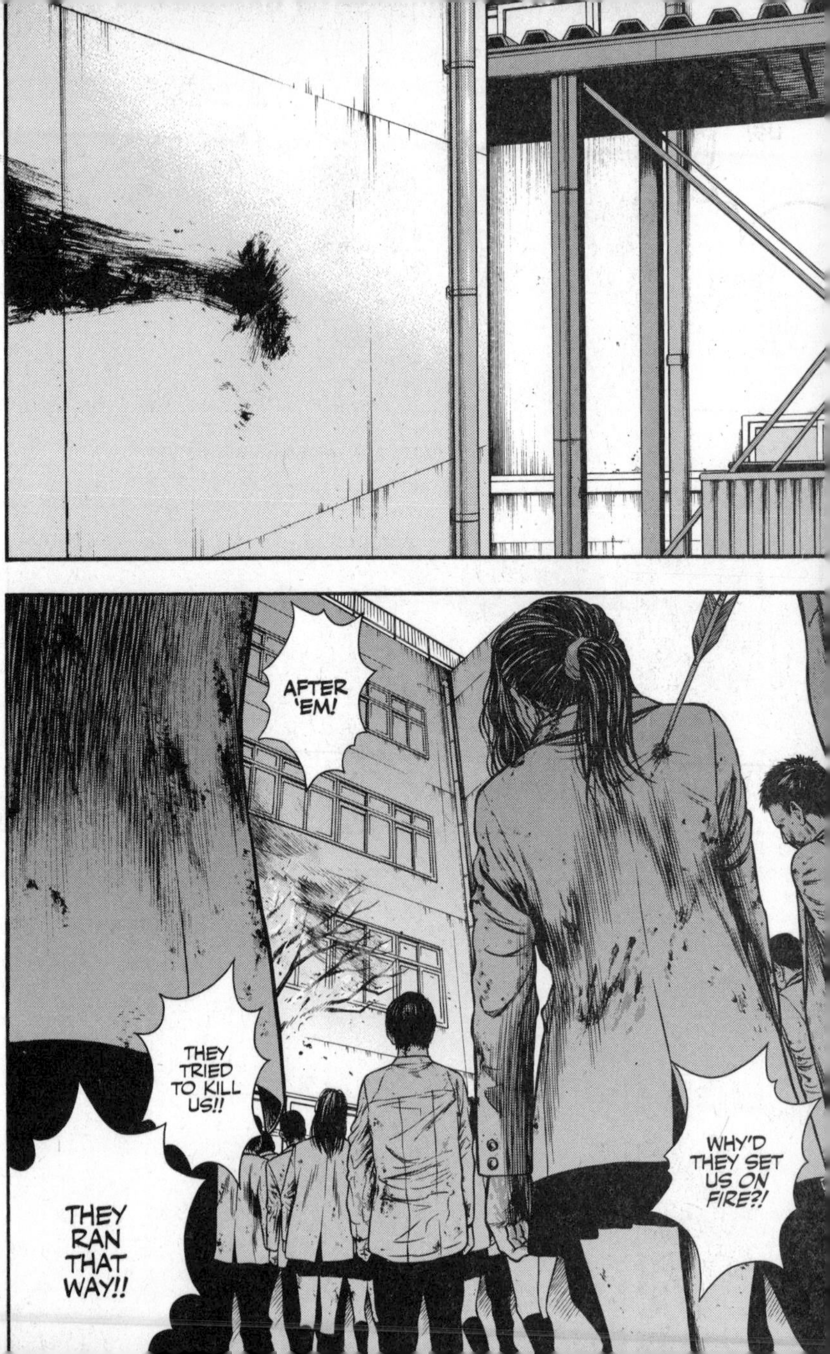
AFTER 'EM!
WHY'D THEY SET US ON FIRE?!
THEY TRIED TO KILL US!!
THEY RAN THAT WAY!!

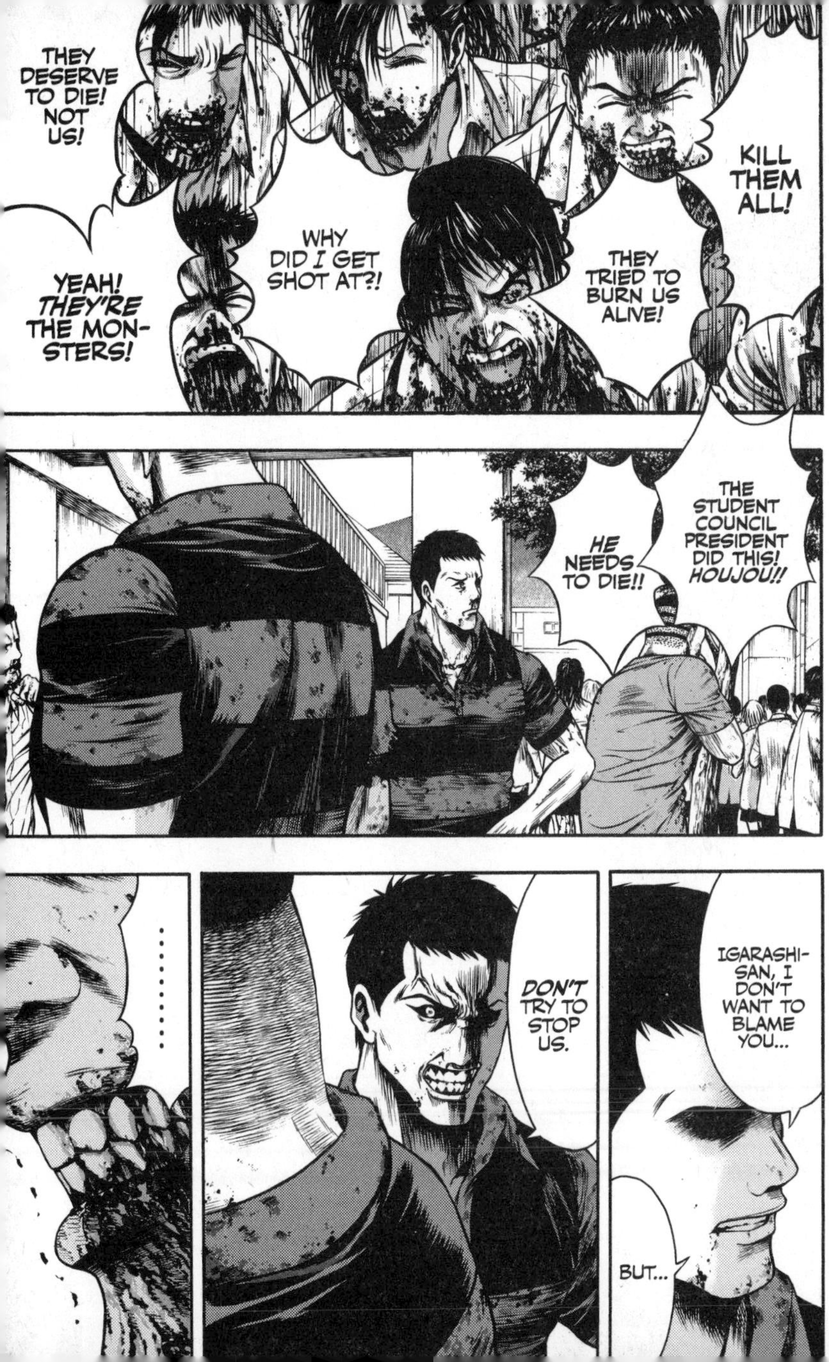
KILL THEM ALL!
THEY TRIED TO BURN US ALIVE!
WHY DID I GET SHOT AT?!
THEY DESERVE TO DIE! NOT US!
YEAH! THEY'RE THE MONSTERS!
THE STUDENT COUNCIL PRESIDENT DID THIS! HOUJOU!!
HE NEEDS TO DIE!!
IGARASHI-SAN, I DON'T WANT TO BLAME YOU...
BUT...
DON'T TRY TO STOP US.
....

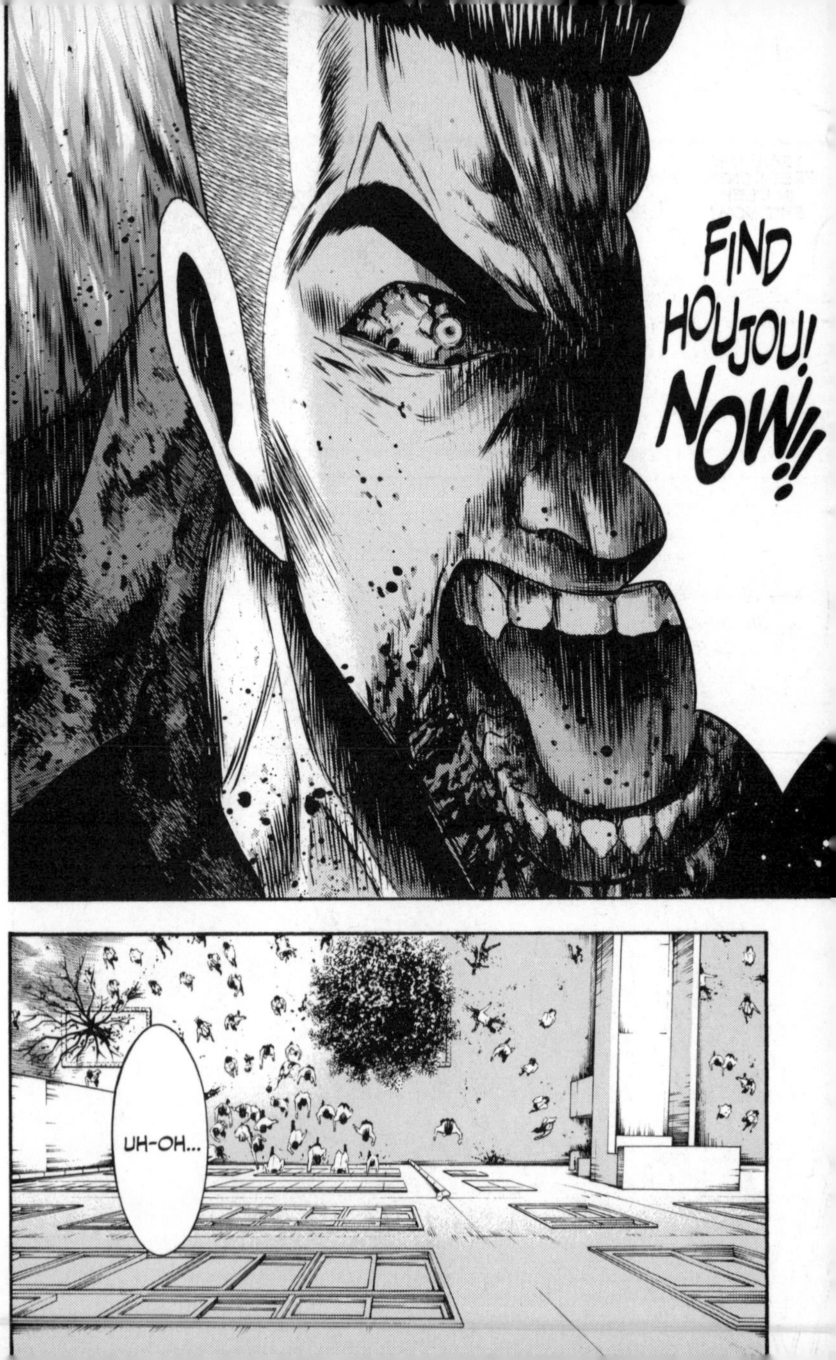
FIND HOUJOU! NOW!!
UH-OH...

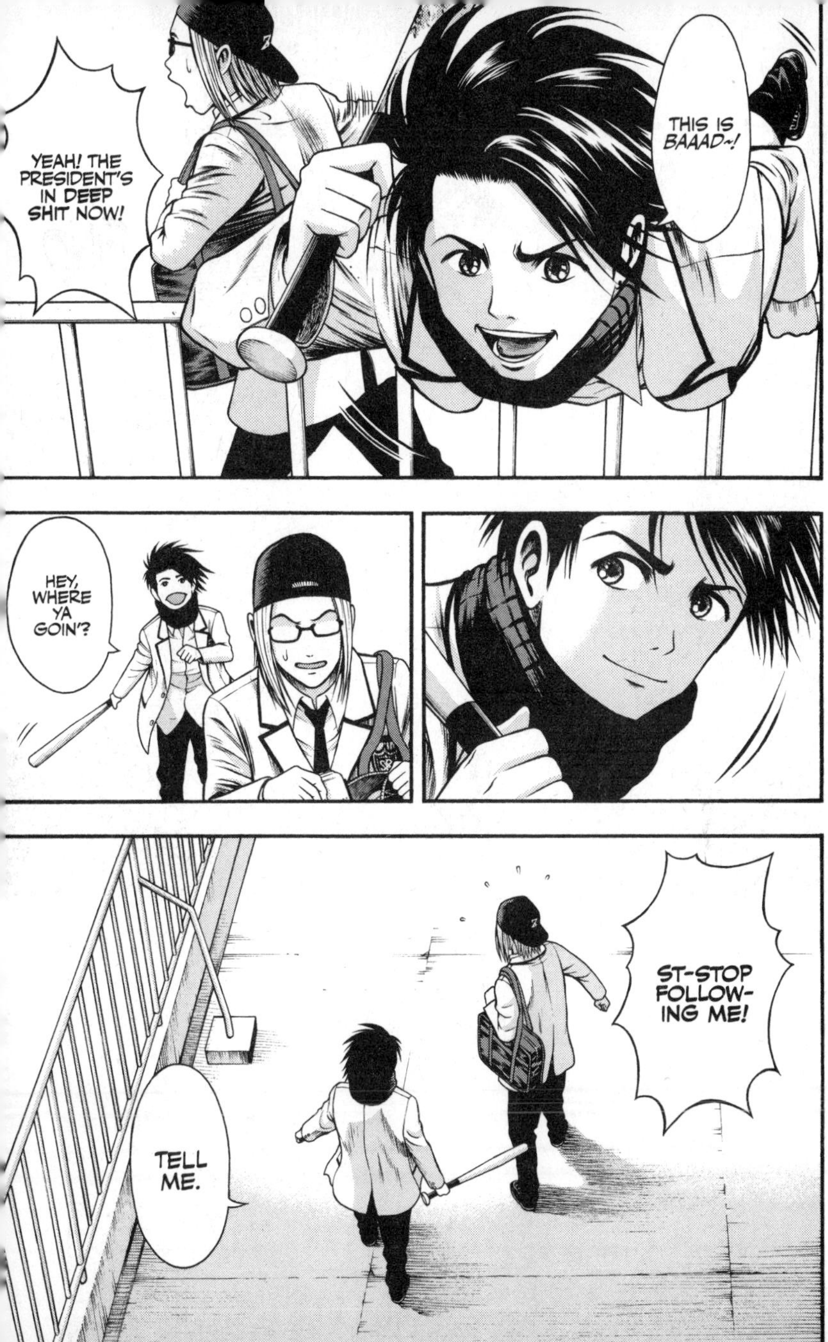
THIS IS BAAAD~!
YEAH! THE PRESIDENT'S IN DEEP SHIT NOW!
HEY, WHERE YA GOIN'?
ST-STOP FOLLOW-ING ME!
TELL ME.

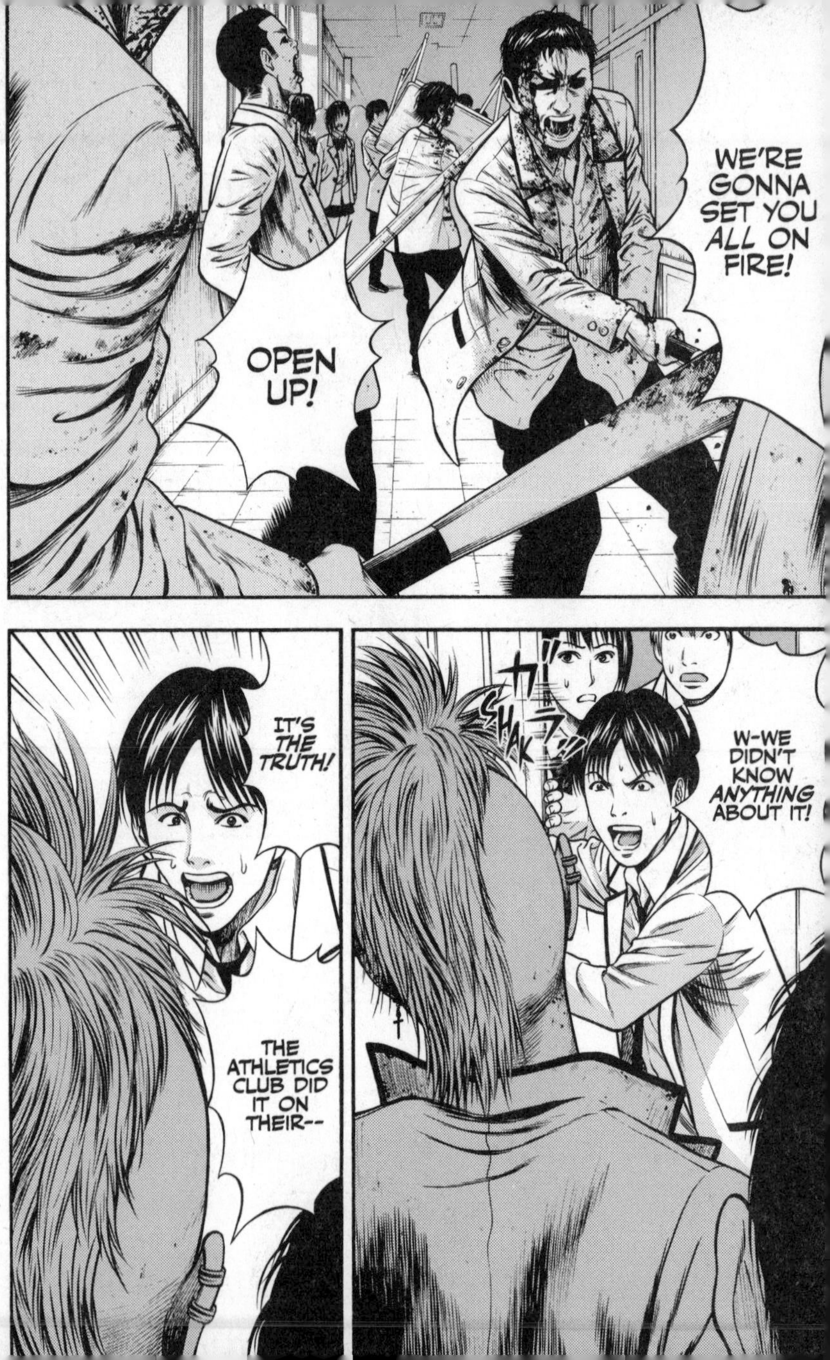
WE'RE GONNA SET YOU ALL ON FIRE!
OPEN UP!
SHAK
W-WE DIDN'T KNOW ANYTHING ABOUT IT!
IT'S THE TRUTH!
THE ATHLETICS CLUB DID IT ON THEIR--

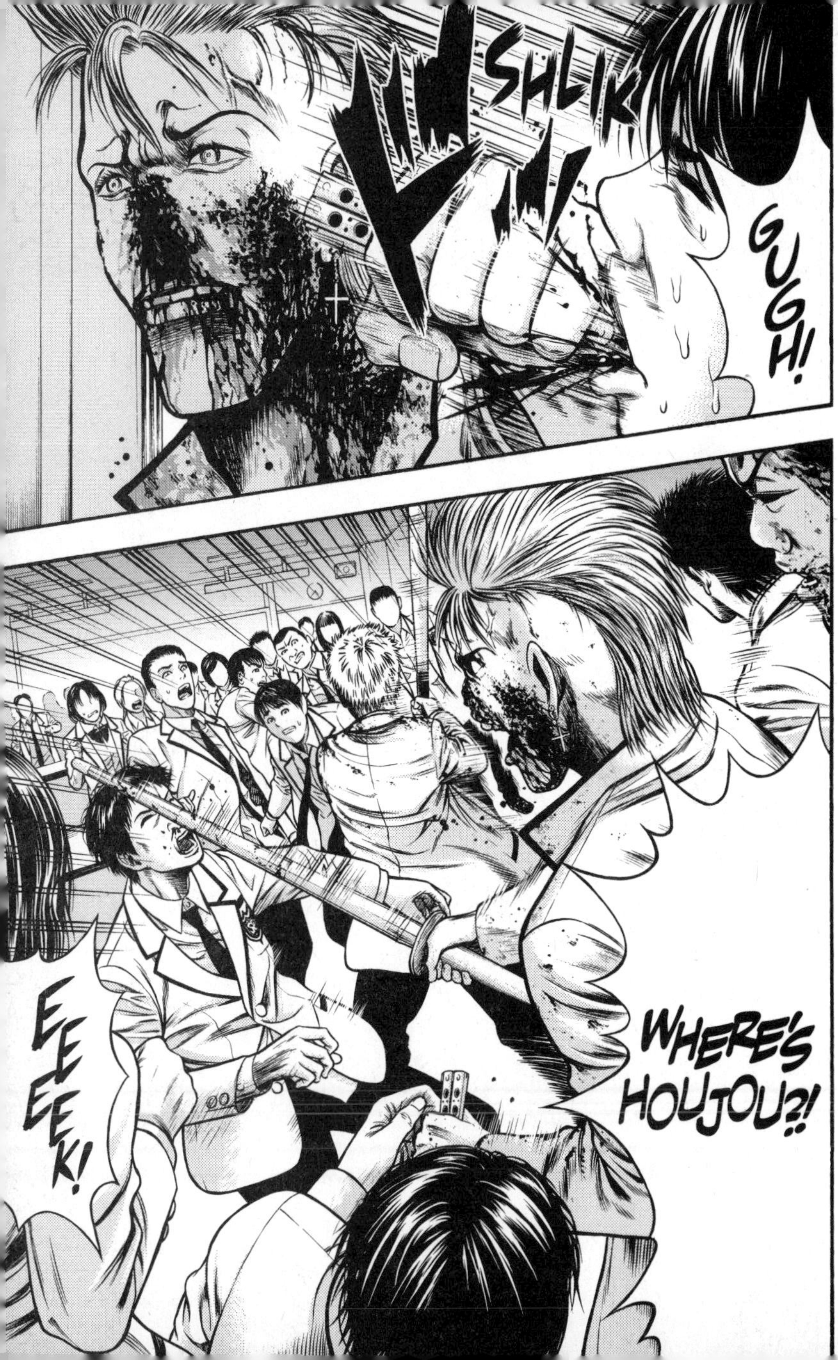
SHLIK
GUGH!
WHERE'S HOUJOU?!
EEEEEK!

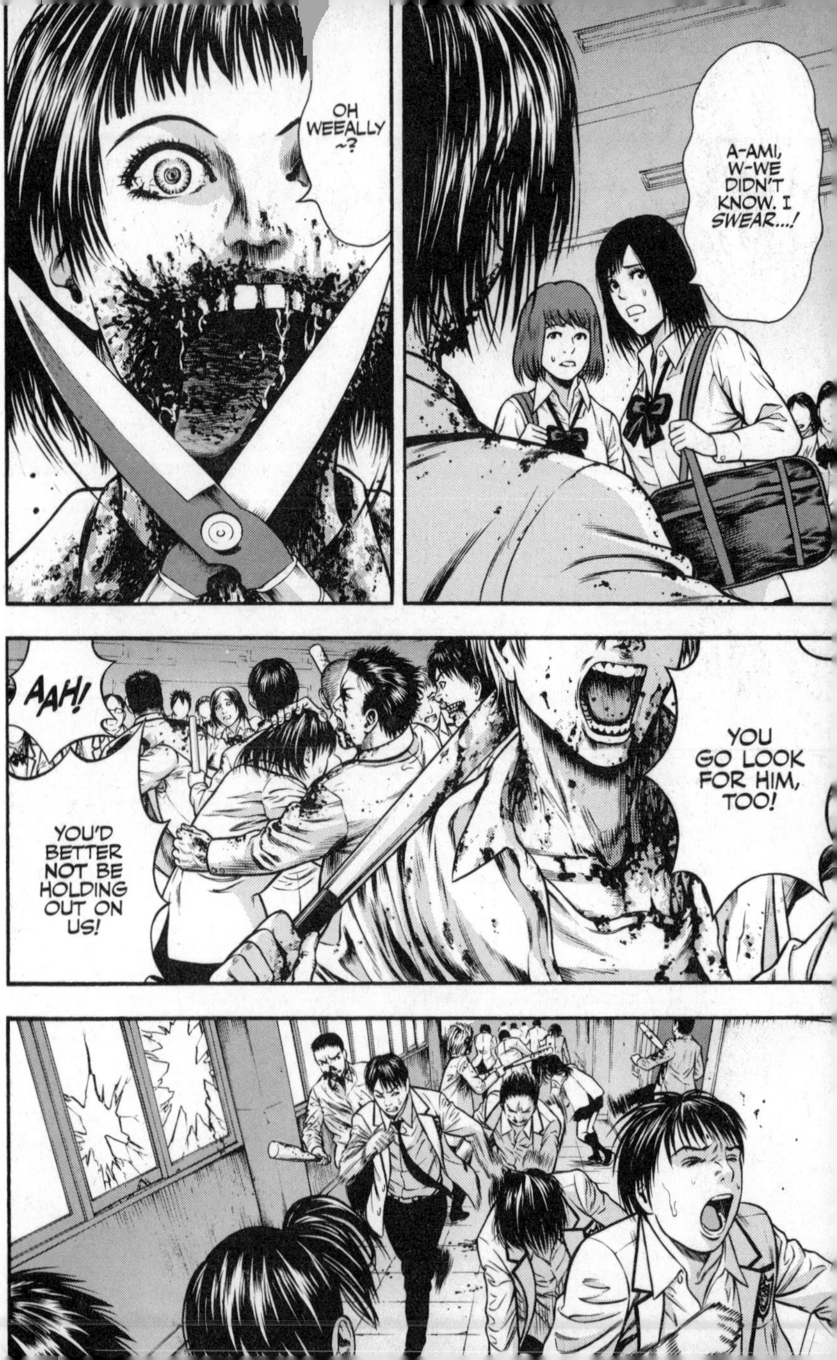
A-AMI, W-WE DIDN'T KNOW. I SWEAR...!
OH WEEALLY ~?
YOU GO LOOK FOR HIM, TOO!
AAH!
YOU'D BETTER NOT BE HOLDING OUT ON US!

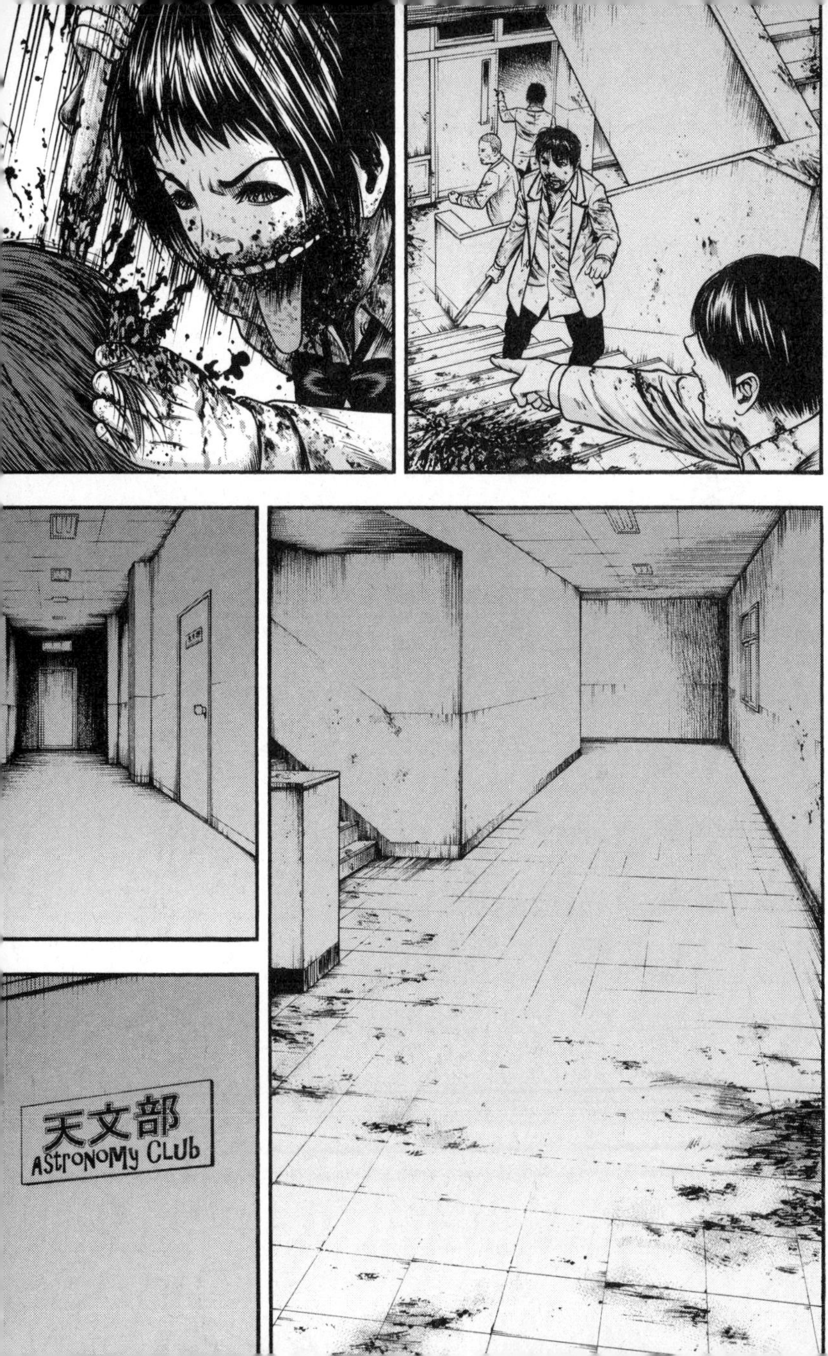
天文部
ASTRONOMY CLUB

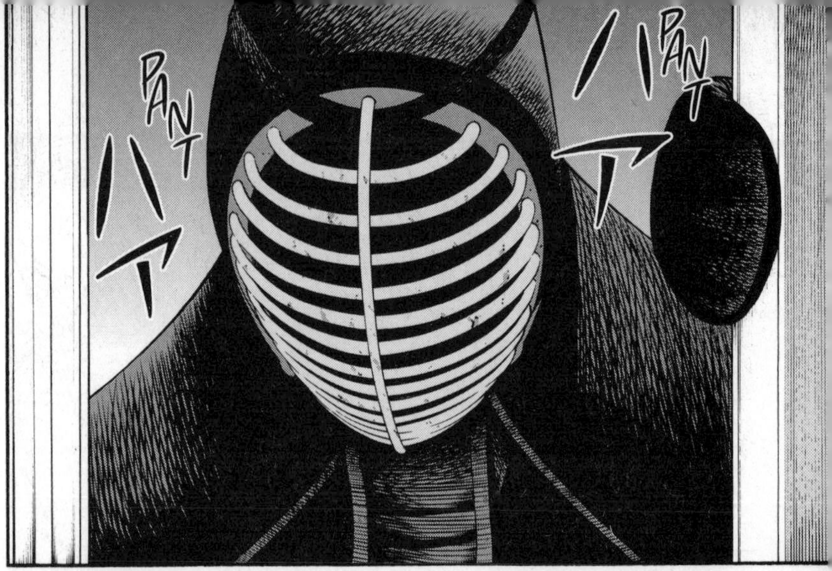
ハァ
PANT
ハァ
PANT

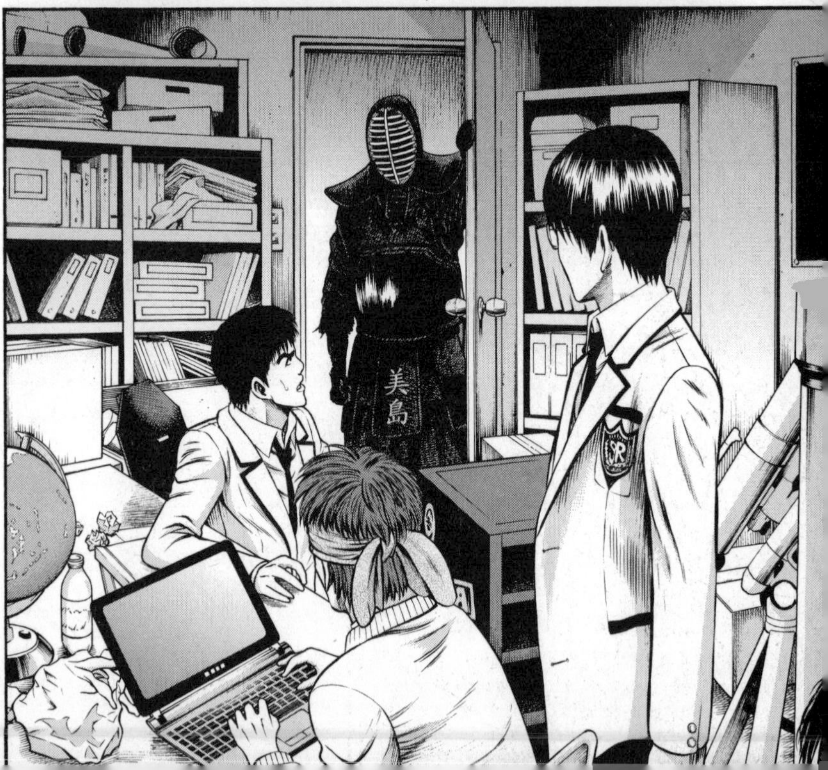
美島

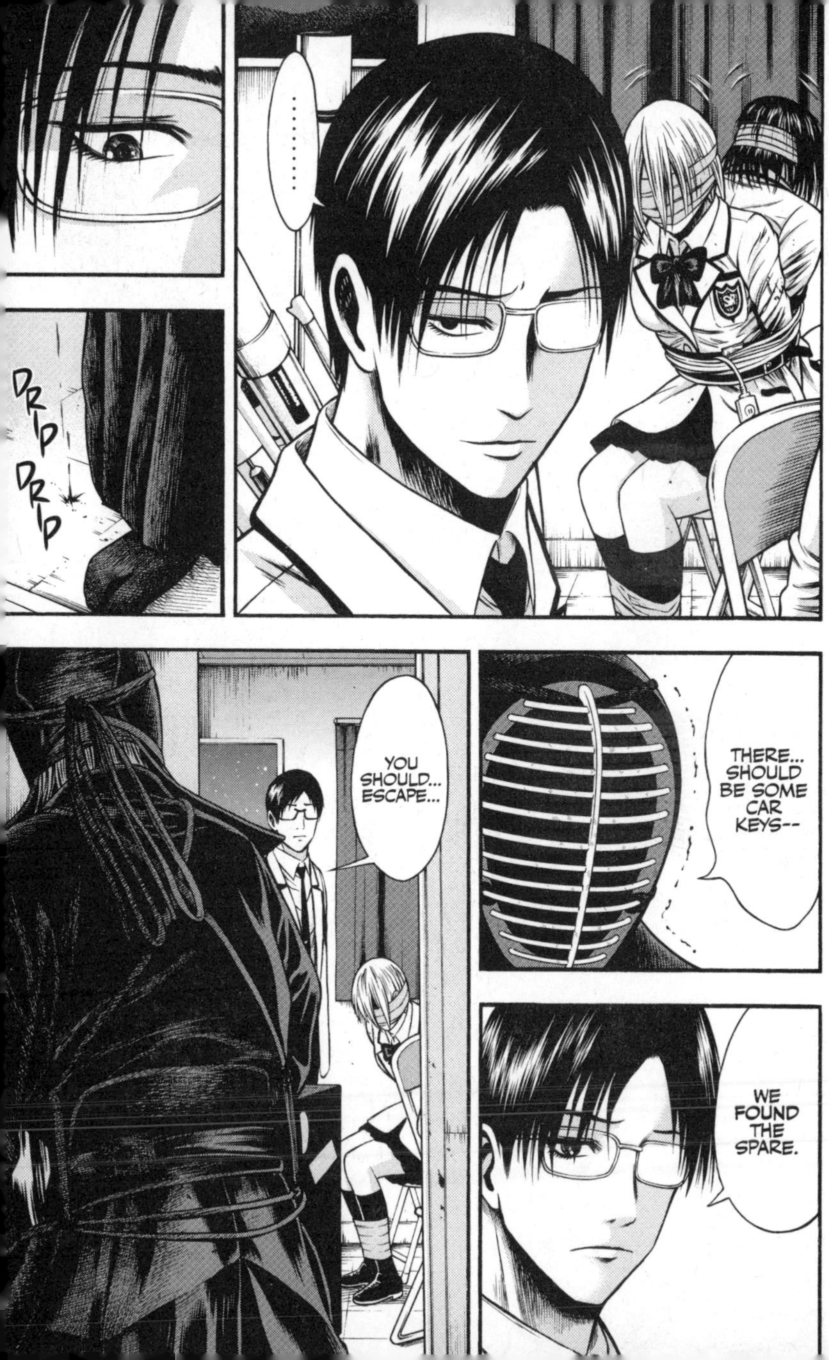
......
DRIP DRIP
DRIP DRIP
YOU SHOULD... ESCAPE...
THERE... SHOULD BE SOME CAR KEYS--
WE FOUND THE SPARE.

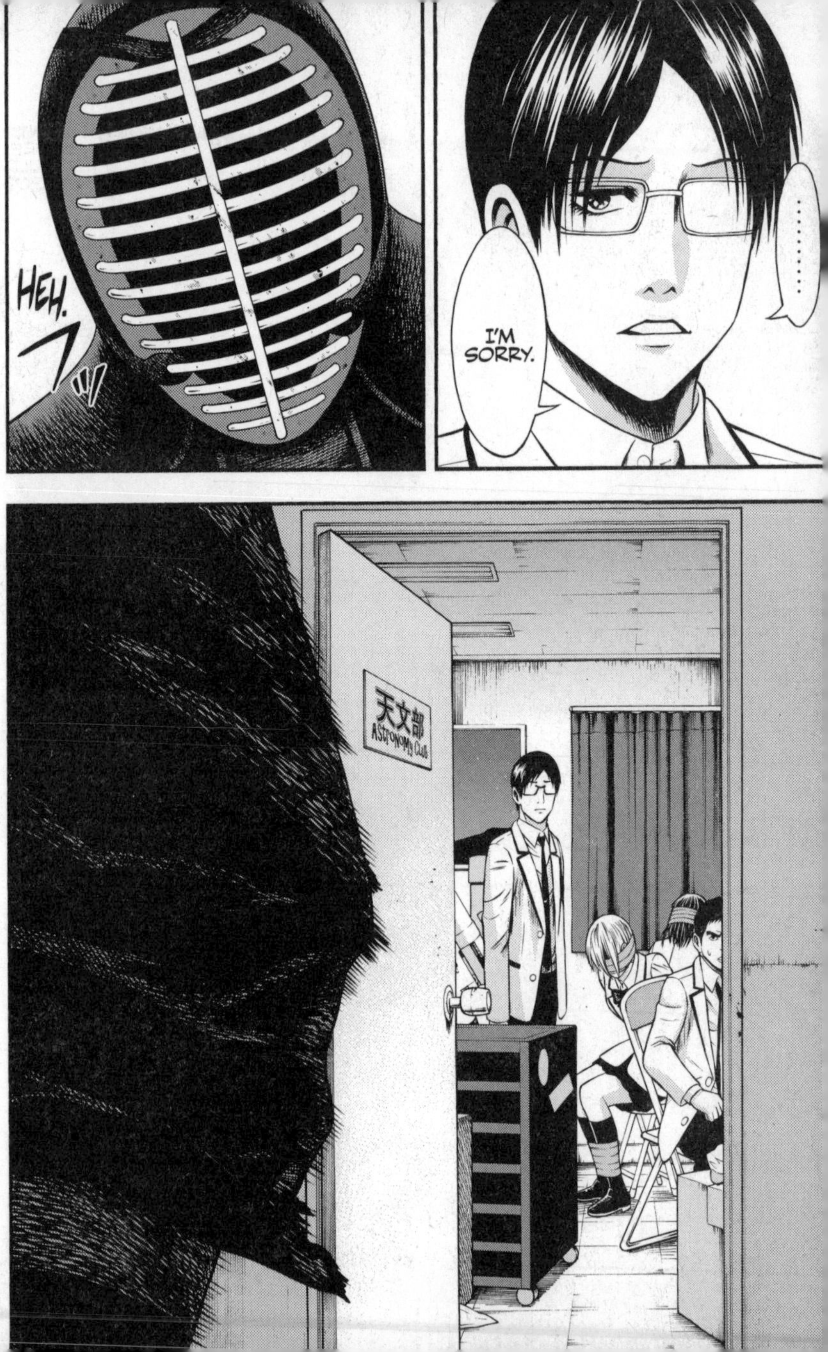

......
I'M SORRY.
HEH.
天文部
ASTRONOMY CLUB

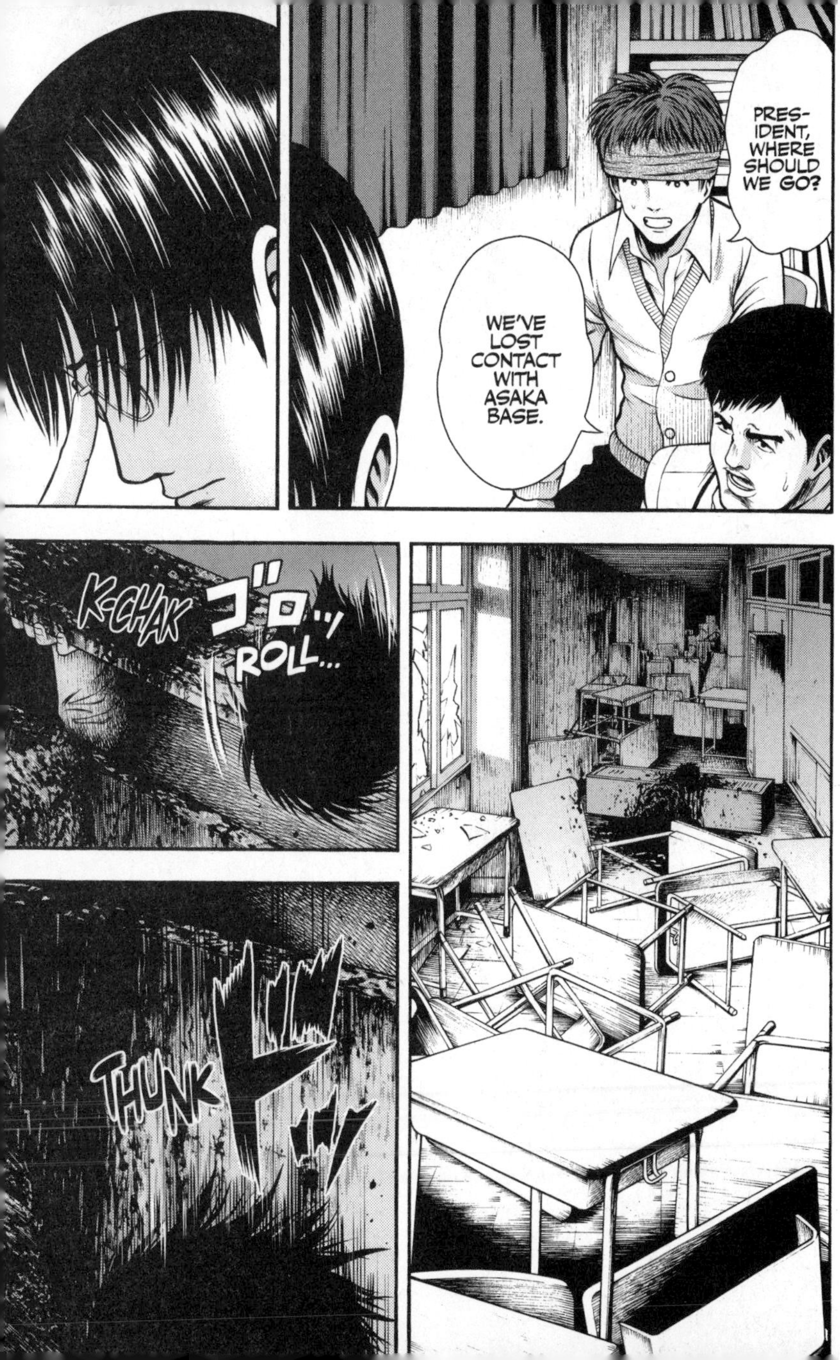
PRES-IDENT, WHERE SHOULD WE GO?
WE'VE LOST CONTACT WITH ASAKA BASE.
K-CHAK
ゴロッ
ROLL...
THUNK

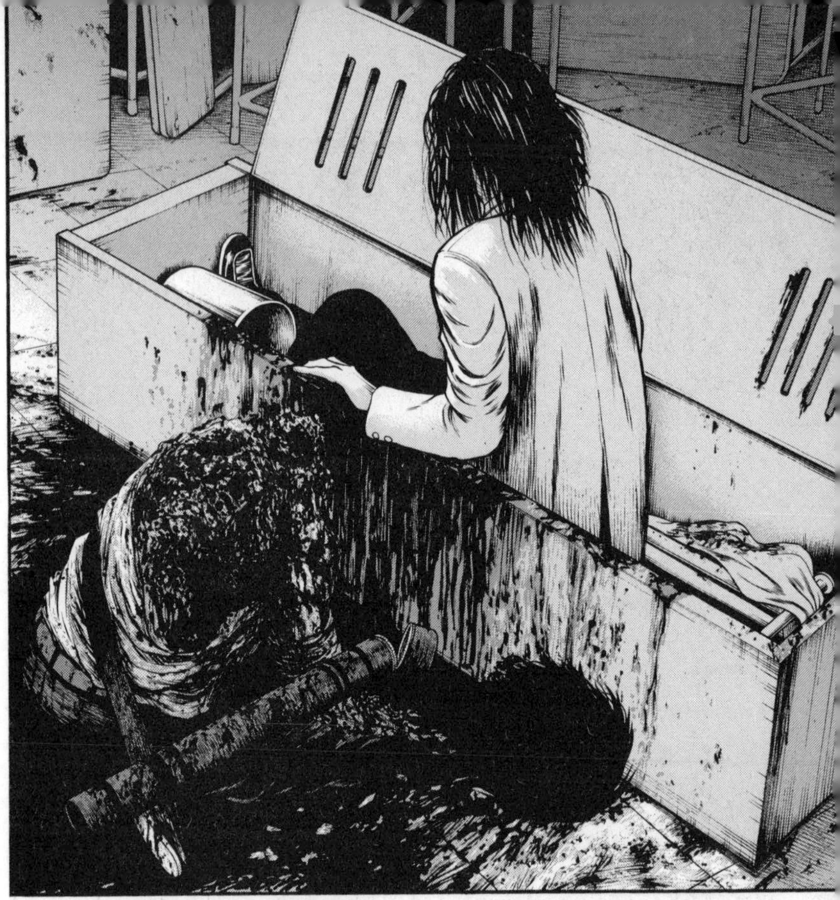
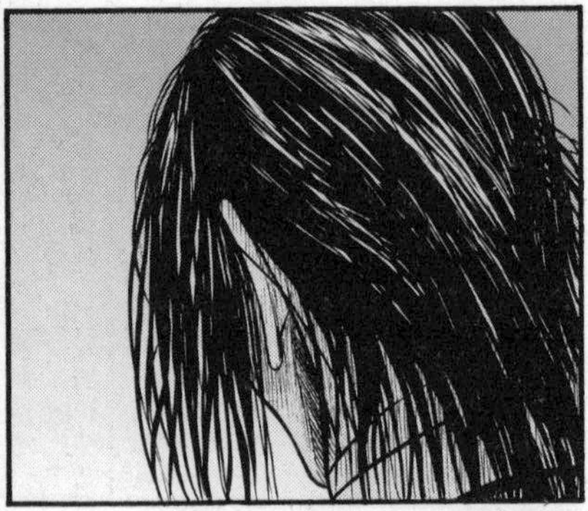
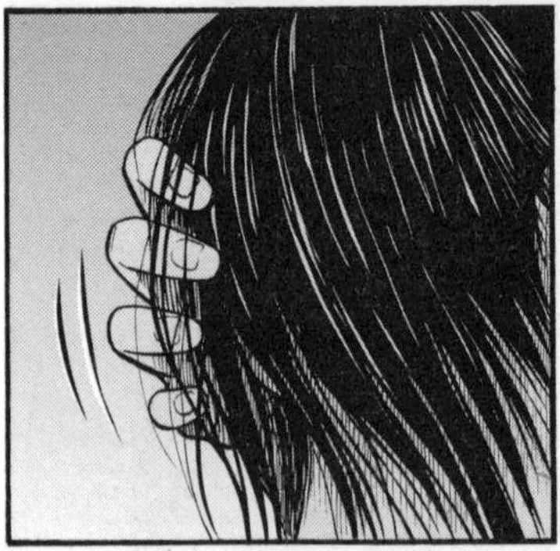

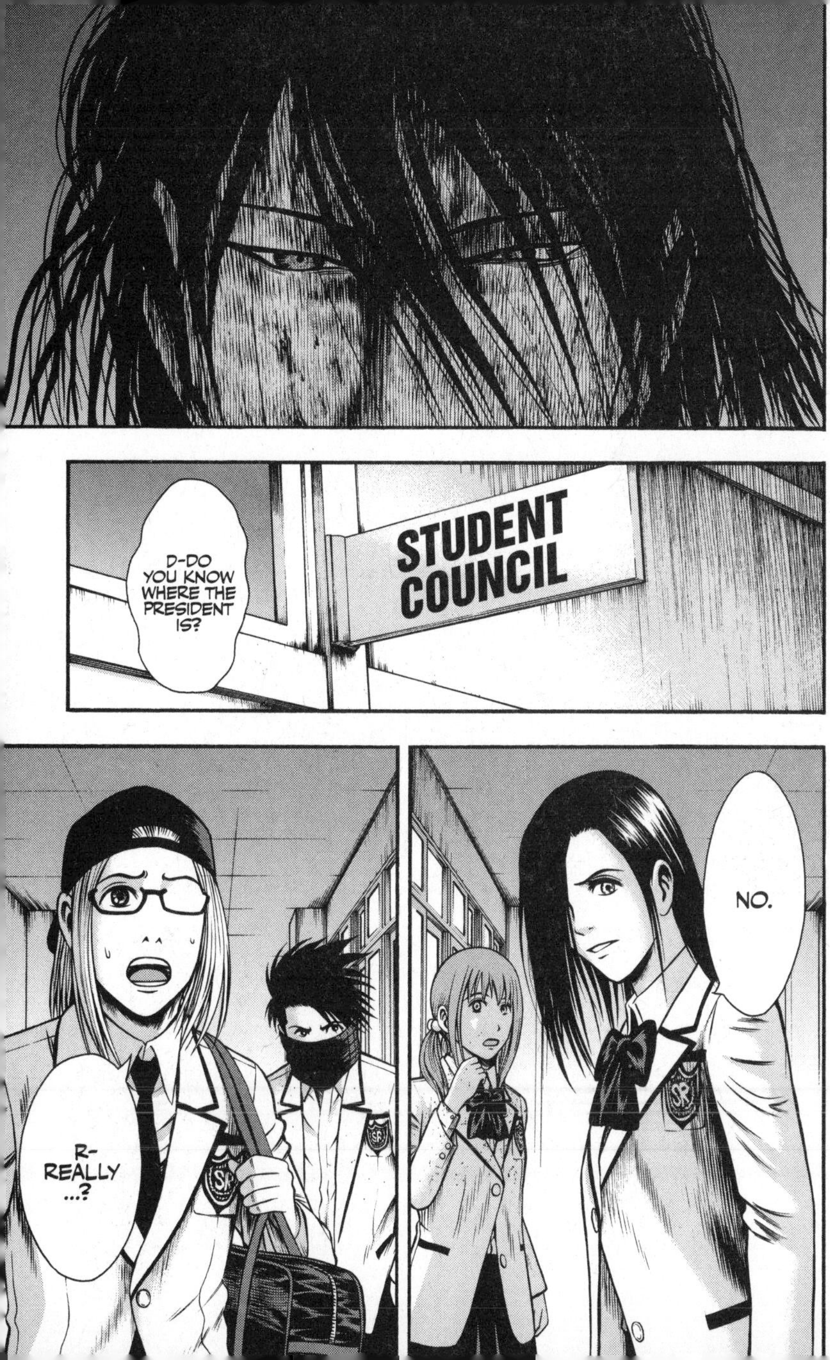
STUDENT COUNCIL
D-DO YOU KNOW WHERE THE PRESIDENT IS?
NO.
R-REALLY ...?

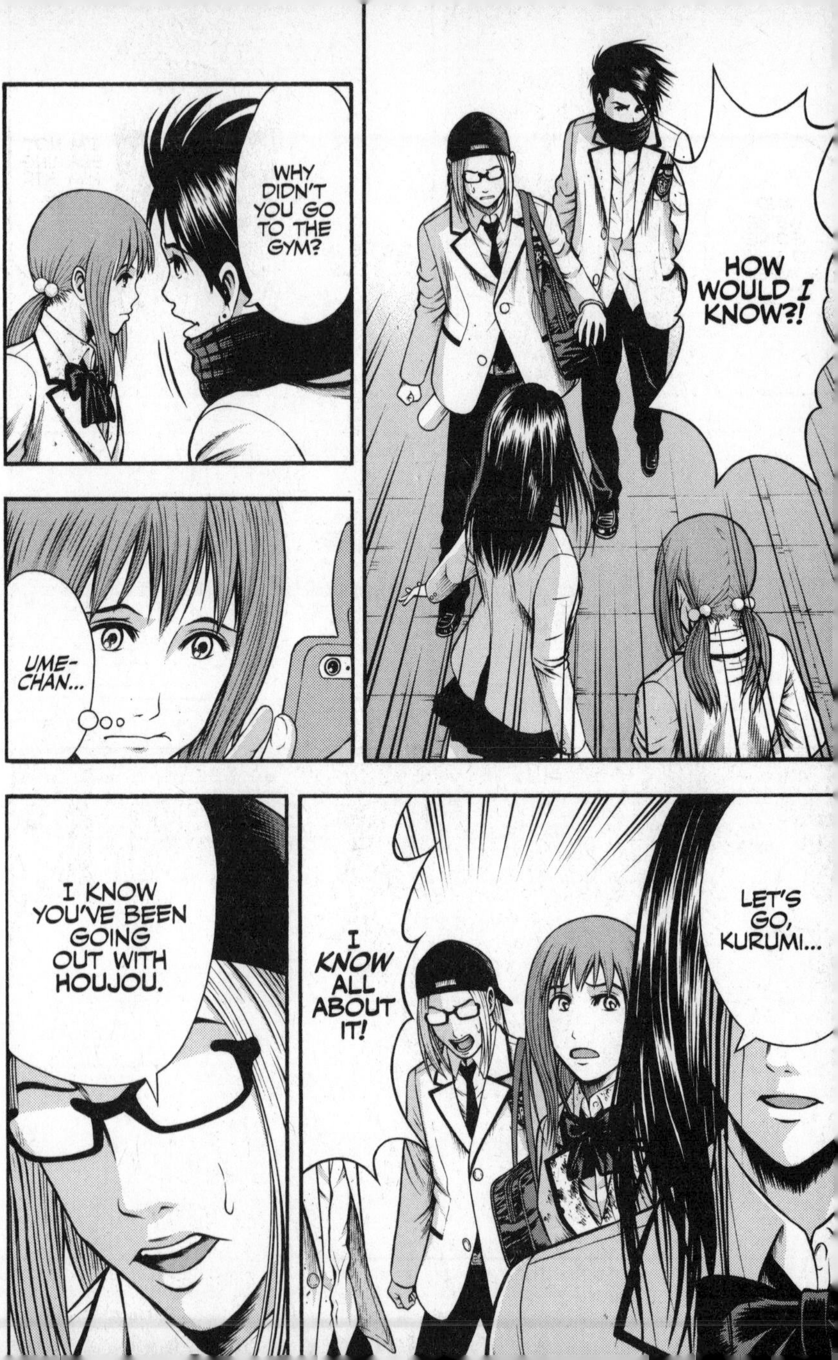
HOW WOULD I KNOW?!
WHY DIDN'T YOU GO TO THE GYM?
UME-CHAN...
LET'S GO, KURUMI...
I KNOW ALL ABOUT IT!
I KNOW YOU'VE BEEN GOING OUT WITH HOUJOU.

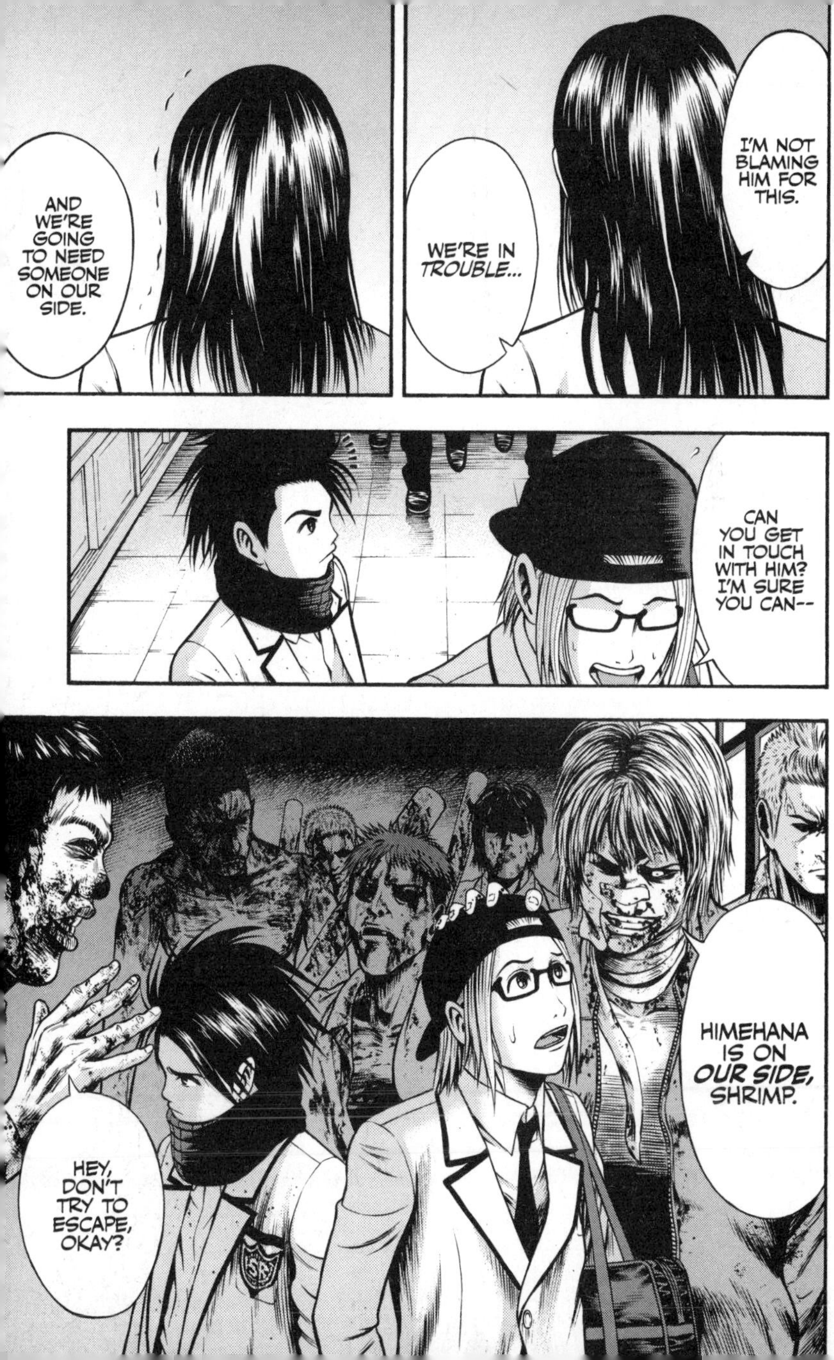
I'M NOT BLAMING HIM FOR THIS.
WE'RE IN *TROUBLE*...
AND WE'RE GOING TO NEED SOMEONE ON OUR SIDE.
CAN YOU GET IN TOUCH WITH HIM? I'M SURE YOU CAN--
HIMEHANA IS ON ***OUR SIDE***, SHRIMP.
HEY, DON'T TRY TO ESCAPE, OKAY?

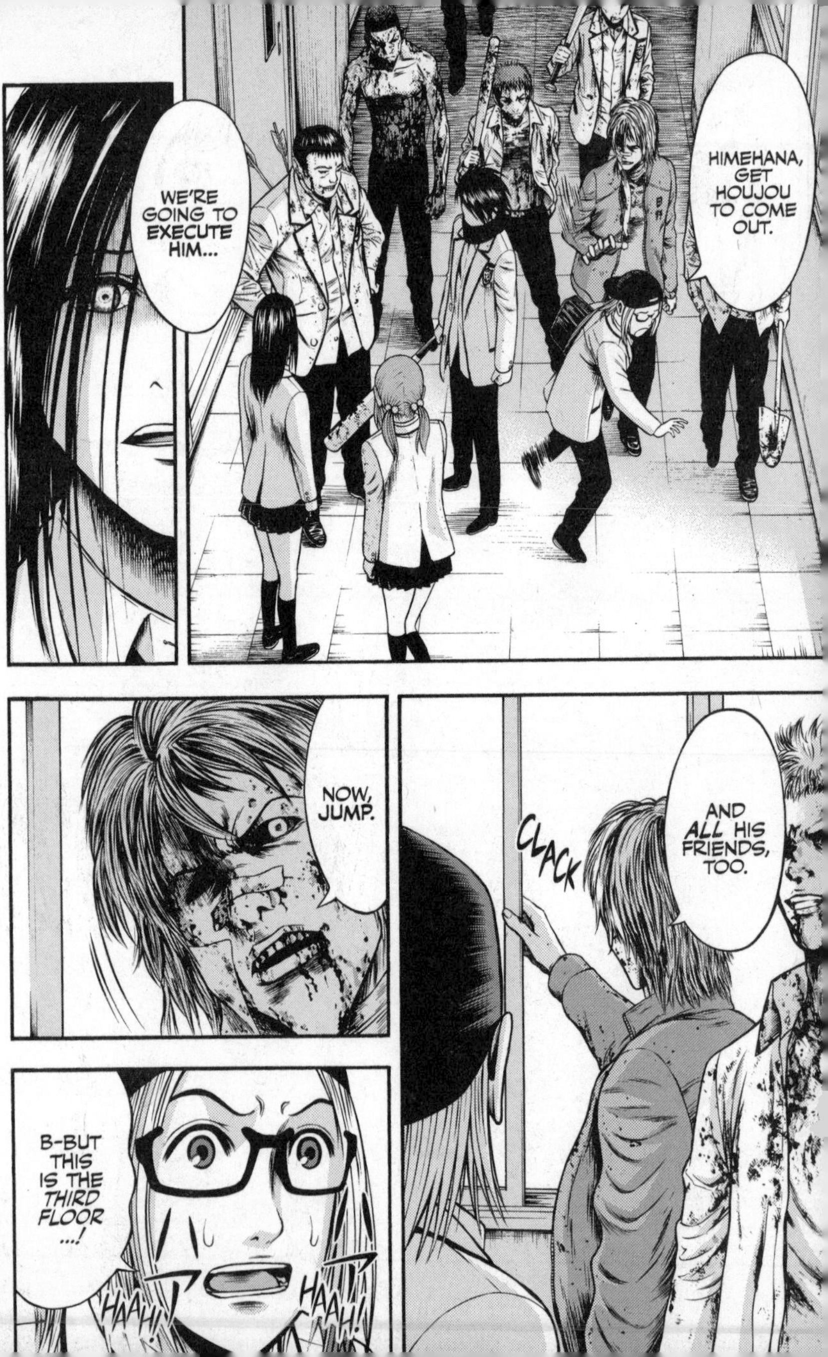
HIMEHANA, GET HOUJOU TO COME OUT.
WE'RE GOING TO EXECUTE HIM...
AND ALL HIS FRIENDS, TOO.
CLACK
NOW, JUMP.
B-BUT THIS IS THE THIRD FLOOR ...!
HAAH!
HAAH!

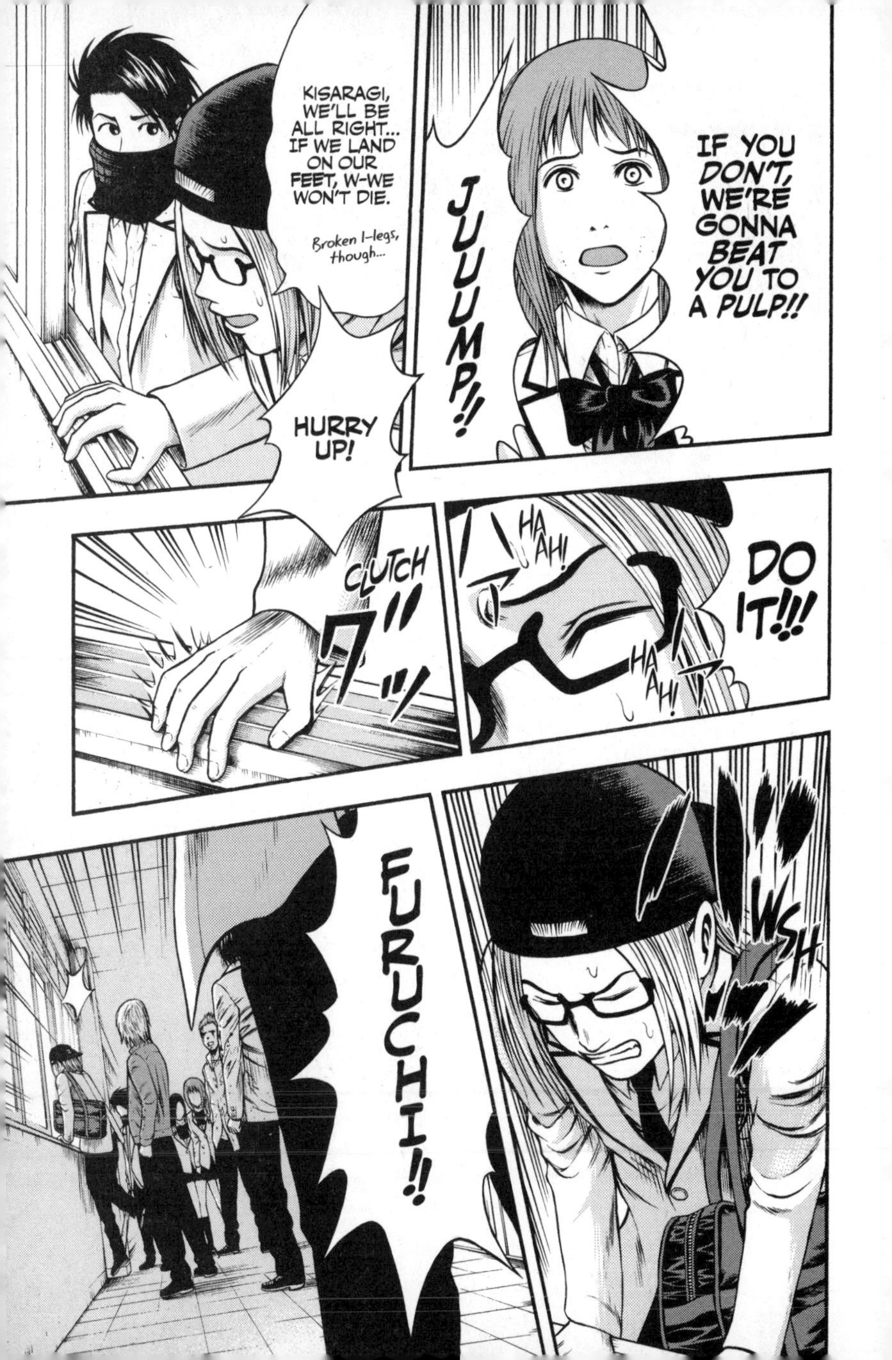
JUUUMP!!
IF YOU DON'T, WE'RE GONNA BEAT YOU TO A PULP!!
HURRY UP!
KISARAGI, WE'LL BE ALL RIGHT... IF WE LAND ON OUR FEET, W-WE WON'T DIE.
Broken l-legs, though...
HA AH!
DO IT!!!
HA AH!
CLUTCH
WSH
FURUCHI!!

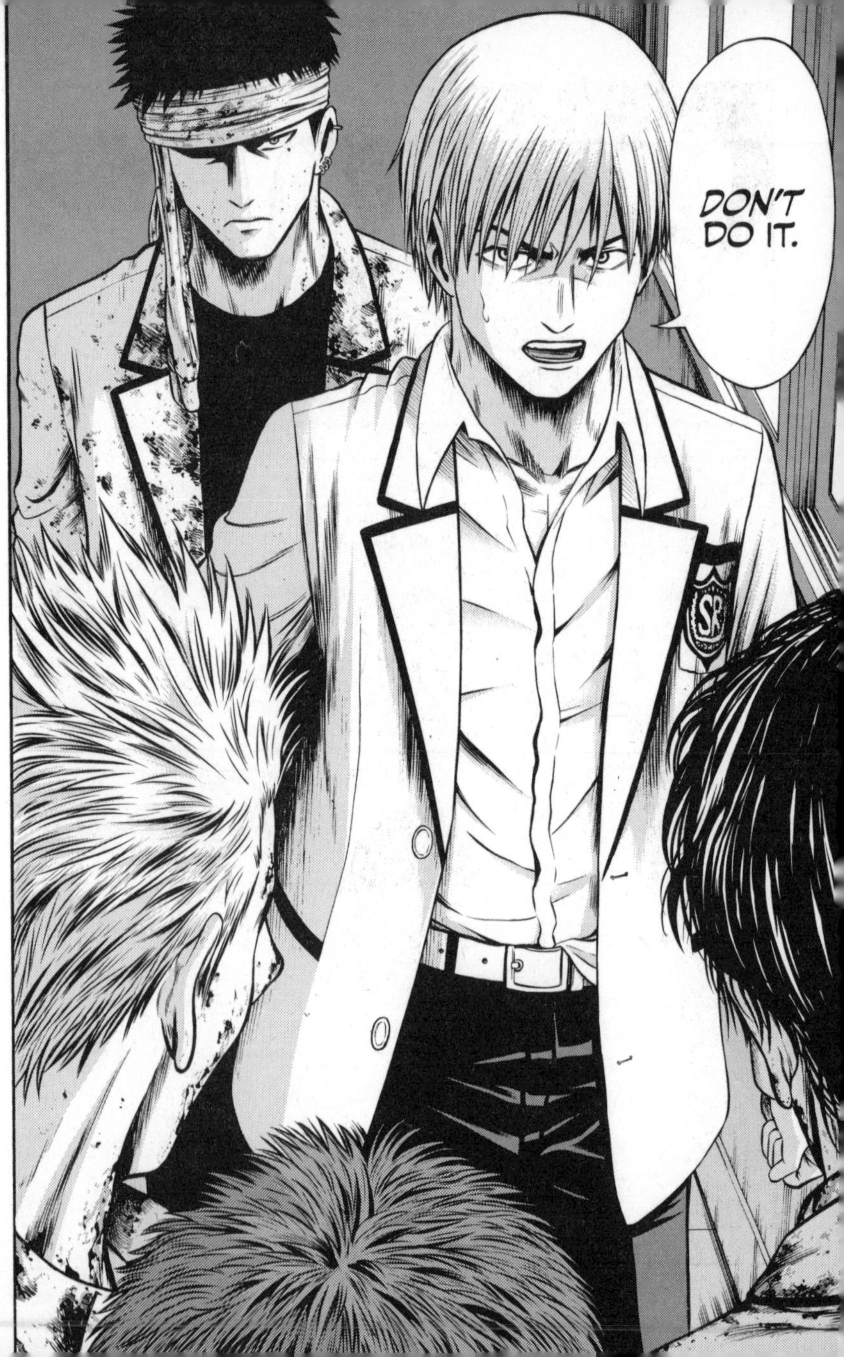
DON'T DO IT.

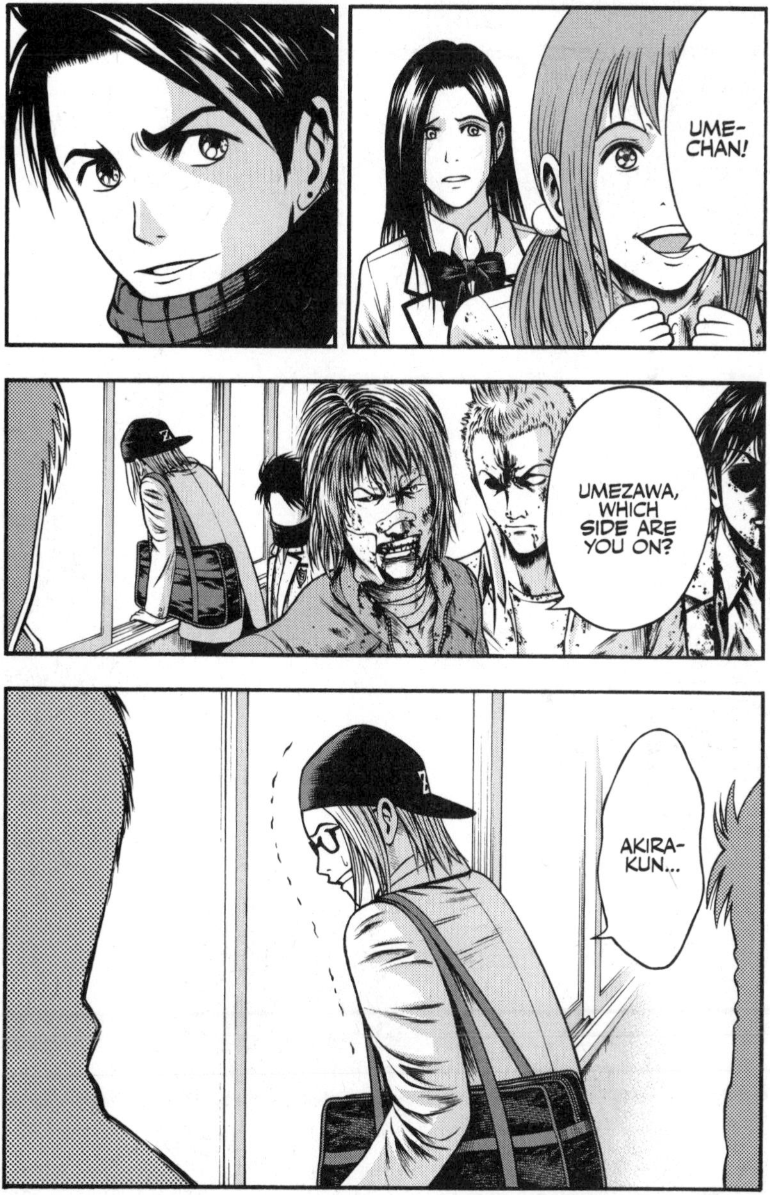
UME-
CHAN!
UMEZAWA, WHICH SIDE ARE YOU ON?
AKIRA-KUN...

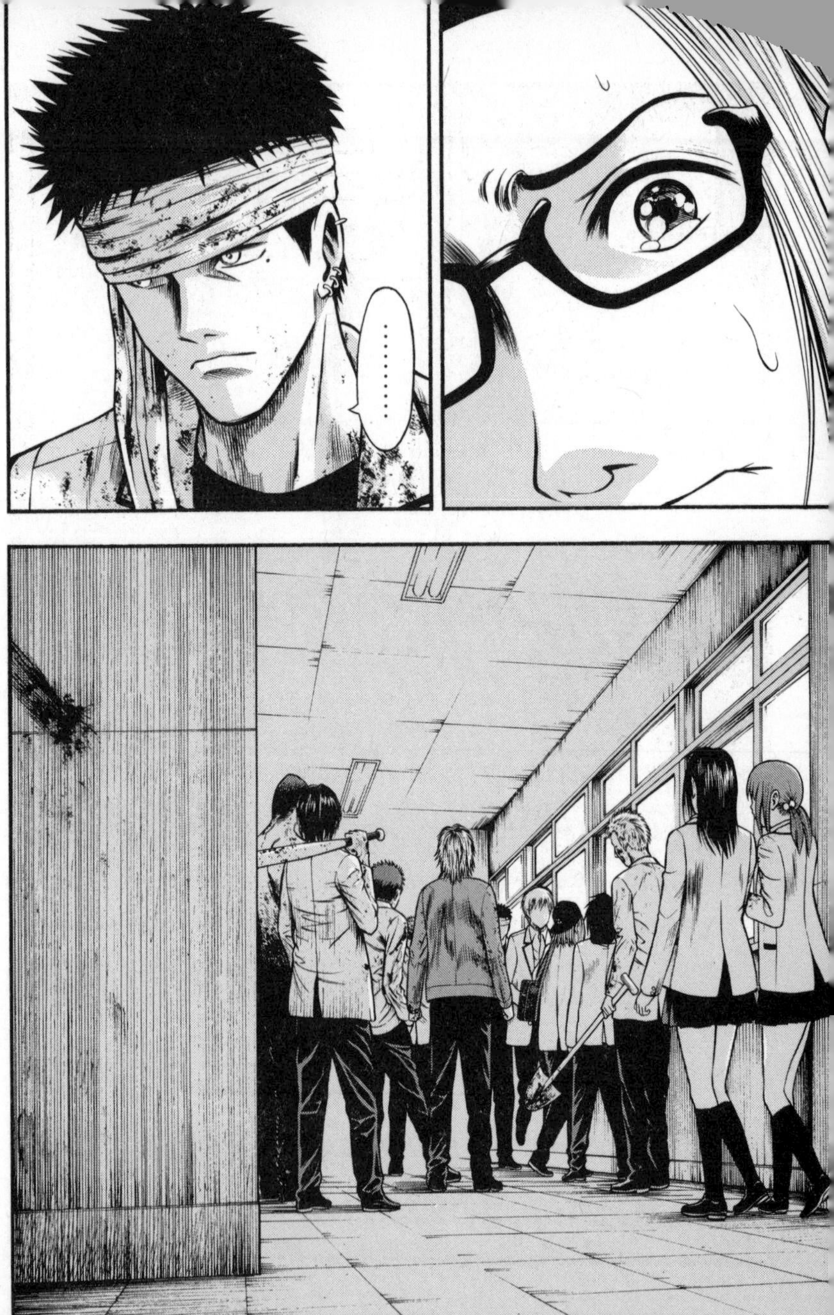
......

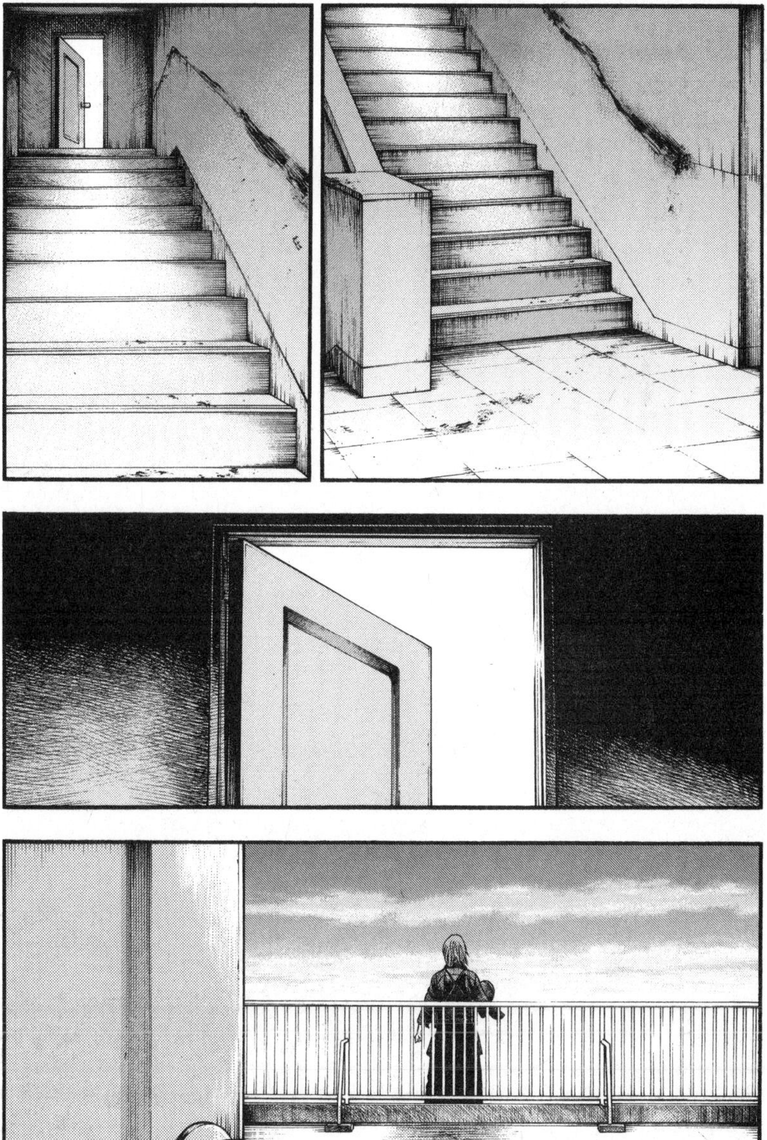

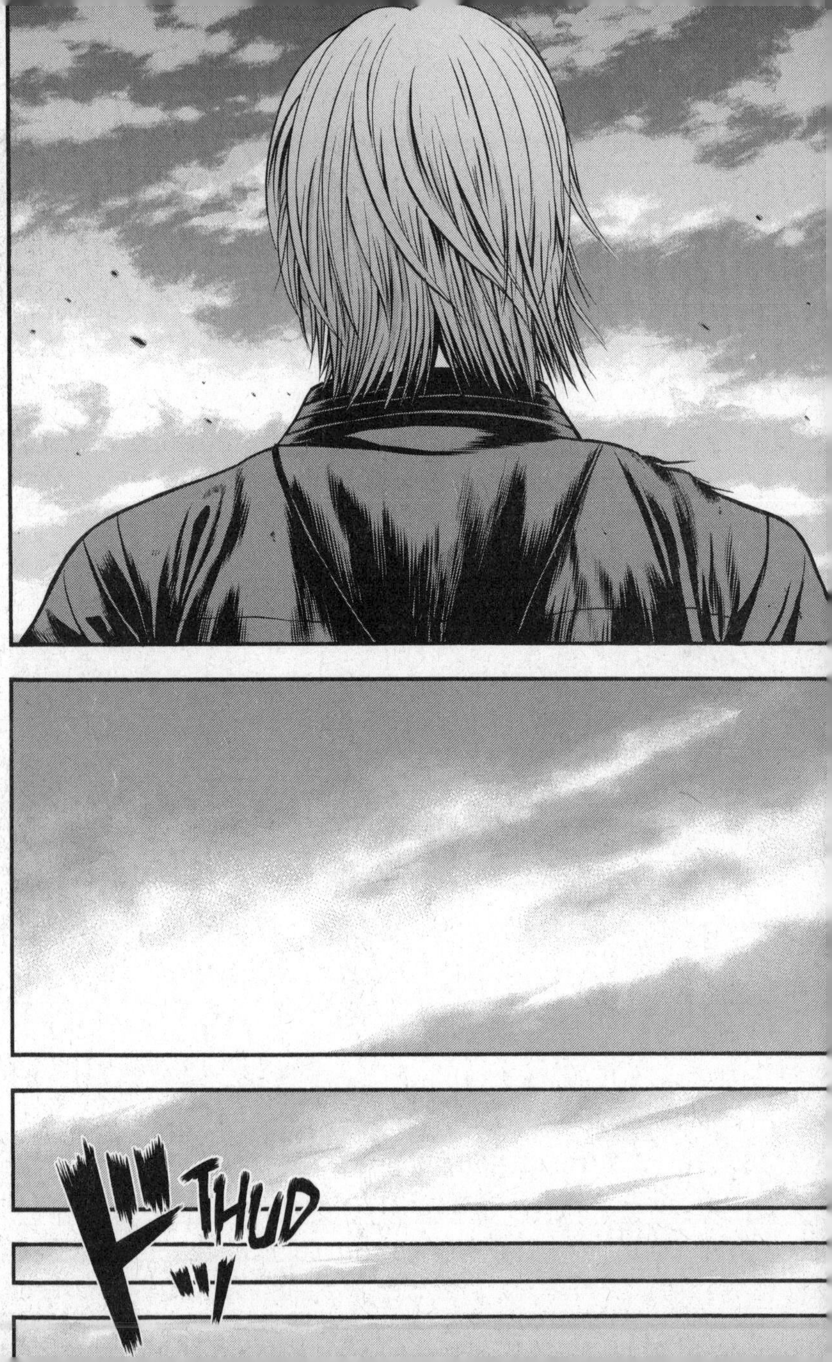
THUD

HOUR OF THE ZOMBIE

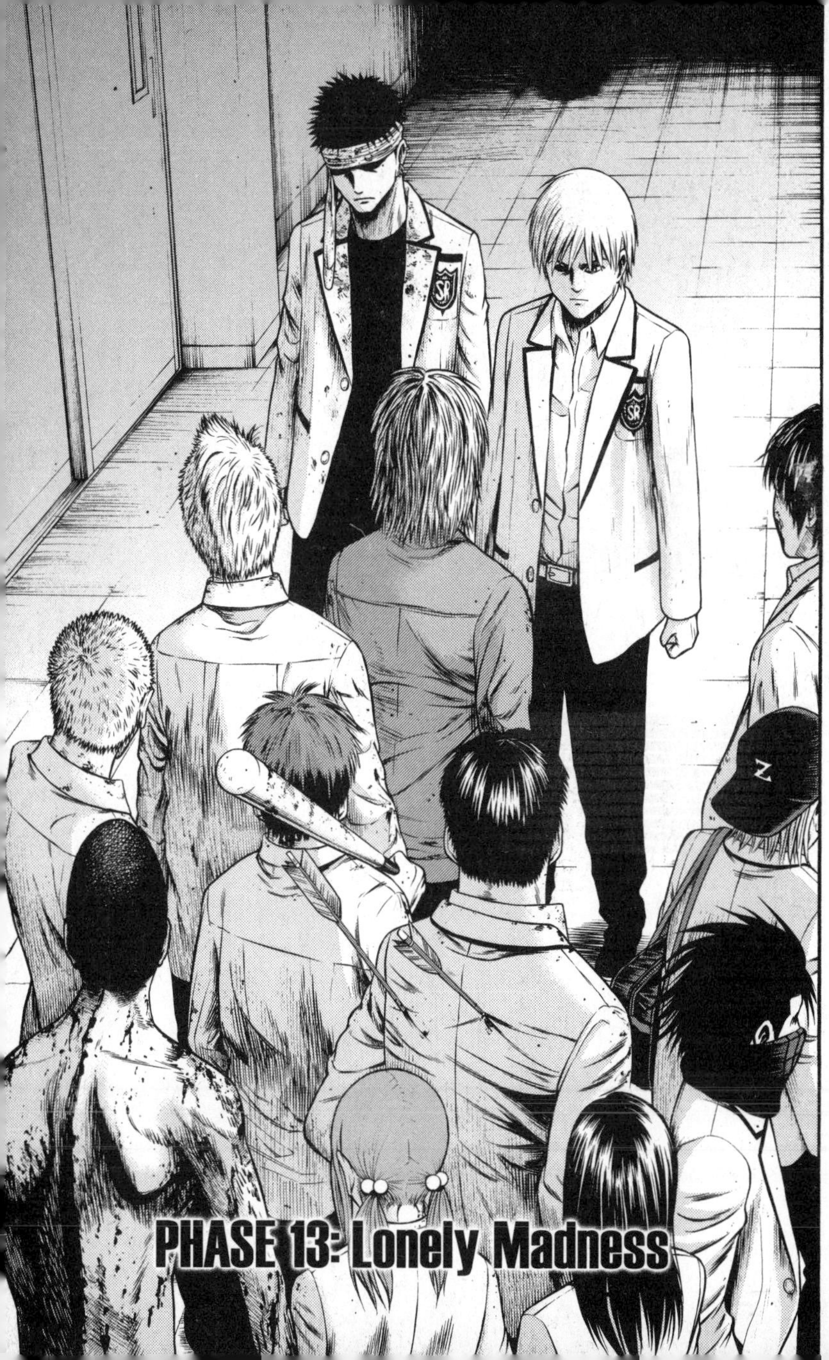
PHASE 13: Lonely Madness

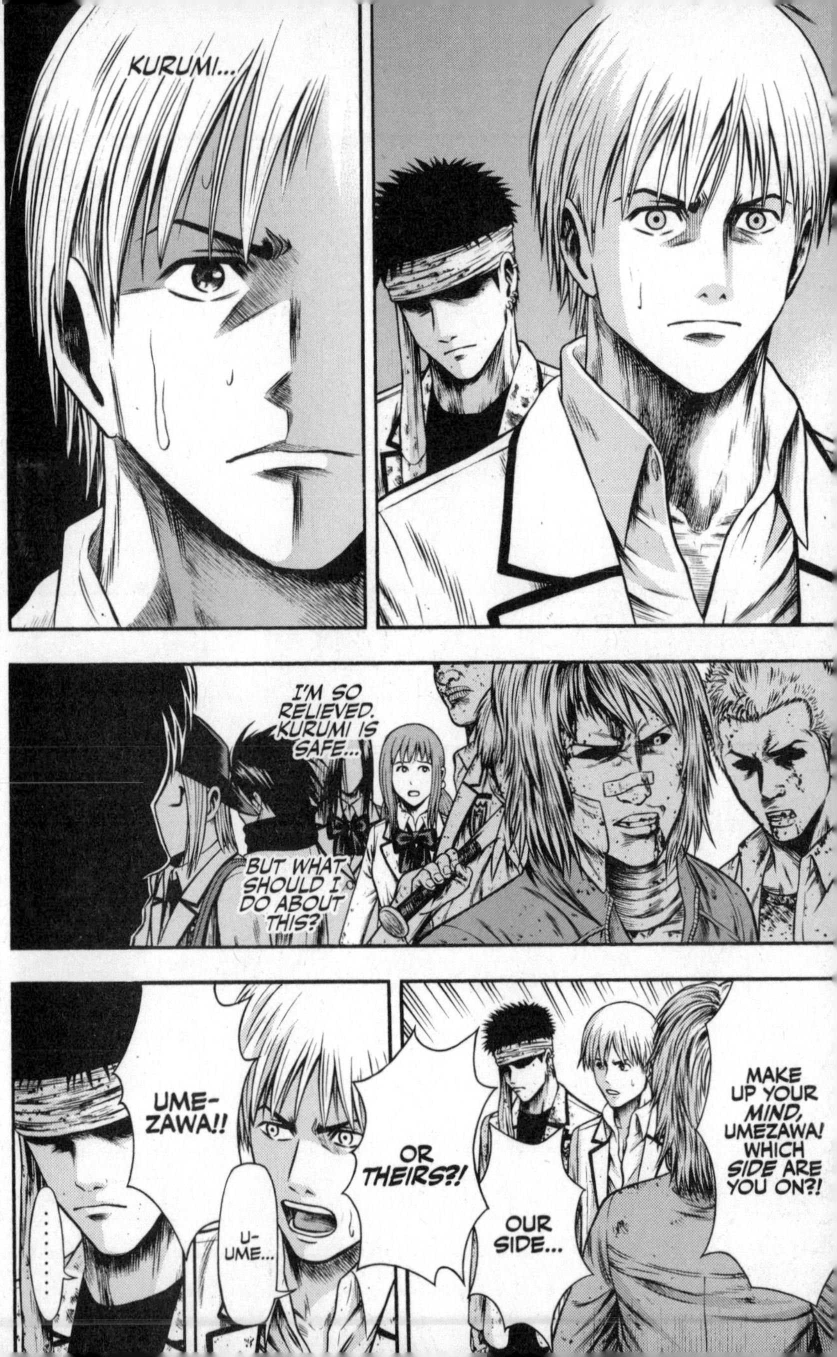
KURUMI...
I'M SO RELIEVED. KURUMI IS SAFE...
BUT WHAT SHOULD I DO ABOUT THIS?
MAKE UP YOUR MIND, UMEZAWA! WHICH SIDE ARE YOU ON?!
OUR SIDE...
OR THEIRS?!
UME-ZAWA!!
U-UME...
......

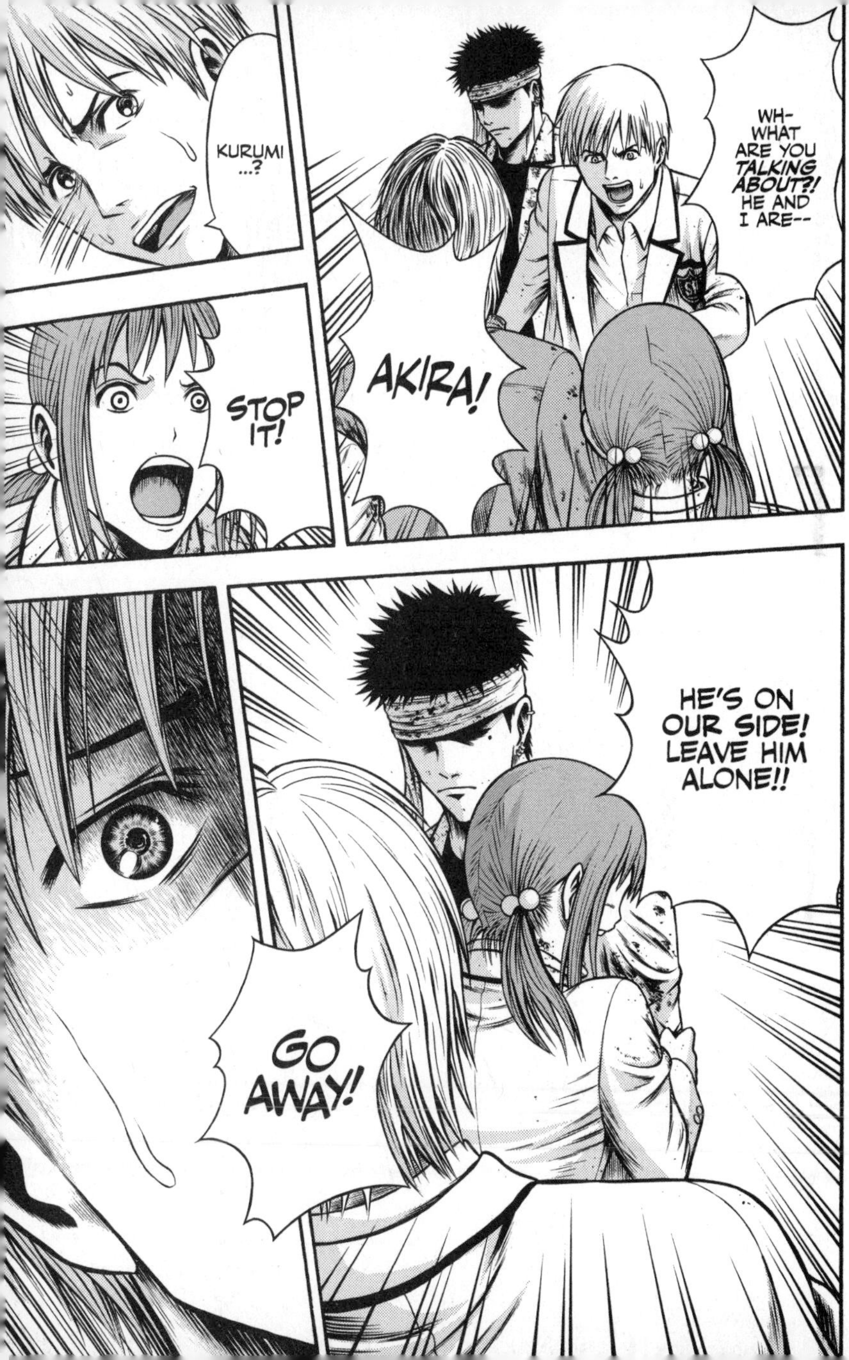
WH- WHAT ARE YOU TALKING ABOUT?! HE AND I ARE--
AKIRA!
KURUMI ...?
STOP IT!
HE'S ON OUR SIDE! LEAVE HIM ALONE!!
GO AWAY!

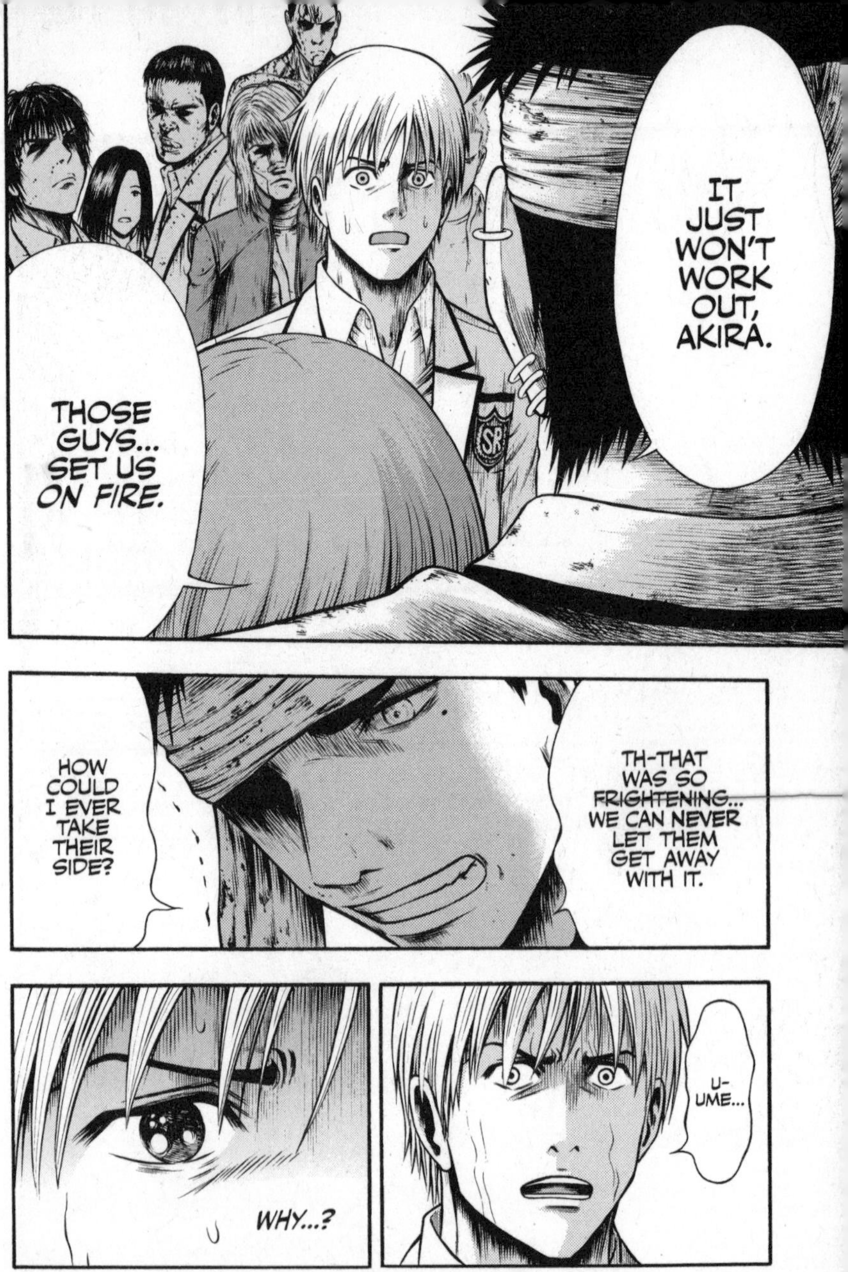
IT JUST WON'T WORK OUT, AKIRA.
THOSE GUYS... SET US ON FIRE.
TH-THAT WAS SO FRIGHTENING... WE CAN NEVER LET THEM GET AWAY WITH IT.
HOW COULD I EVER TAKE THEIR SIDE?
U-UME...
WHY...?

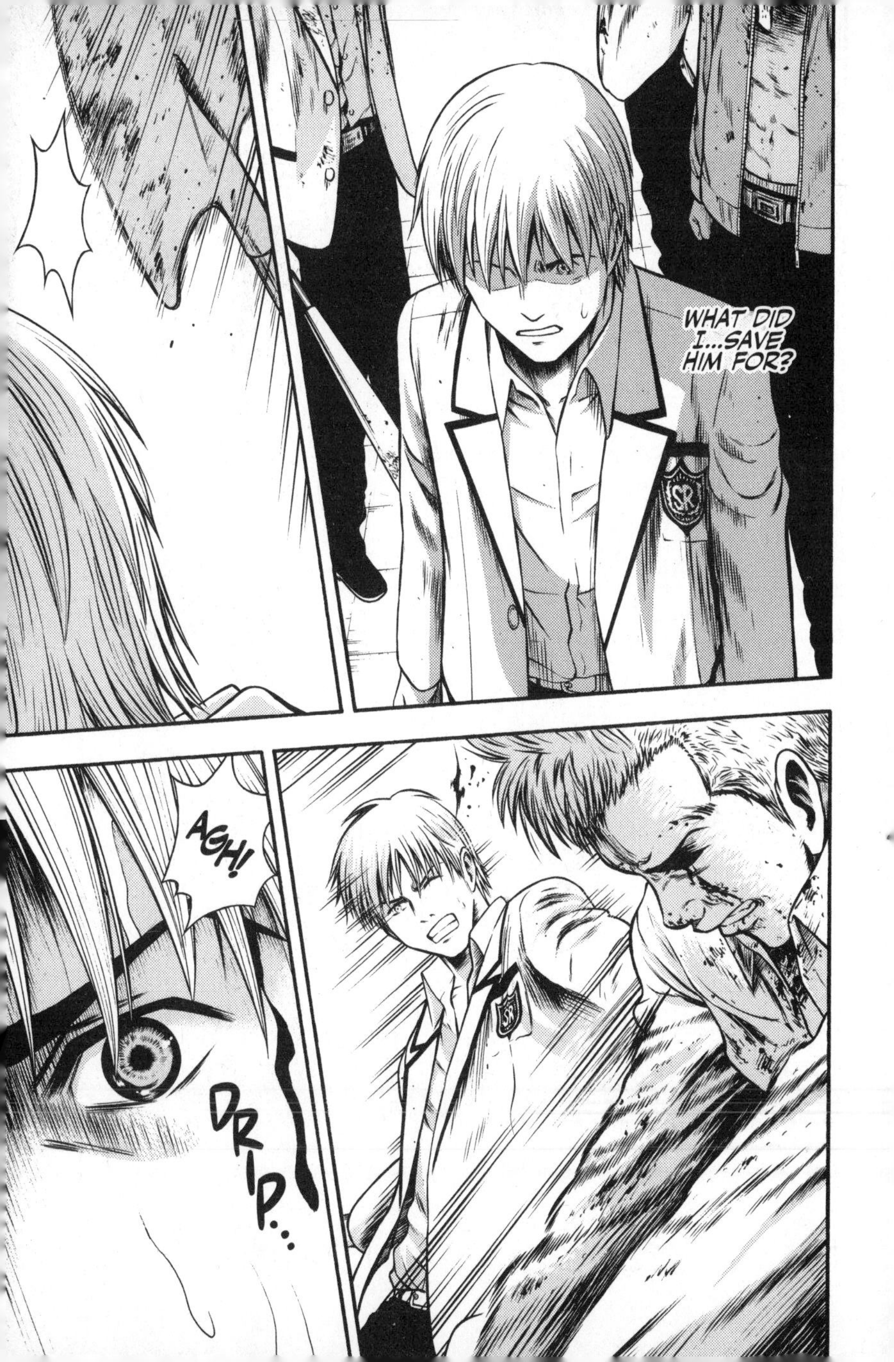
WHAT DID I...SAVE HIM FOR?
AGH!
DRIP...

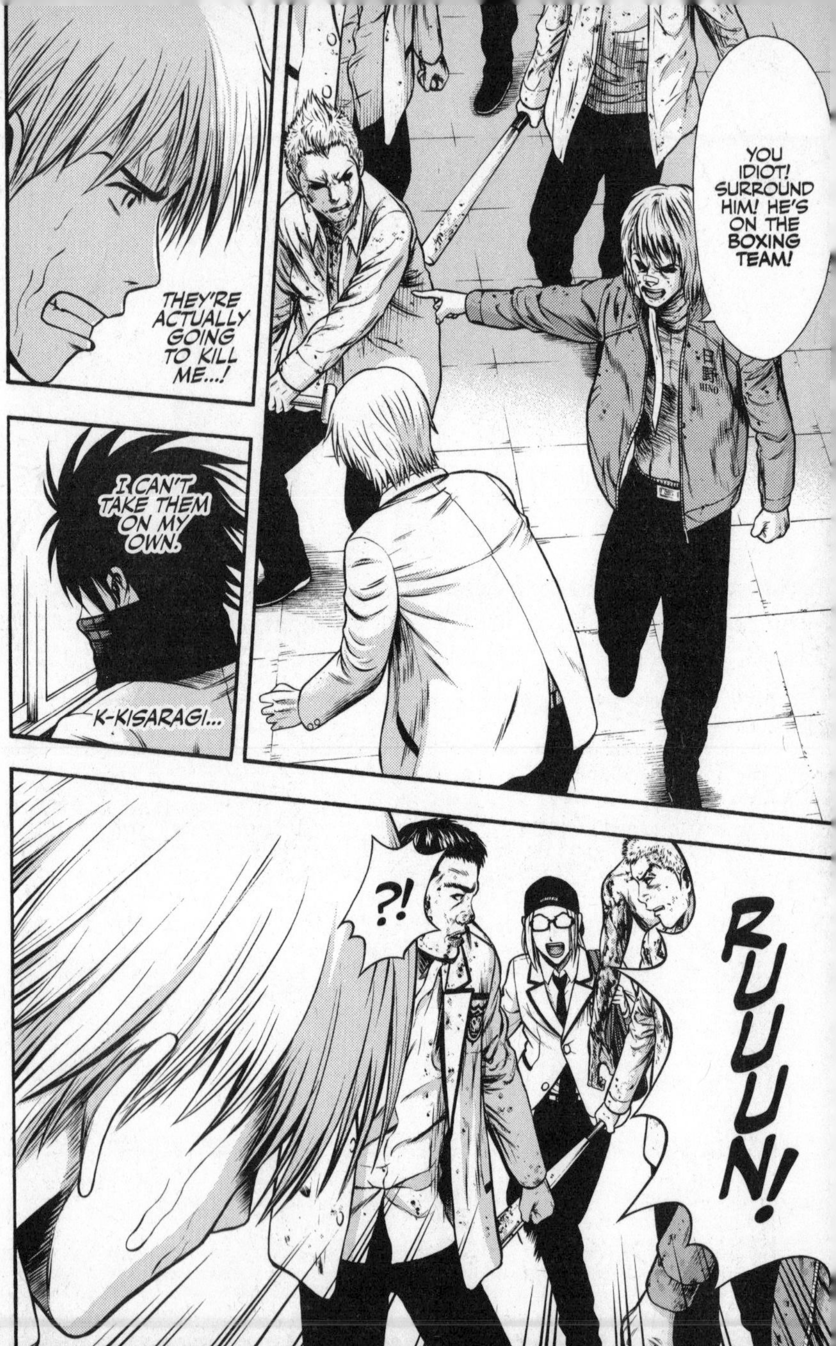
YOU IDIOT! SURROUND HIM! HE'S ON THE BOXING TEAM!
THEY'RE ACTUALLY GOING TO KILL ME...!
I CAN'T TAKE THEM ON MY OWN.
K-KISARAGI...
?!
RUUUN!

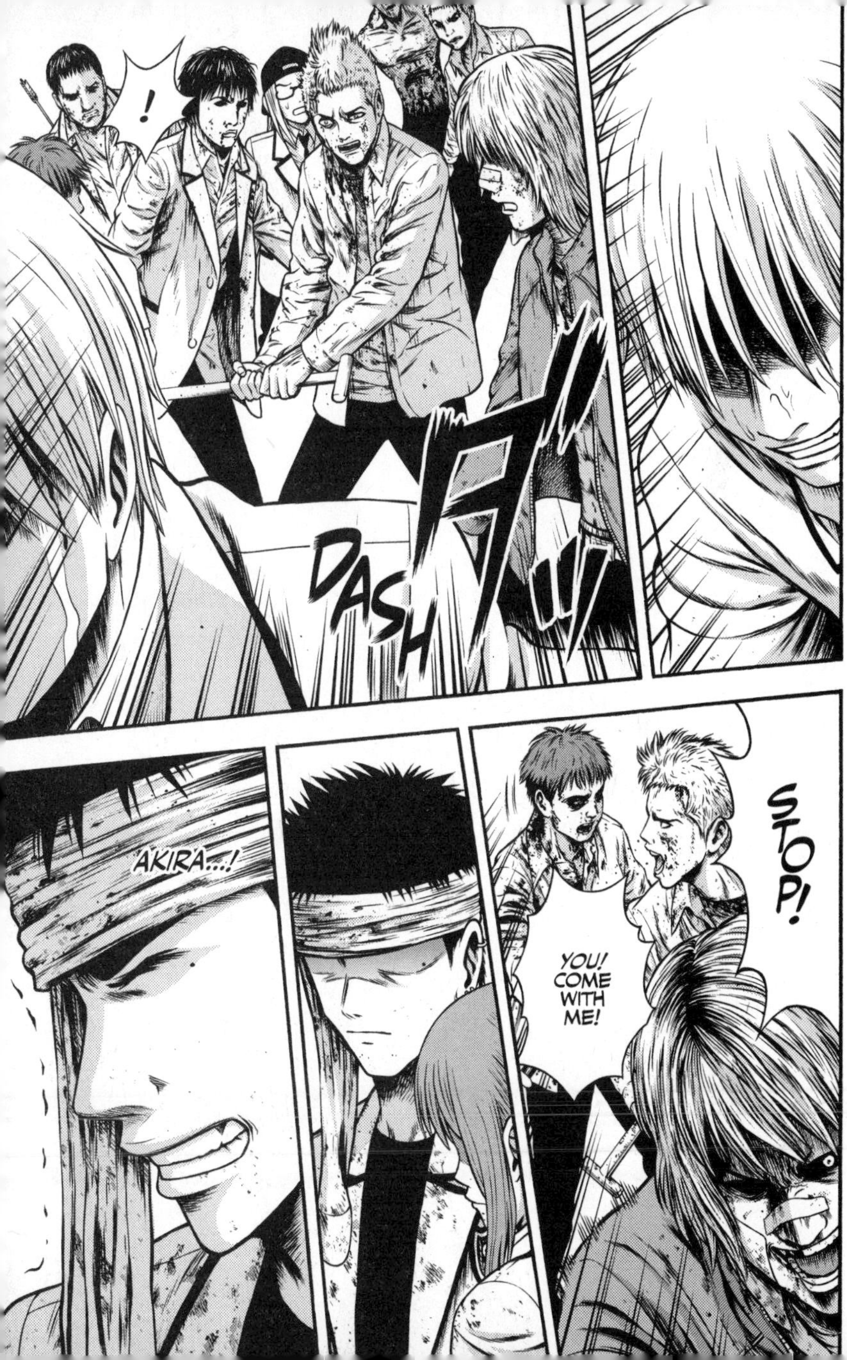
!
DASH
STOP!
YOU! COME WITH ME!
AKIRA...!

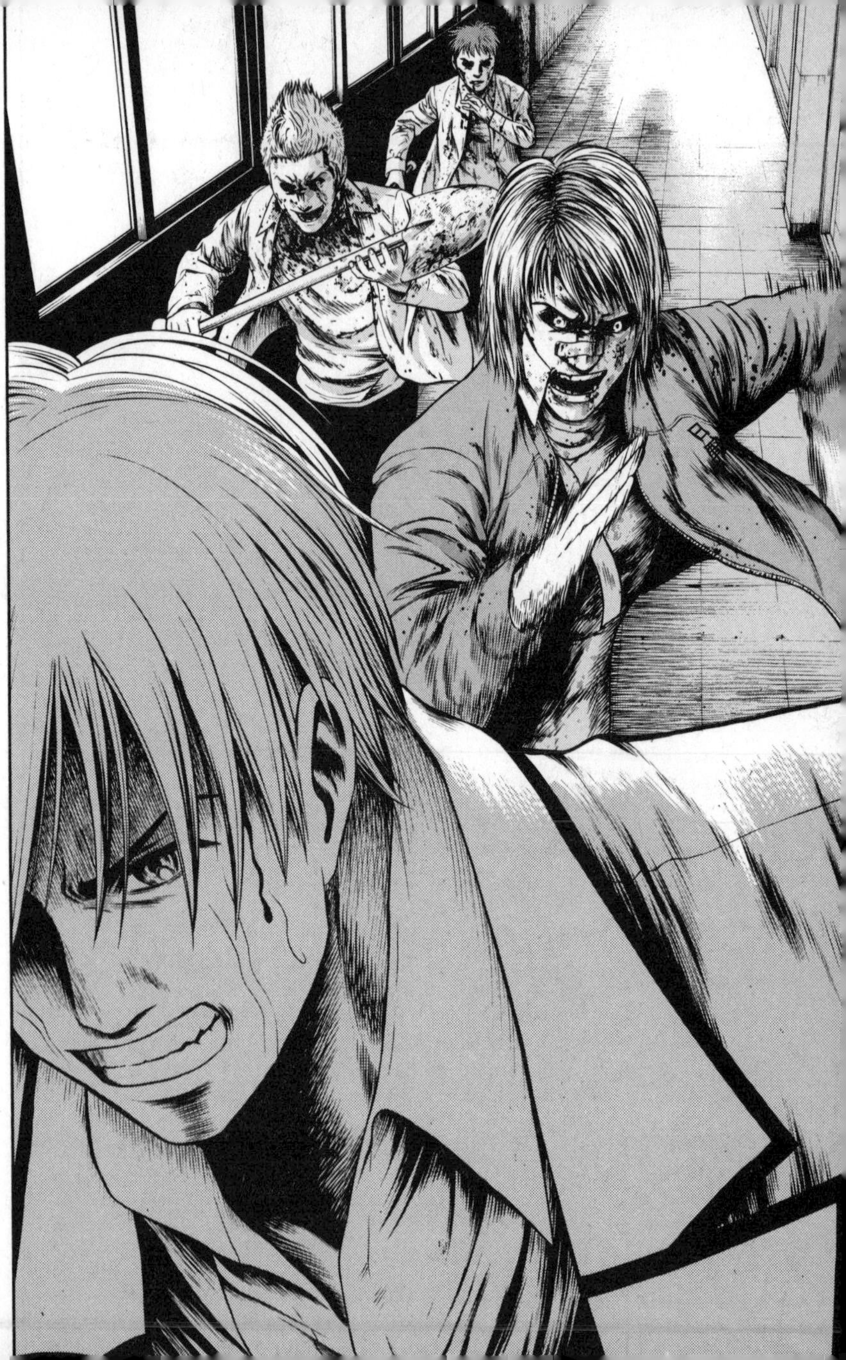

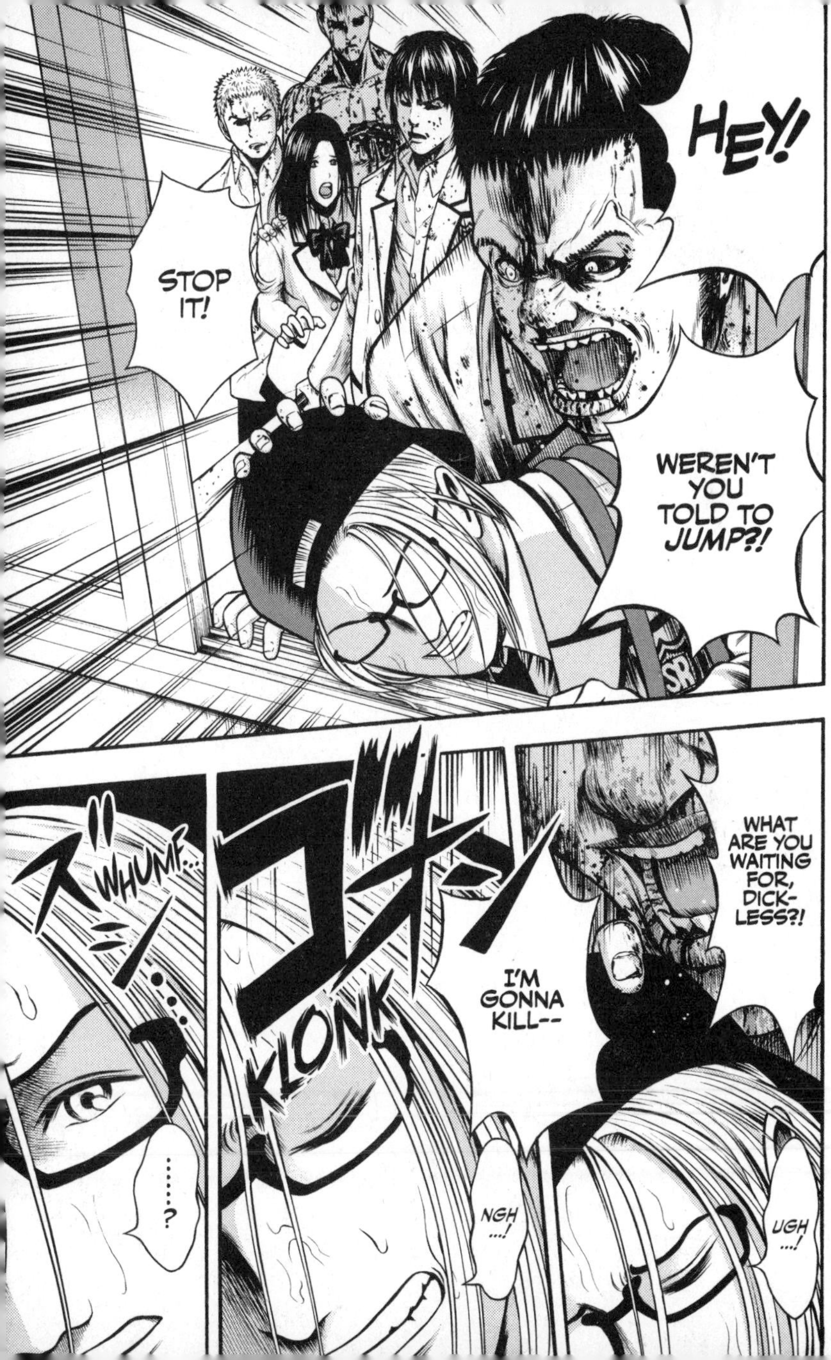
HEY!
WEREN'T YOU TOLD TO JUMP?!
STOP IT!
WHAT ARE YOU WAITING FOR, DICK-LESS?!
I'M GONNA KILL--
UGH ...!
KLONK
NGH ...!
WHUMF...
......?

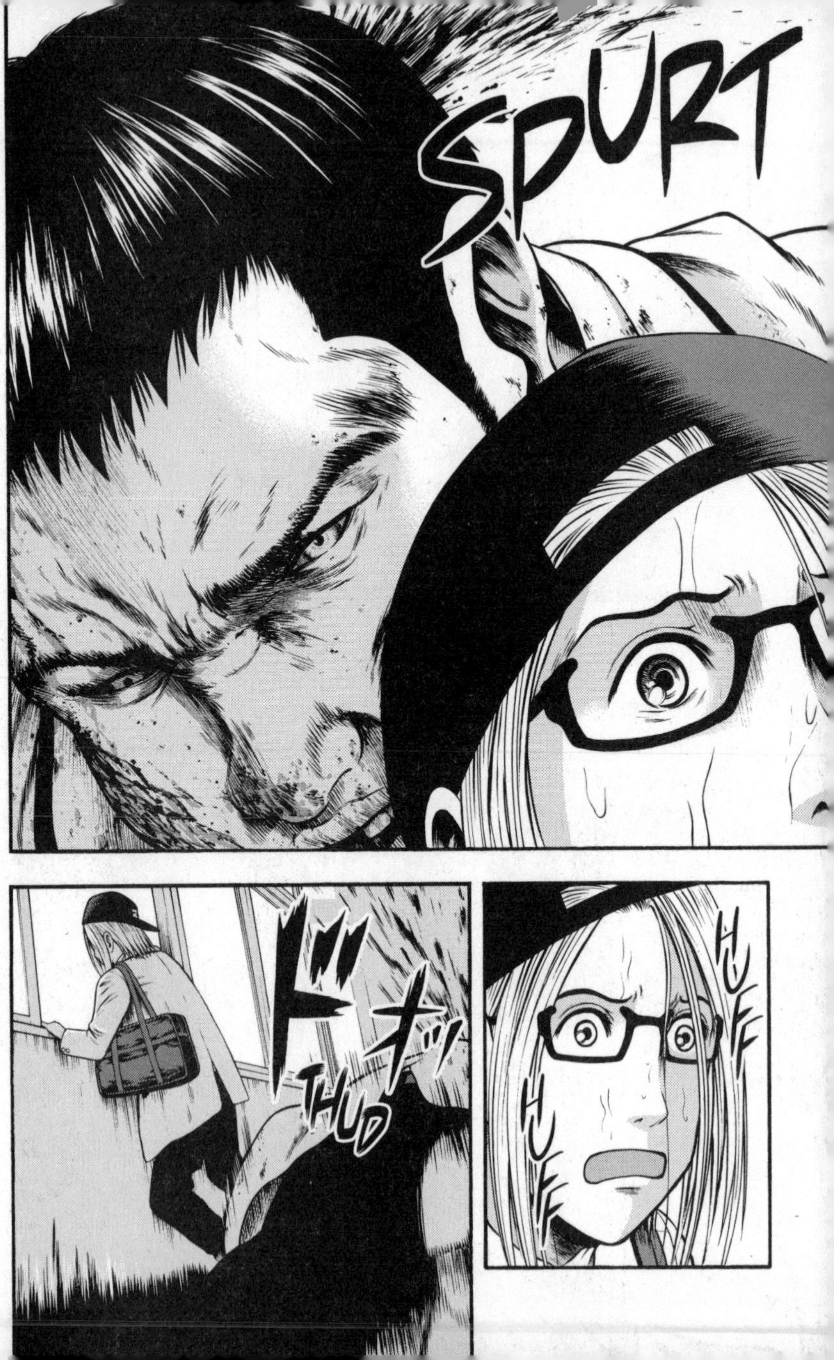
SPURT
HUFF HUFF
HUFF HUFF
ドオッ
THUD

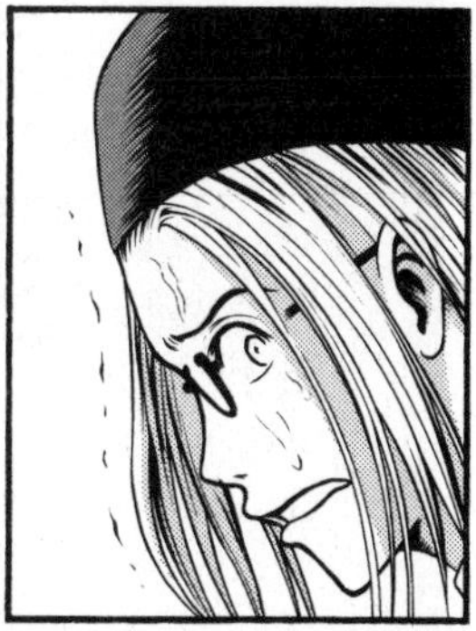
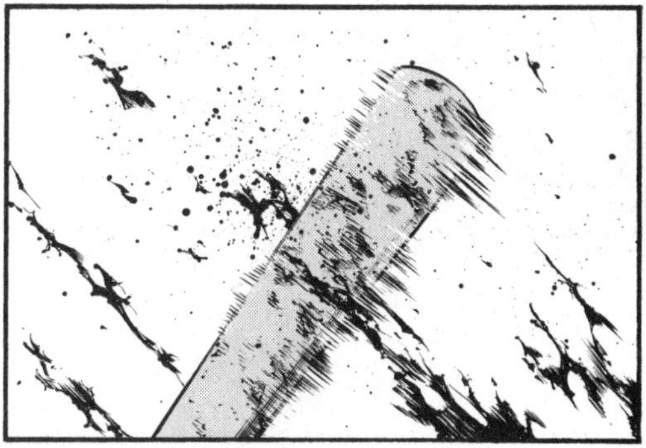
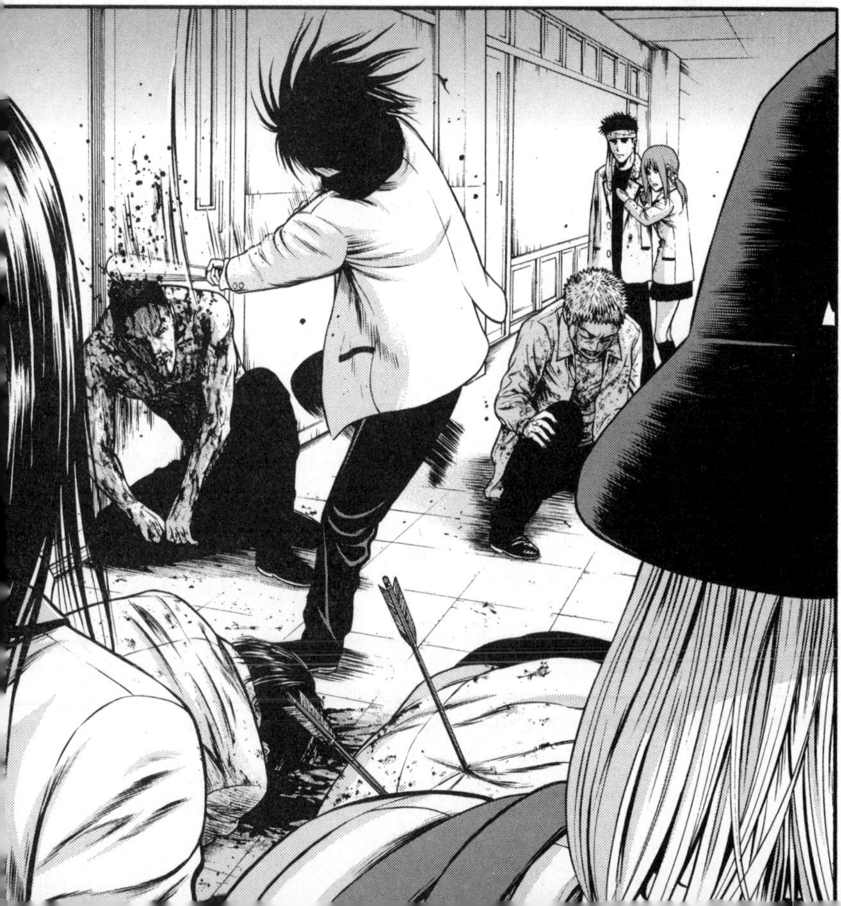

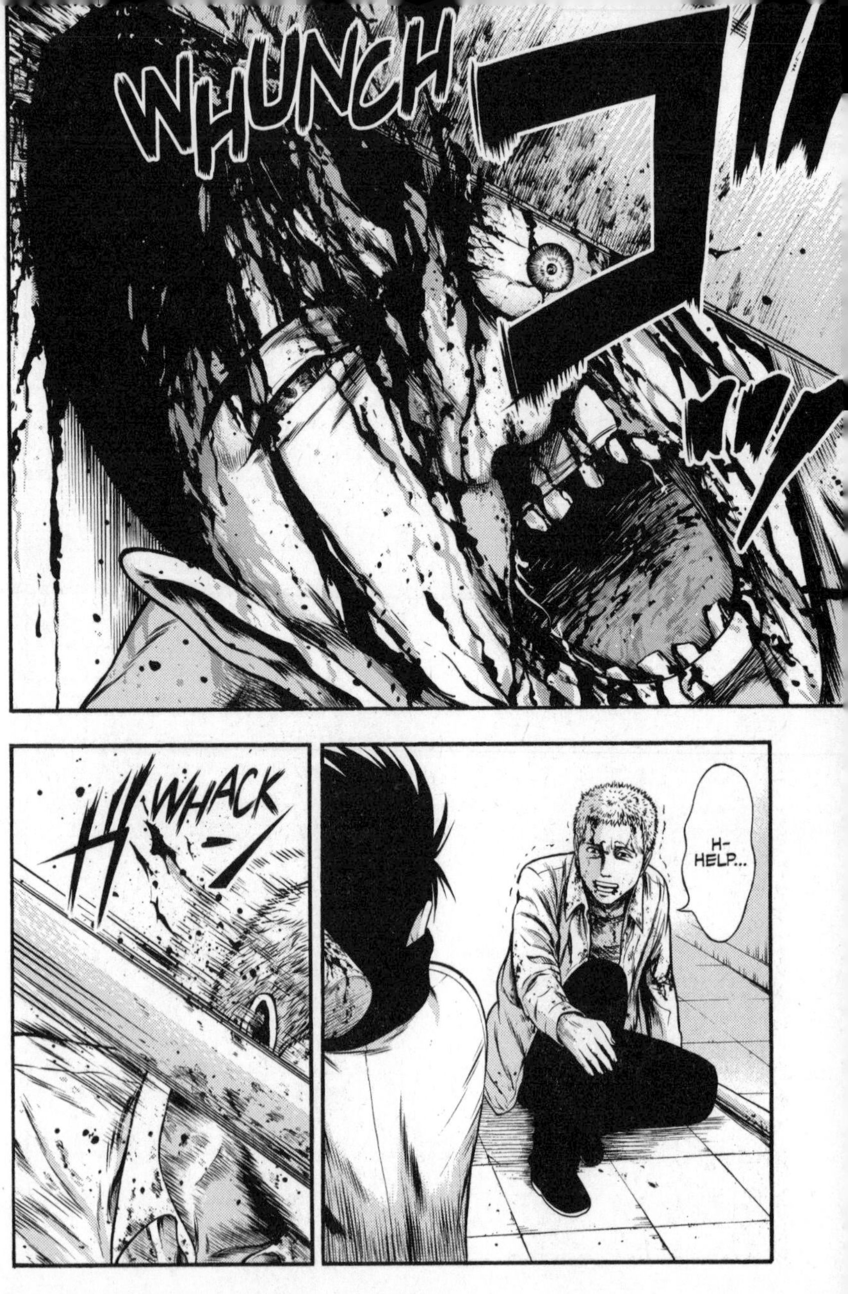
WHUNCH
H-
HELP...
WHACK

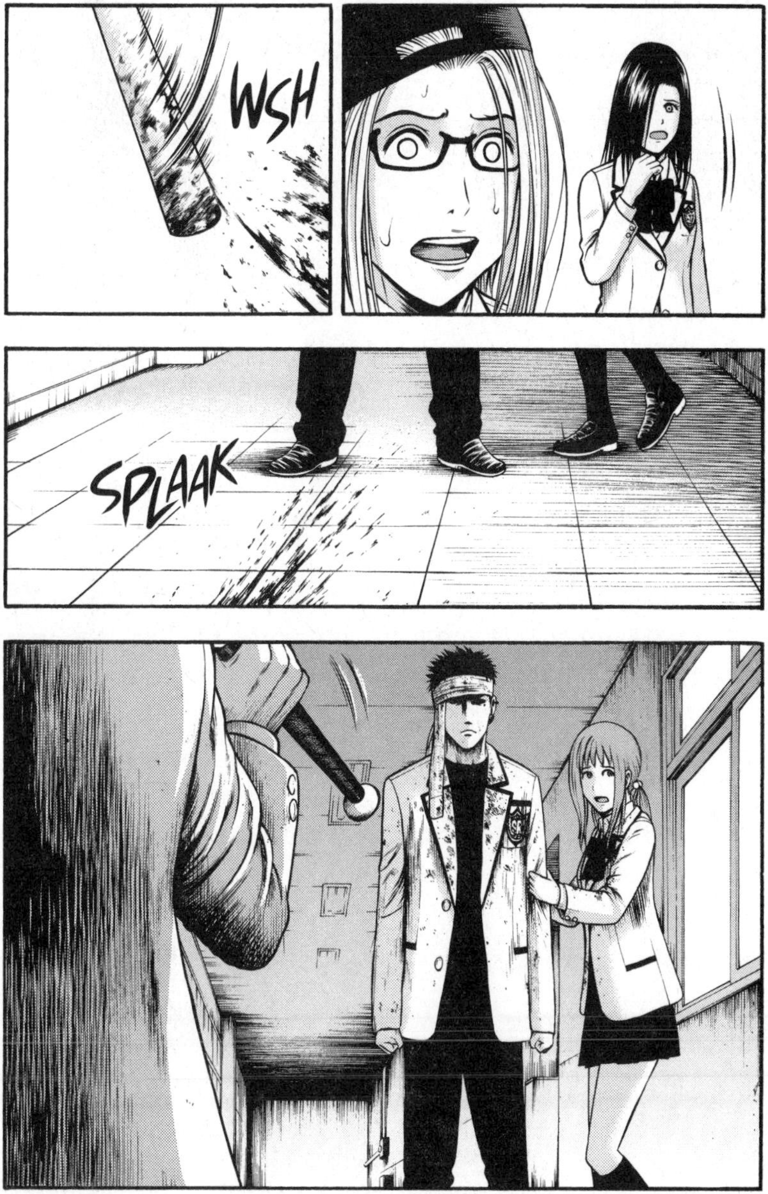
WSH
SPLAAK

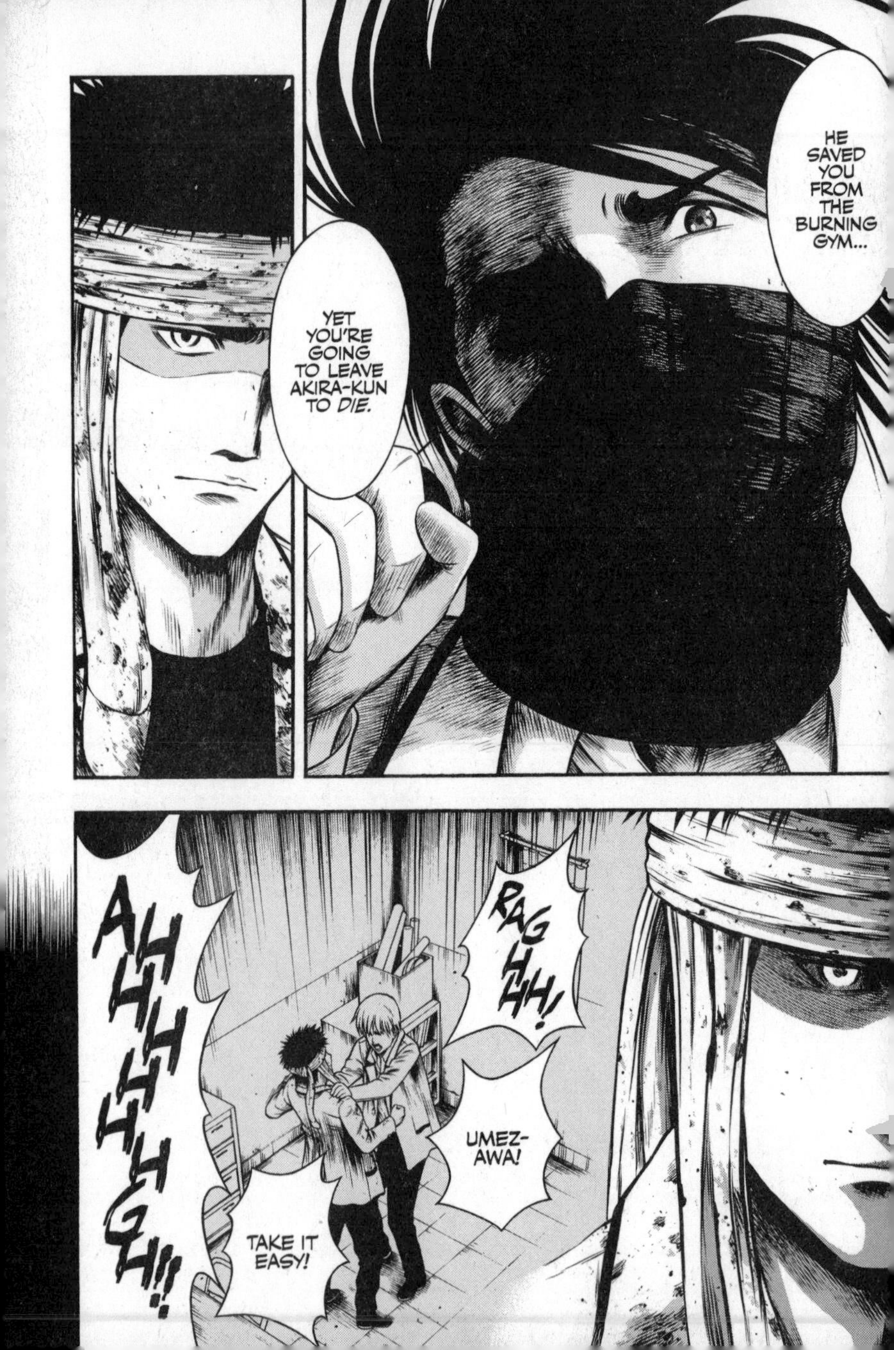
HE SAVED YOU FROM THE BURNING GYM...
YET YOU'RE GOING TO LEAVE AKIRA-KUN TO *DIE*.
RAGHHH!
UMEZ-AWA!
TAKE IT EASY!
AHHHHHHHHGH!!!

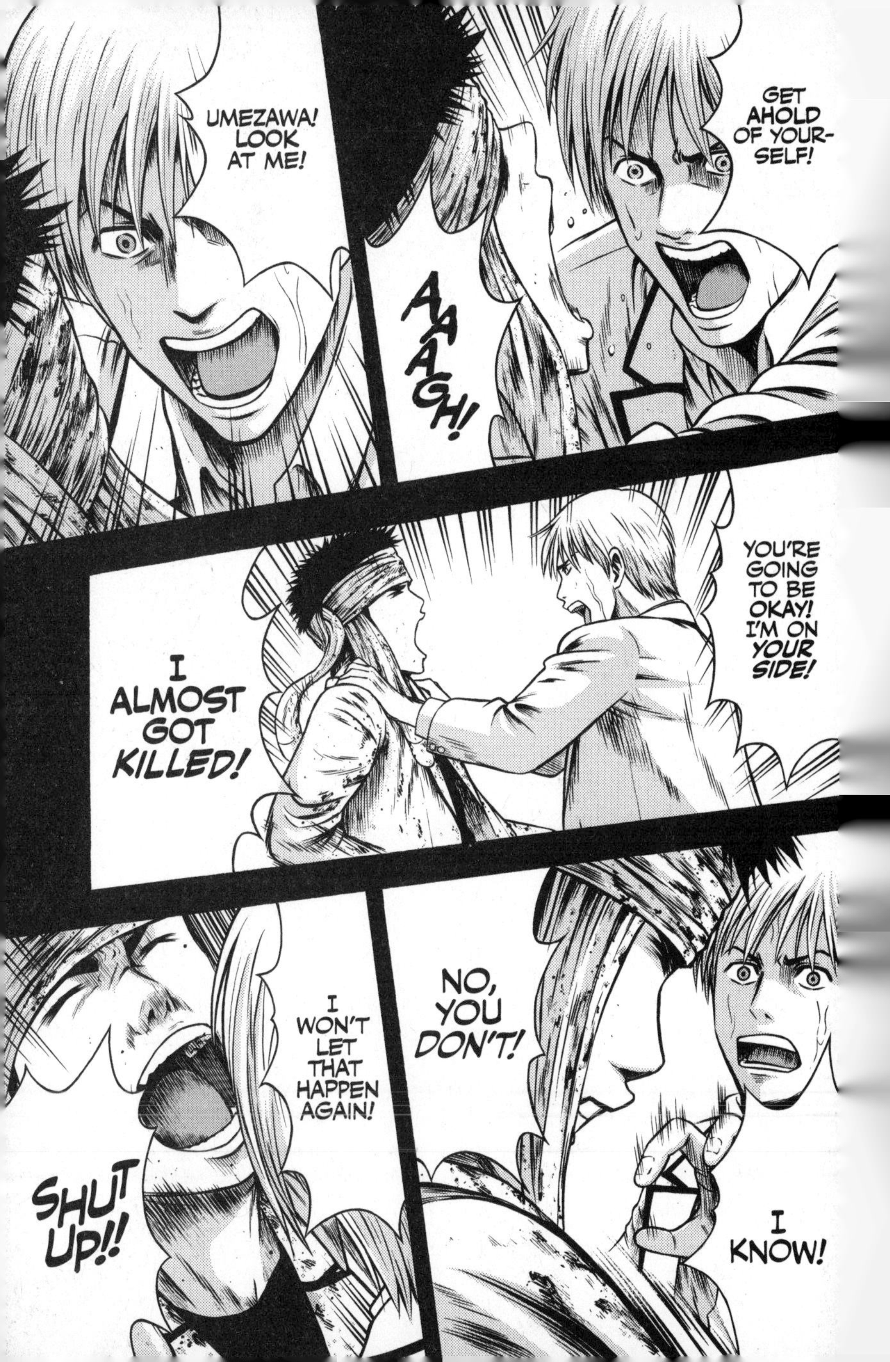
GET AHOLD OF YOUR-SELF!
AAAGH!
UMEZAWA! LOOK AT ME!
YOU'RE GOING TO BE OKAY! I'M ON YOUR SIDE!
I ALMOST GOT KILLED!
I KNOW!
NO, YOU DON'T!
I WON'T LET THAT HAPPEN AGAIN!
SHUT UP!!

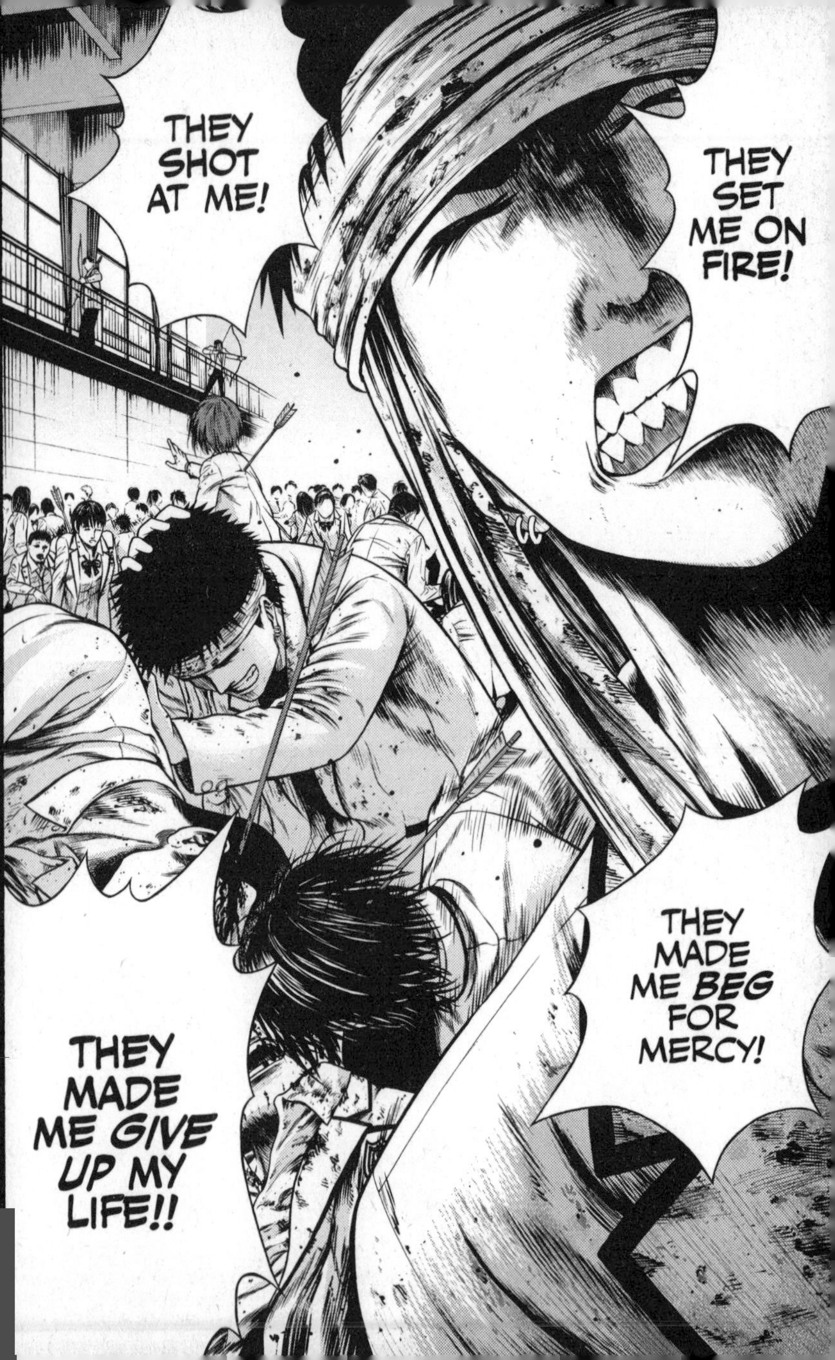
THEY SET ME ON FIRE!
THEY SHOT AT ME!
THEY MADE ME BEG FOR MERCY!
THEY MADE ME GIVE UP MY LIFE!!

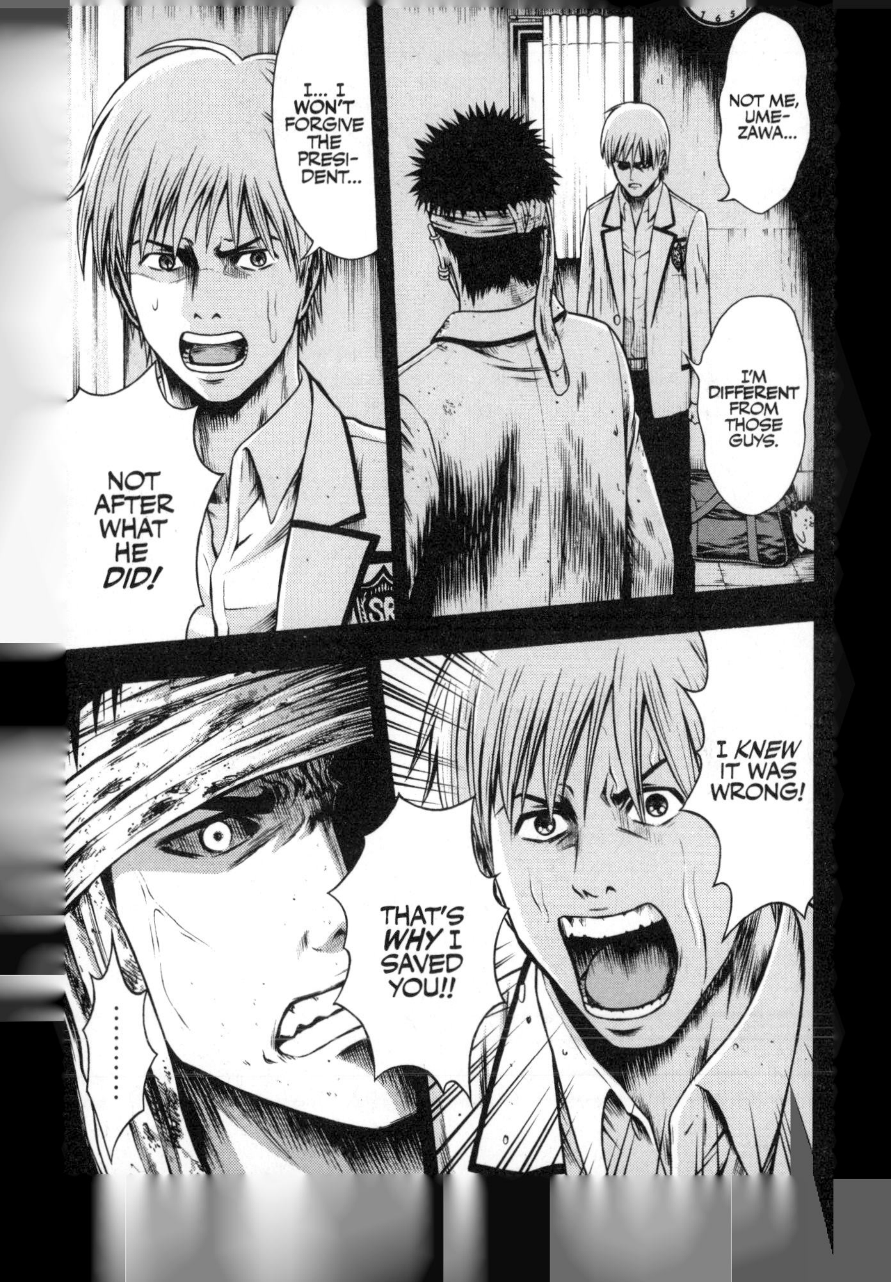
NOT ME, UME-ZAWA...
I'M DIFFERENT FROM THOSE GUYS.
I... I WON'T FORGIVE THE PRESI-DENT...
NOT AFTER WHAT HE *DID*!
I *KNEW* IT WAS WRONG!
THAT'S *WHY* I SAVED YOU!!
......

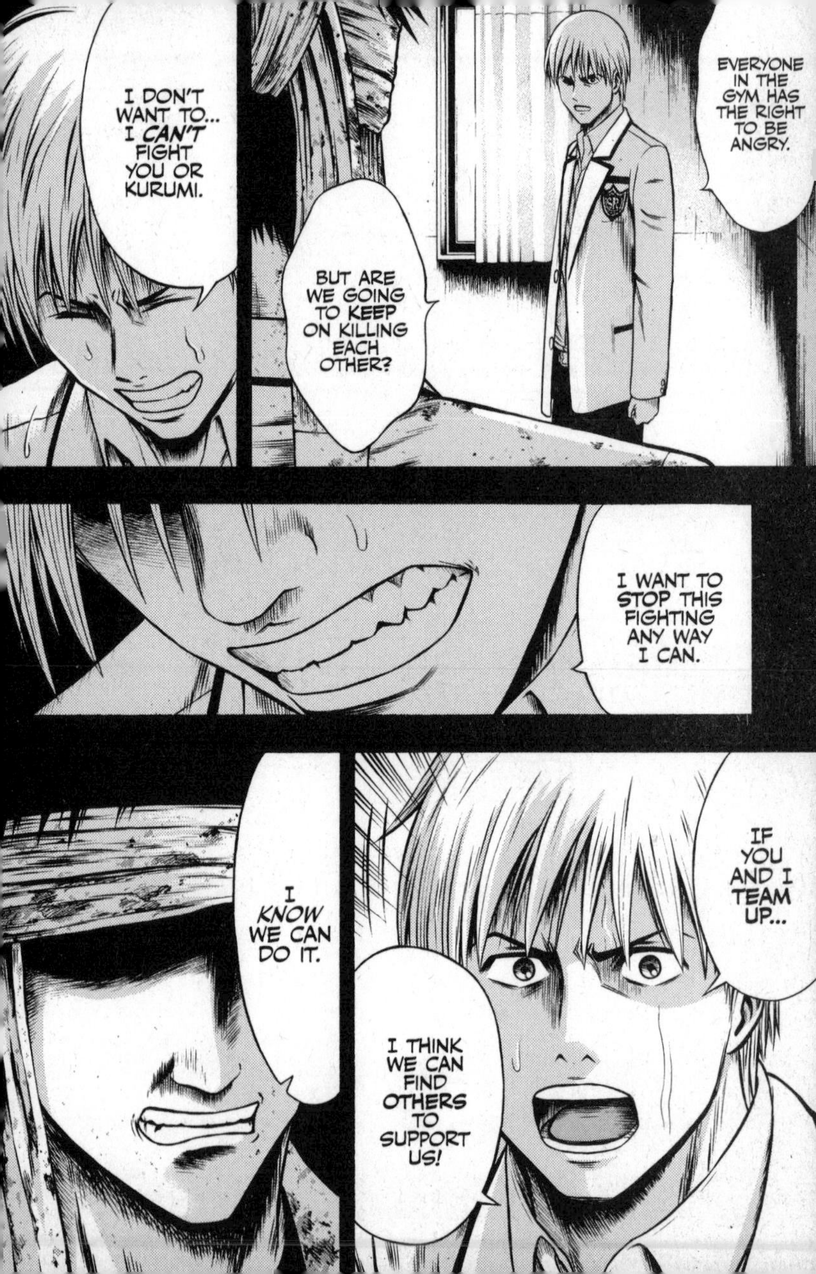
EVERYONE IN THE GYM HAS THE RIGHT TO BE ANGRY.
BUT ARE WE GOING TO KEEP ON KILLING EACH OTHER?
I DON'T WANT TO... I *CAN'T* FIGHT YOU OR KURUMI.
I WANT TO STOP THIS FIGHTING ANY WAY I CAN.
IF YOU AND I TEAM UP...
I THINK WE CAN FIND OTHERS TO SUPPORT US!
I *KNOW* WE CAN DO IT.

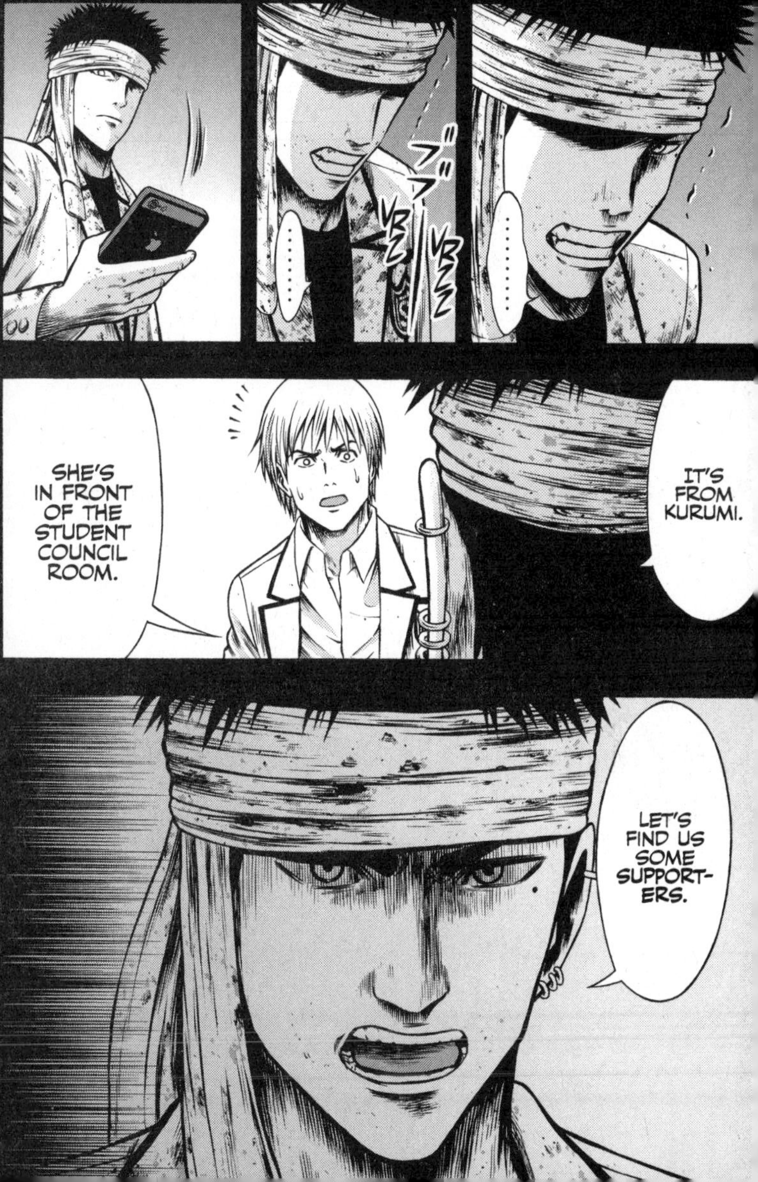
……
……
ブブ
VRZZ
VRZZ
IT'S FROM KURUMI.
SHE'S IN FRONT OF THE STUDENT COUNCIL ROOM.
LET'S FIND US SOME SUPPORTERS.

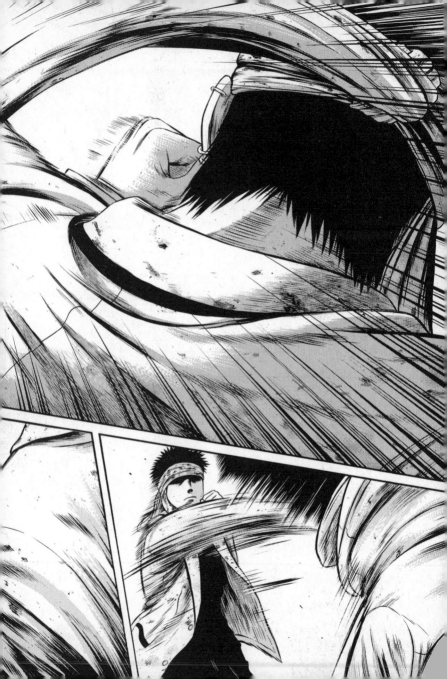

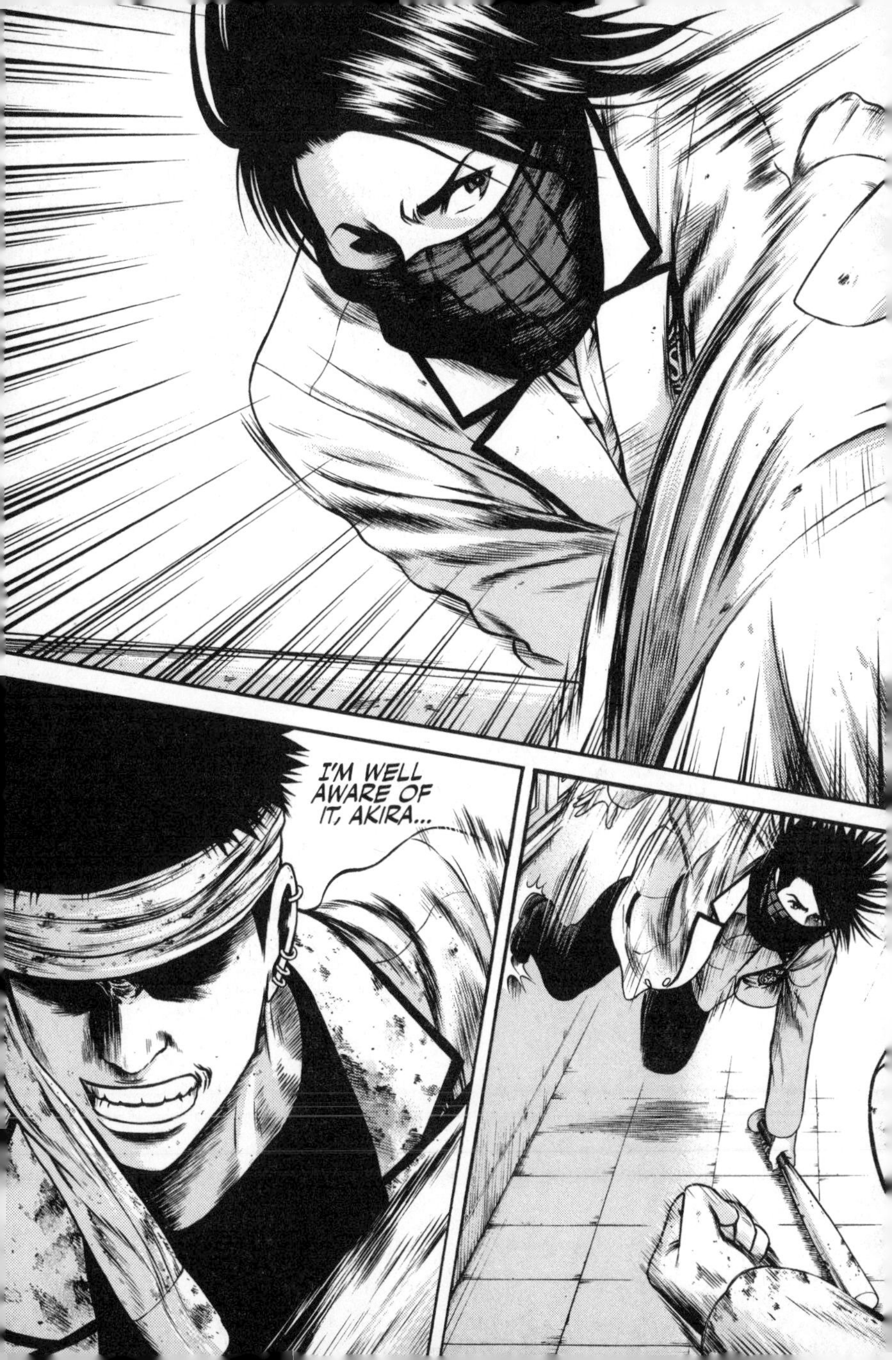
I'M WELL AWARE OF IT, AKIRA...

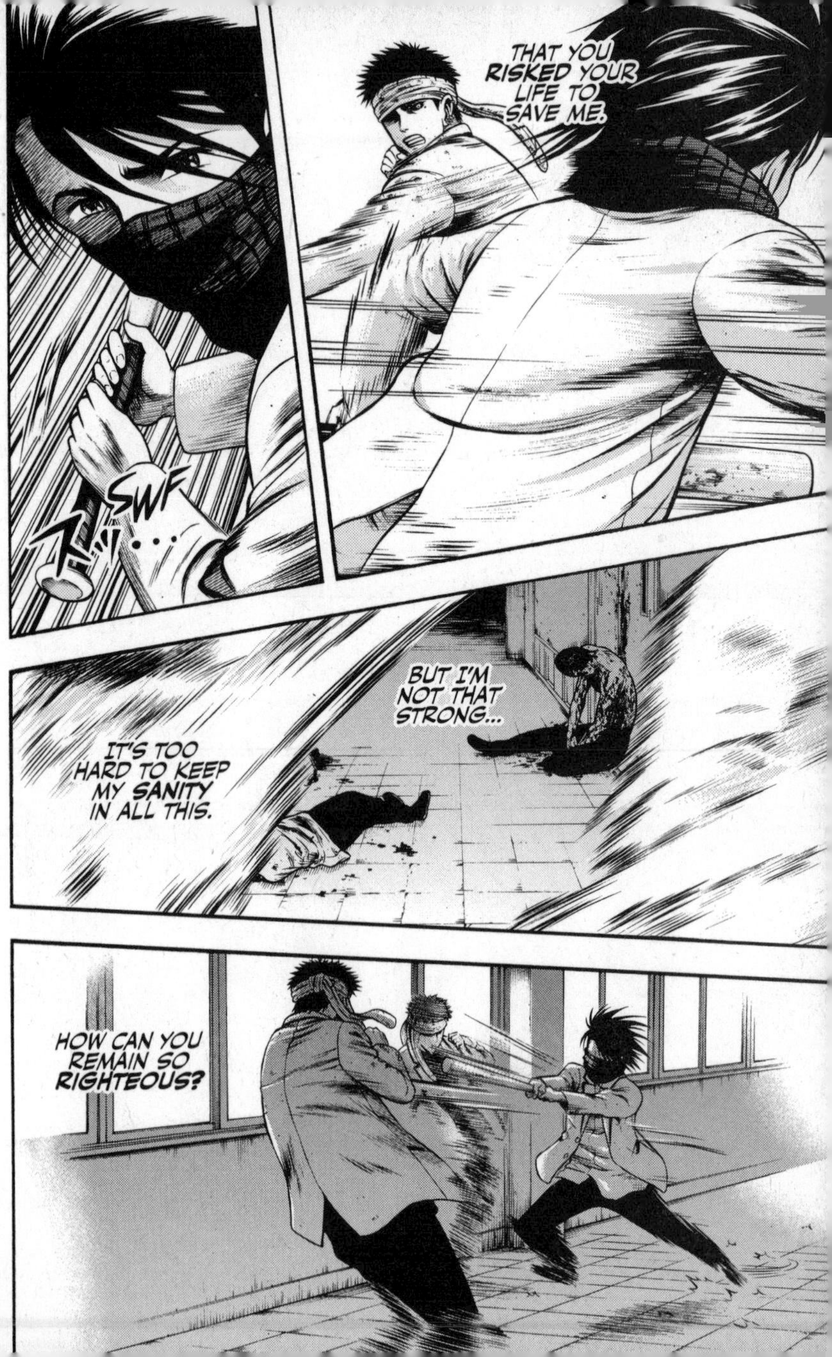
THAT YOU RISKED YOUR LIFE TO SAVE ME.
SWF
...
BUT I'M NOT THAT STRONG...
IT'S TOO HARD TO KEEP MY SANITY IN ALL THIS.
HOW CAN YOU REMAIN SO RIGHTEOUS?

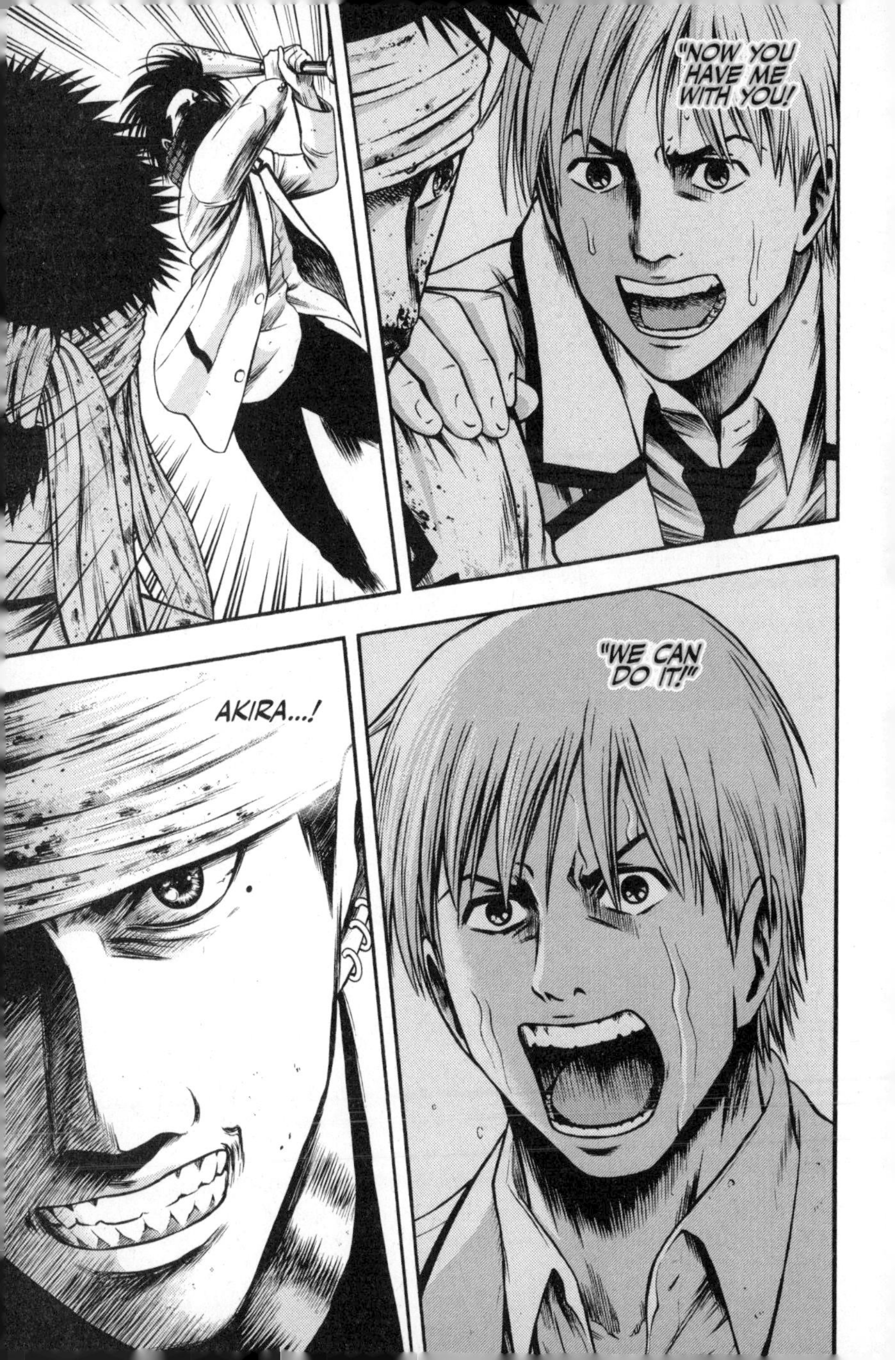
"NOW YOU HAVE ME WITH YOU!
"WE CAN DO IT!"
AKIRA...!

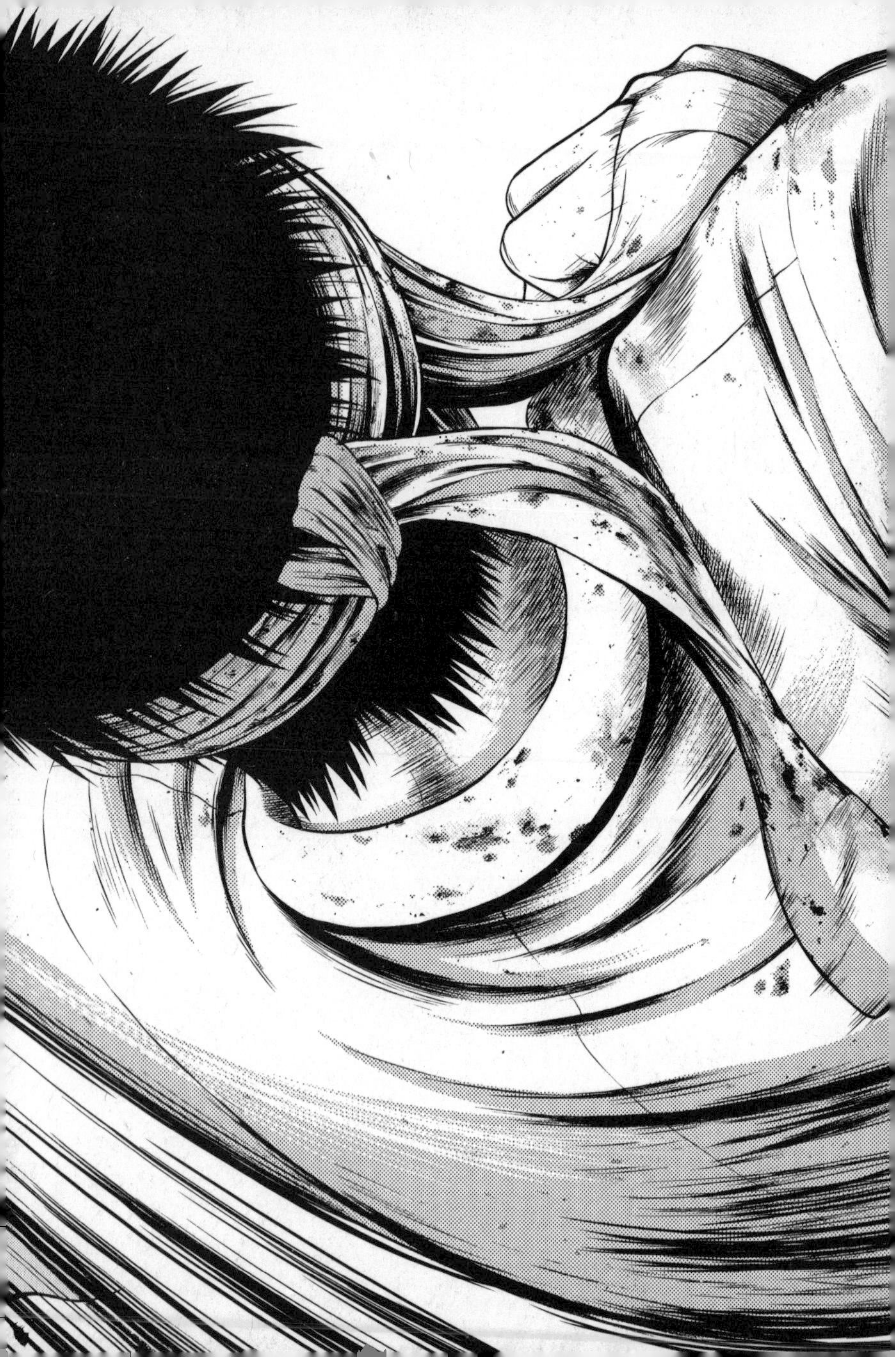

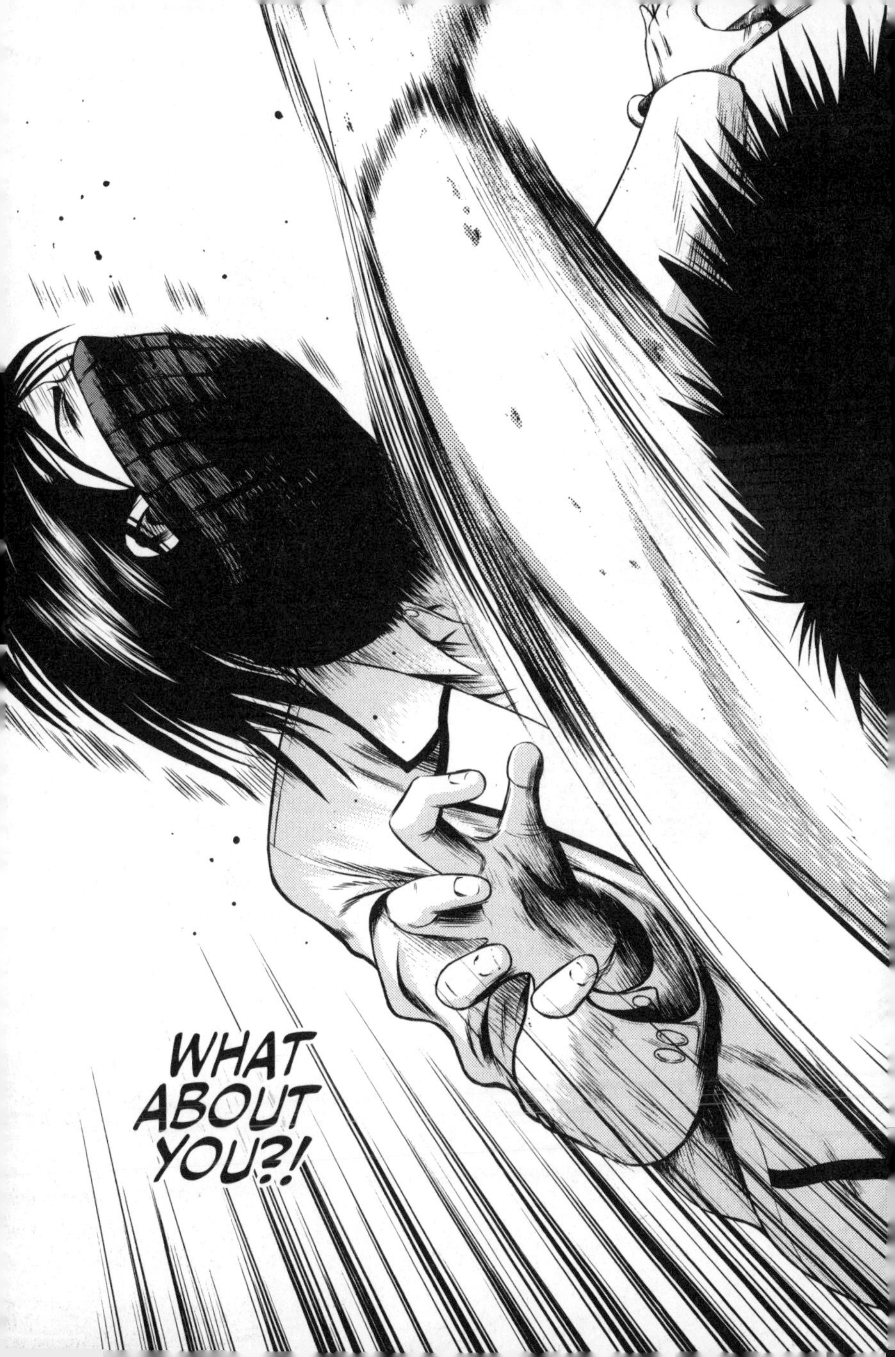
WHAT ABOUT YOU?!

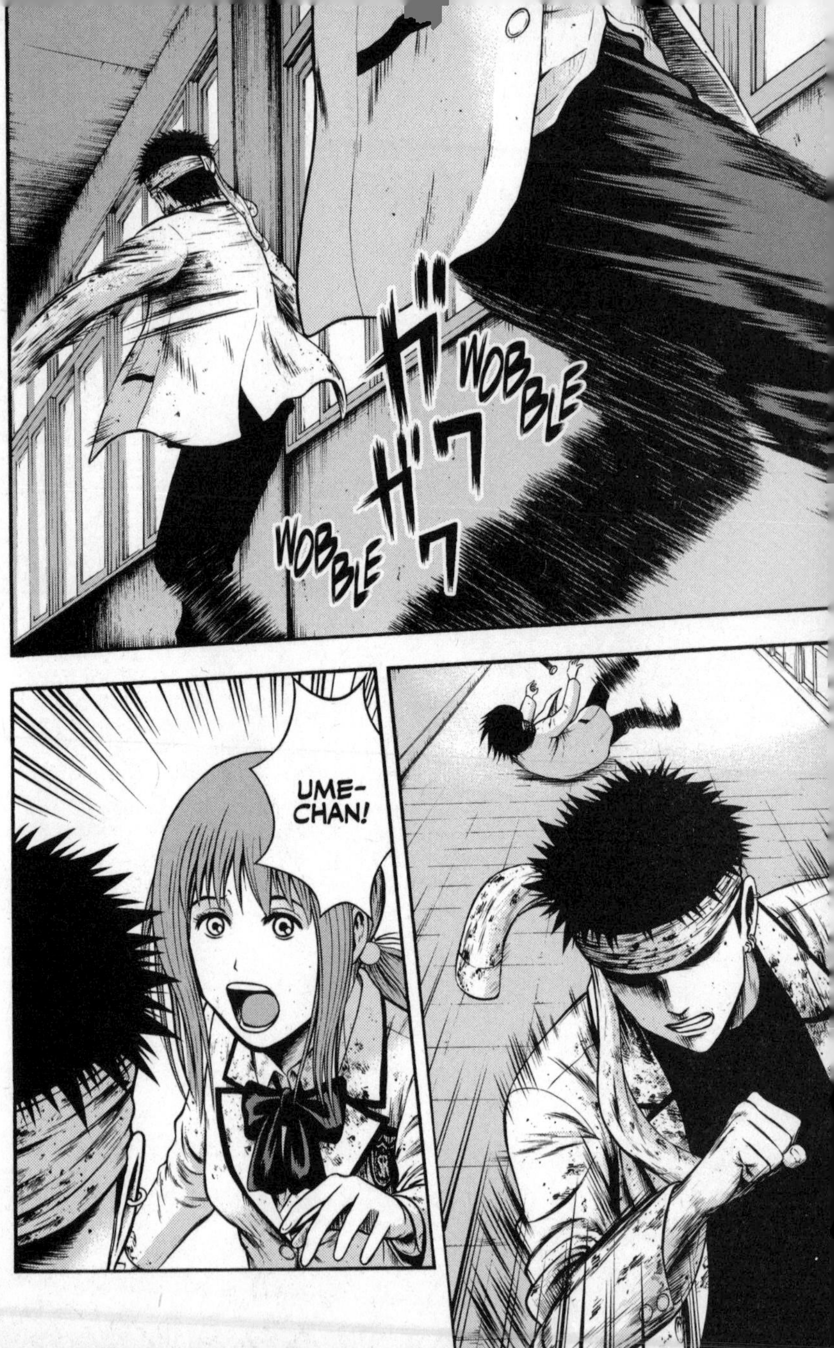
ガク
WOBBLE
ガク
WOBBLE
UME-CHAN!

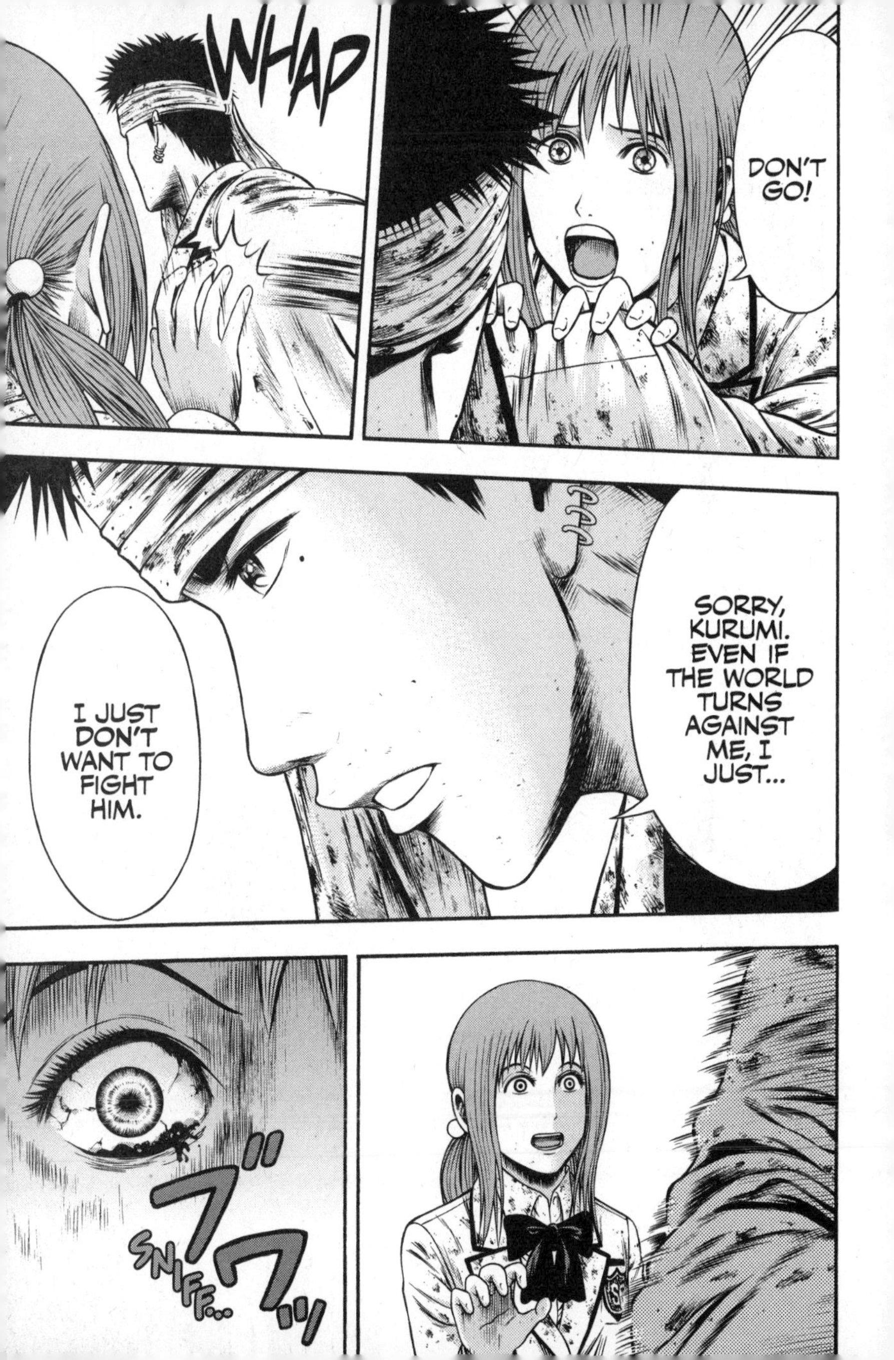
DON'T GO!
WHAP
SORRY, KURUMI. EVEN IF THE WORLD TURNS AGAINST ME, I JUST...
I JUST DON'T WANT TO FIGHT HIM.
ブワッ
SNIFF...

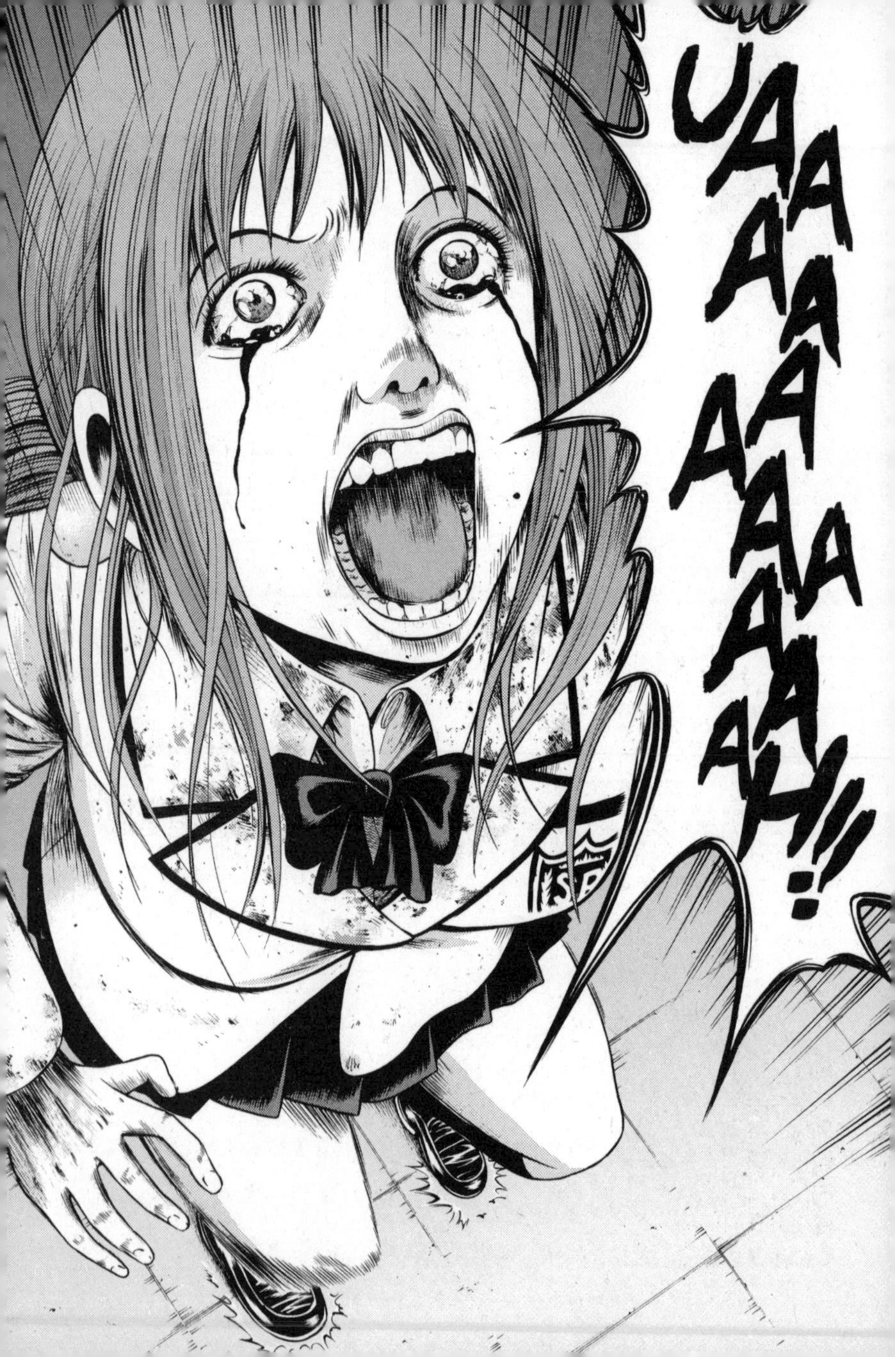
UAAAAAAAAAAAAH!!

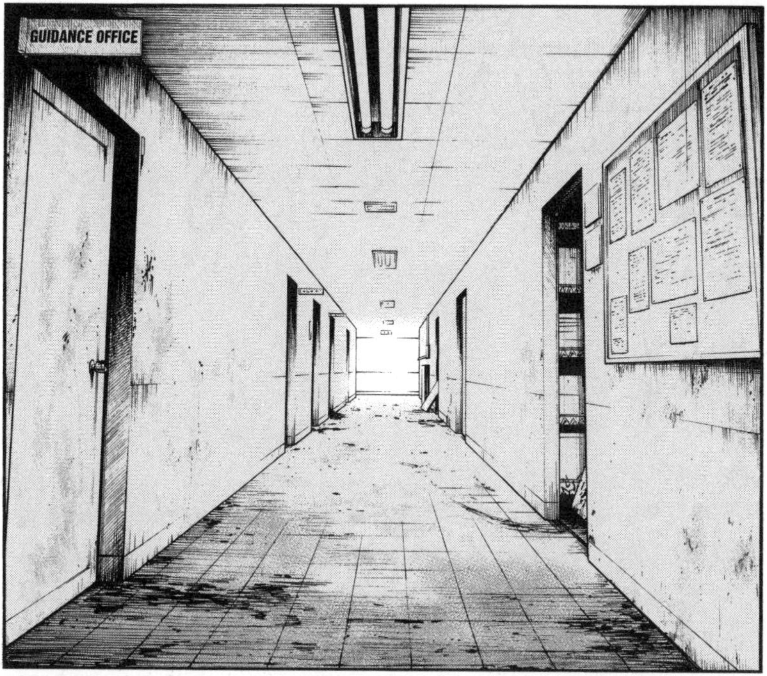
GUIDANCE OFFICE
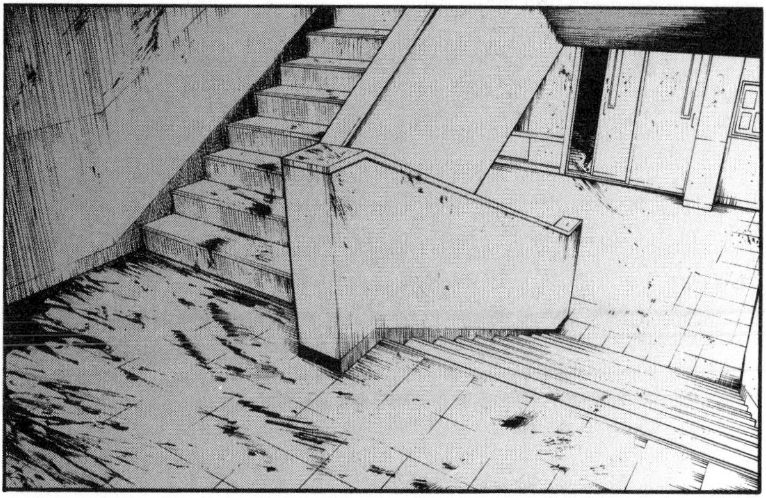

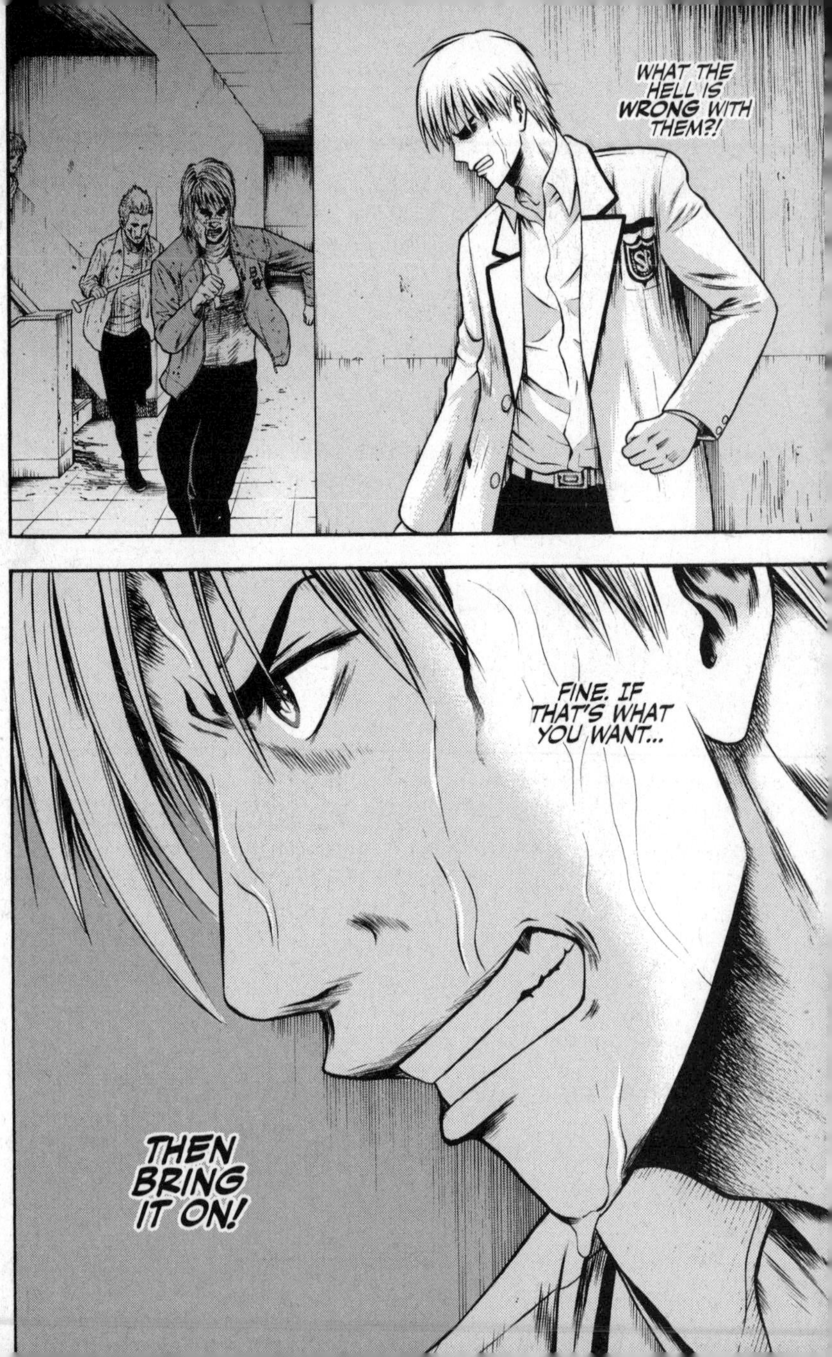
WHAT THE HELL IS WRONG WITH THEM?!
FINE. IF THAT'S WHAT YOU WANT...
THEN BRING IT ON!

HOUR OF THE ZOMBIE

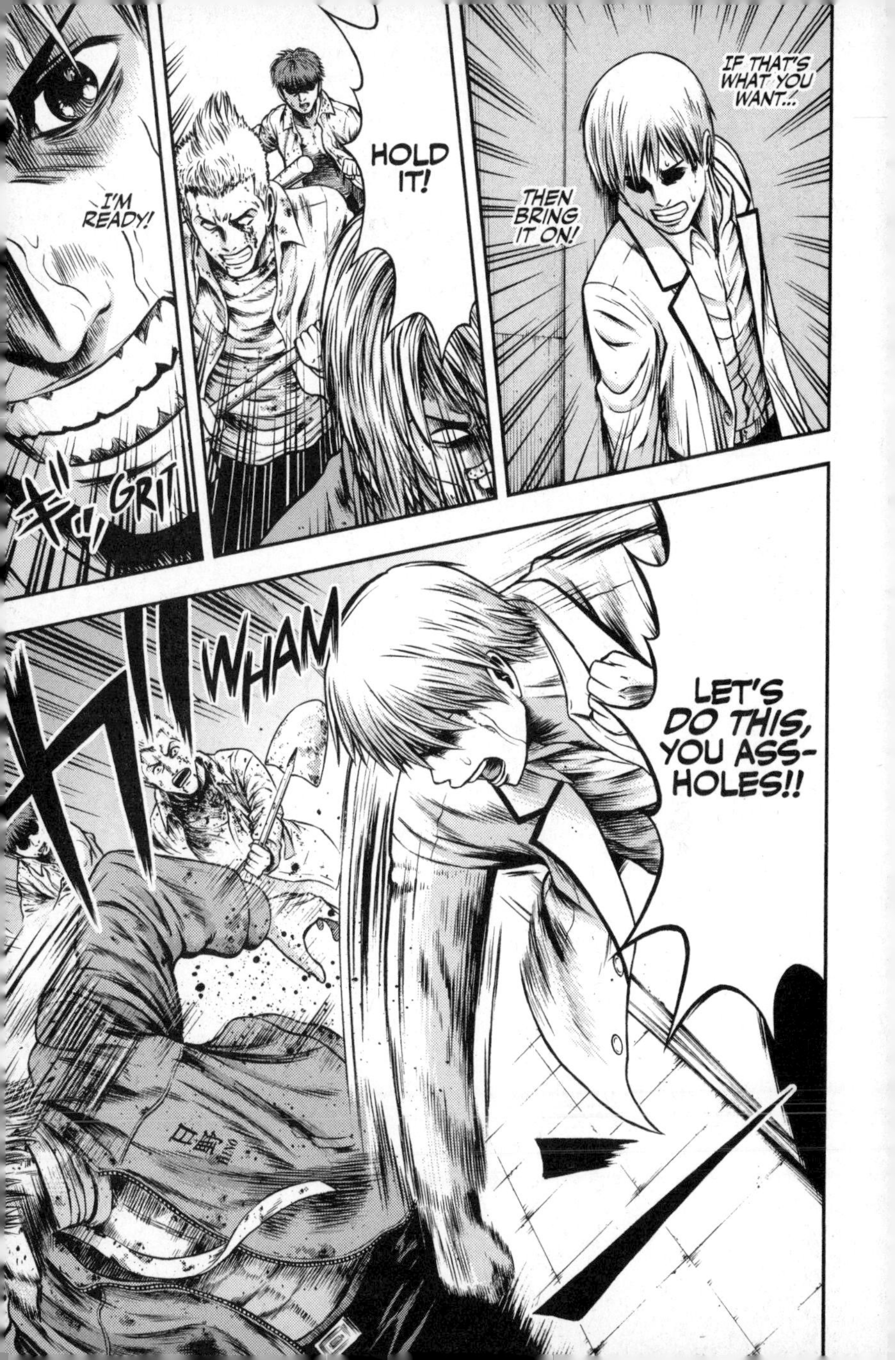
IF THAT'S WHAT YOU WANT...
THEN BRING IT ON!
HOLD IT!
I'M READY!
ギッ
GRIT
LET'S DO THIS, YOU ASS-HOLES!!
WHAM

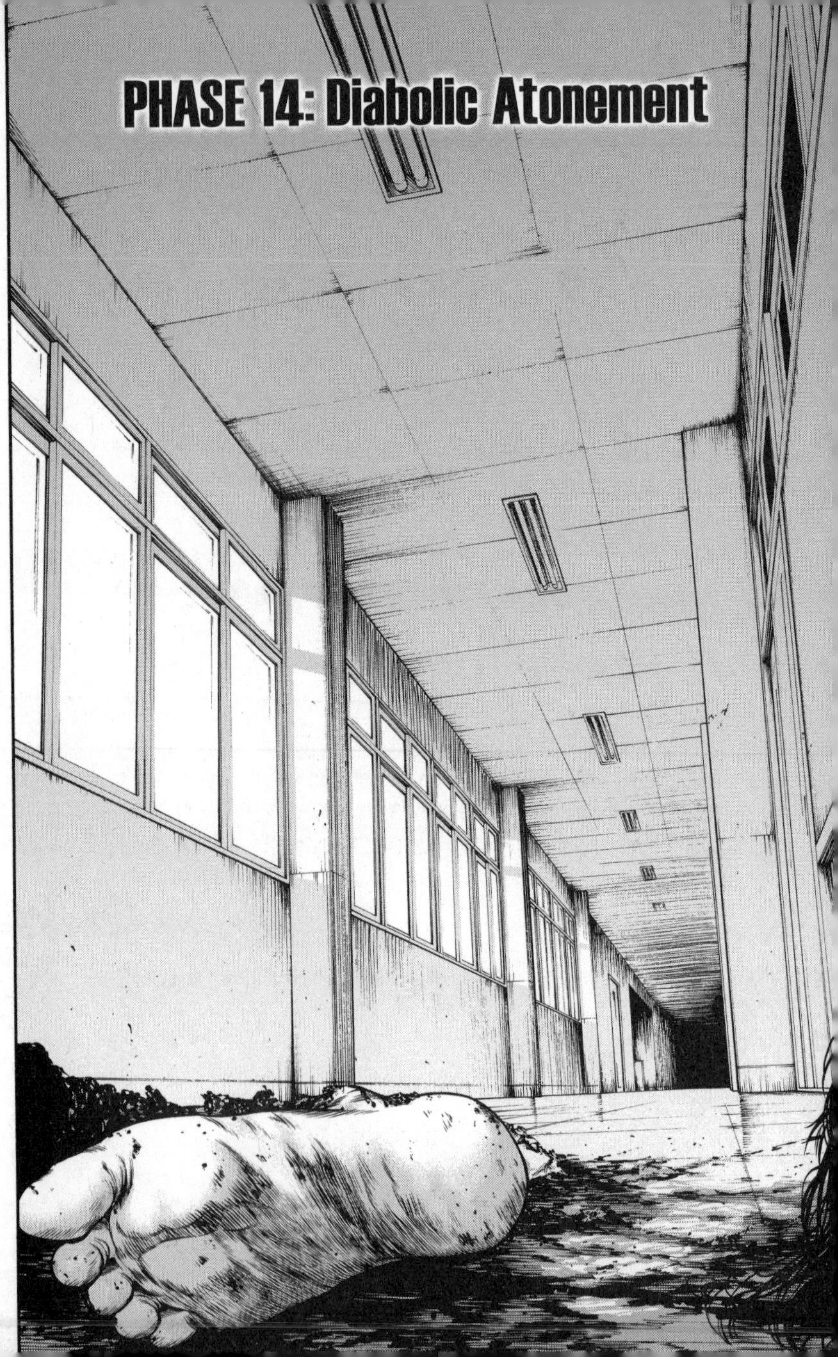
PHASE 14: Diabolic Atonement

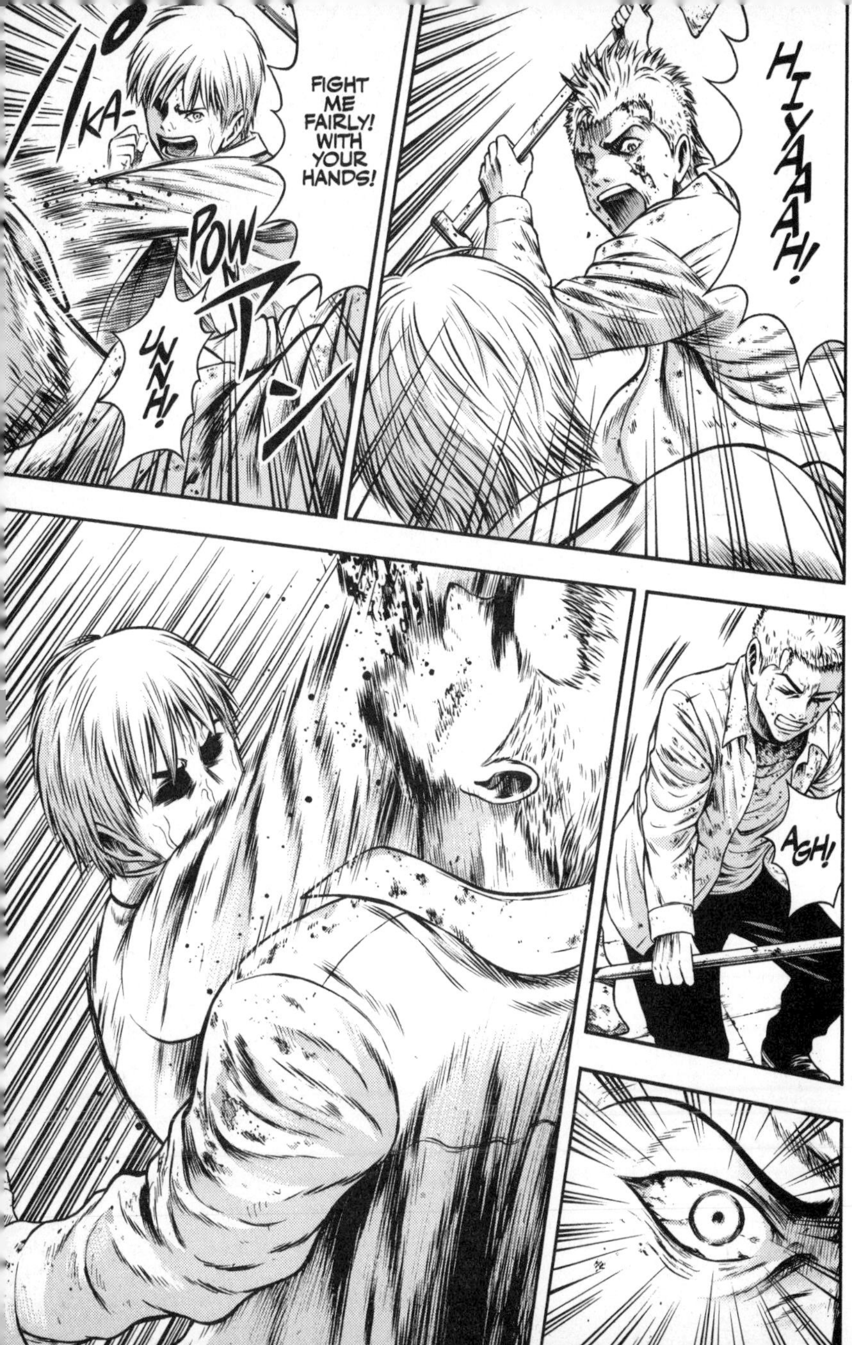
HIYAAAH!
KA-
FIGHT ME FAIRLY! WITH YOUR HANDS!
POW
UNNH!
AGH!

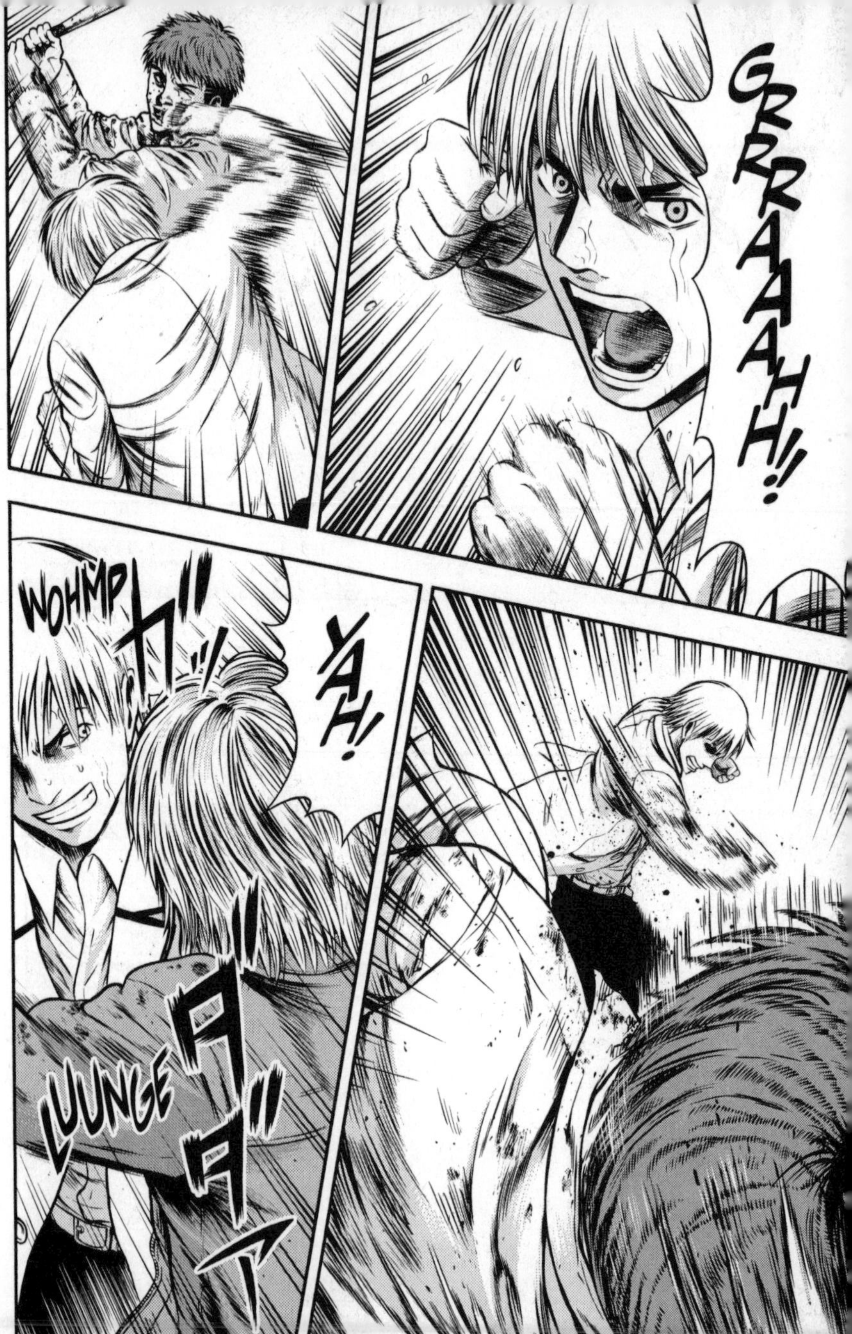
GRRAAAAHH!!
YAH!
WOHMP
LUNGE

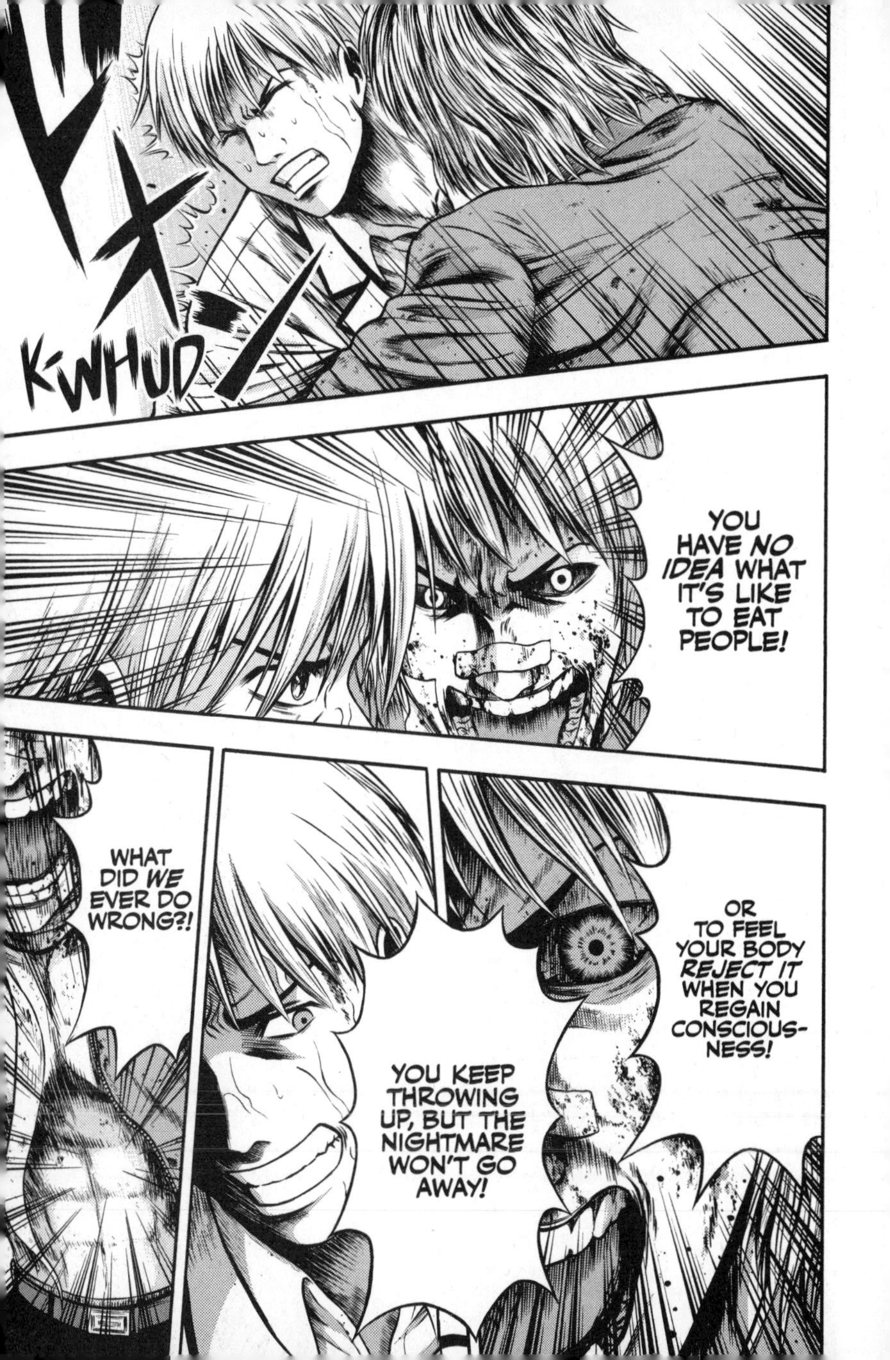
K-WHUD
YOU HAVE NO IDEA WHAT IT'S LIKE TO EAT PEOPLE!
OR TO FEEL YOUR BODY REJECT IT WHEN YOU REGAIN CONSCIOUS-NESS!
YOU KEEP THROWING UP, BUT THE NIGHTMARE WON'T GO AWAY!
WHAT DID WE EVER DO WRONG?!

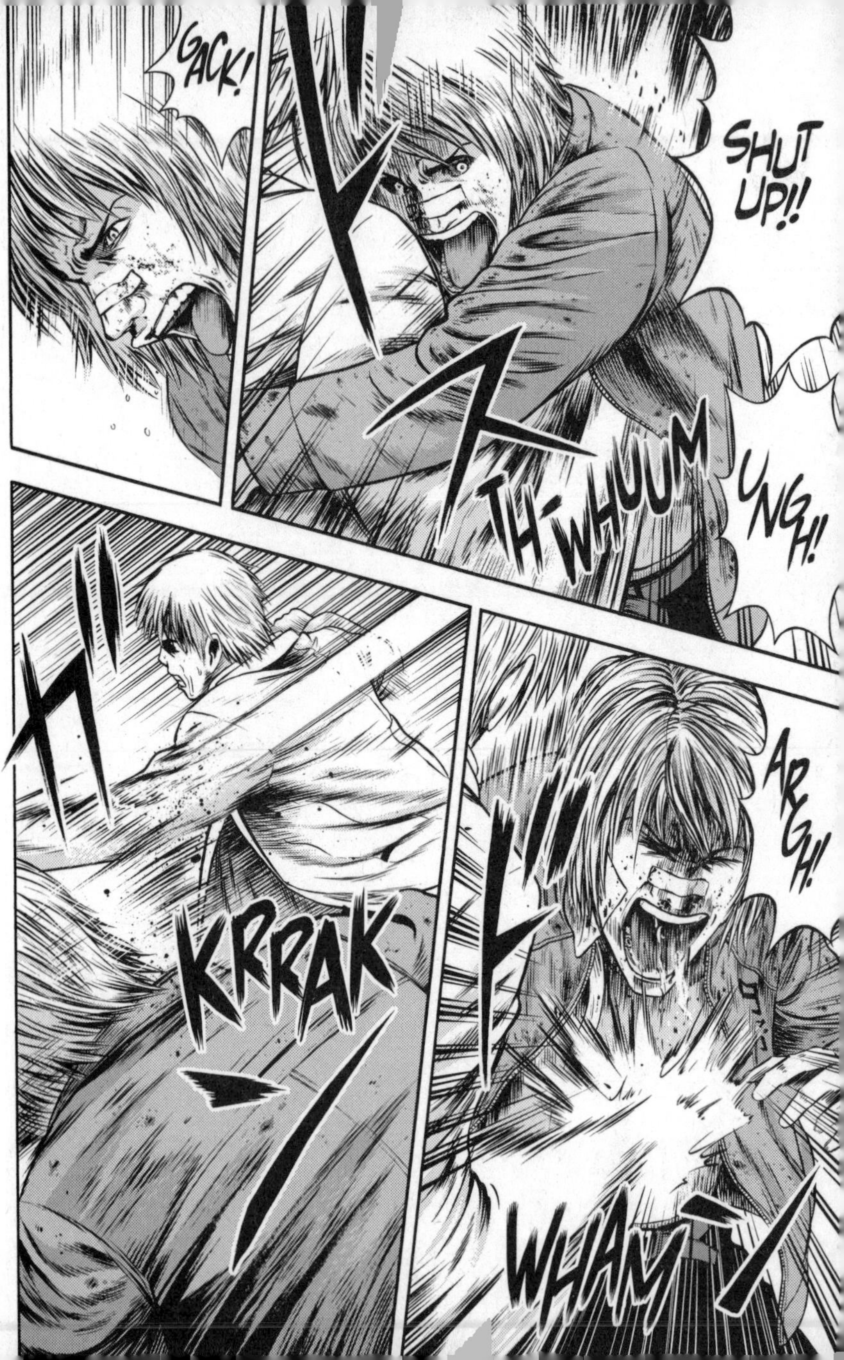
SHUT UP!!
TH-WHUUM
UNGH!
GACK!
ARGH!
WHAM
KRRAK

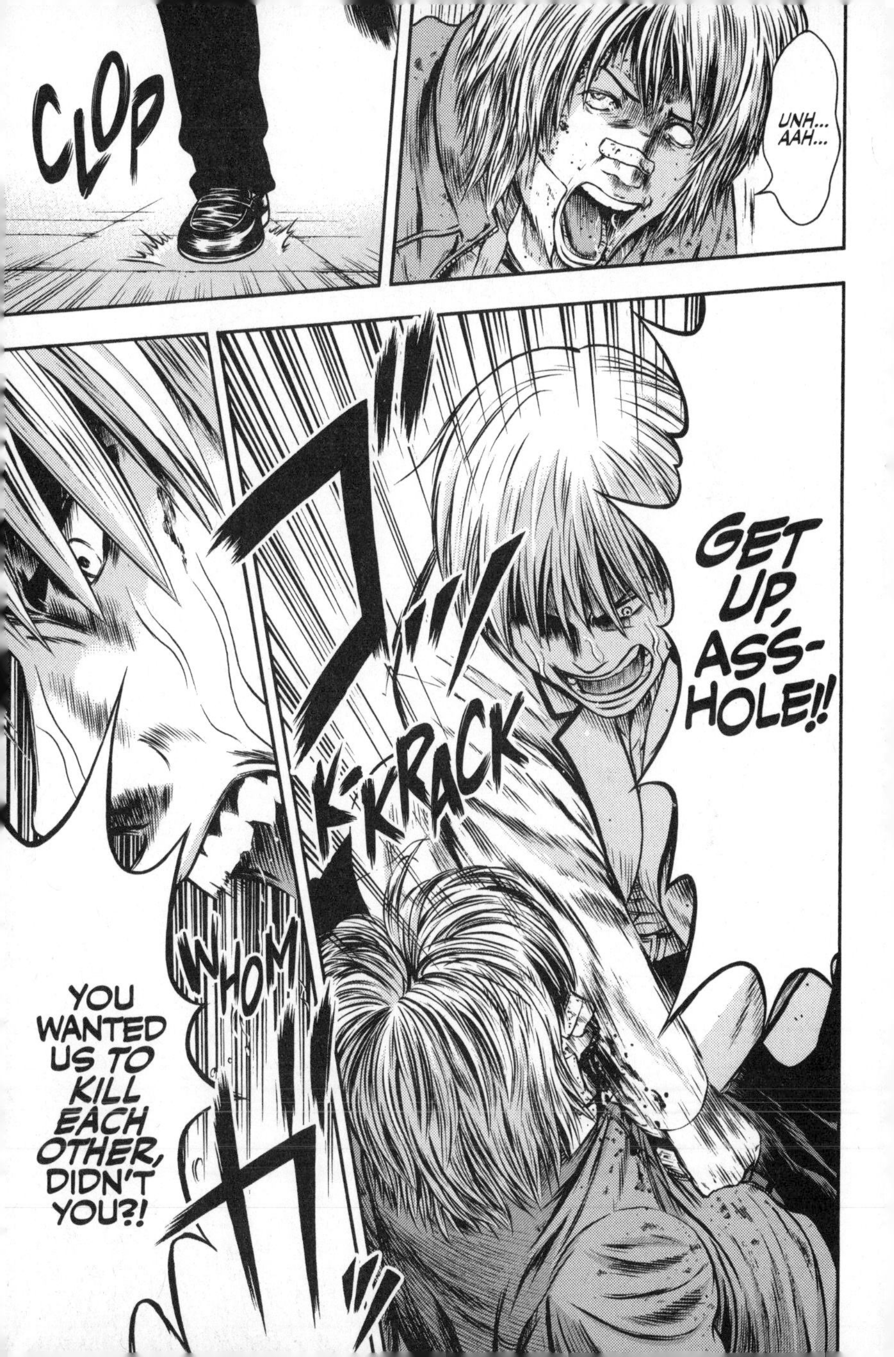
UNH... AAH...
CLOP
GET UP, ASS-HOLE!!
K-KRACK
WHOM
YOU WANTED US TO KILL EACH OTHER, DIDN'T YOU?!

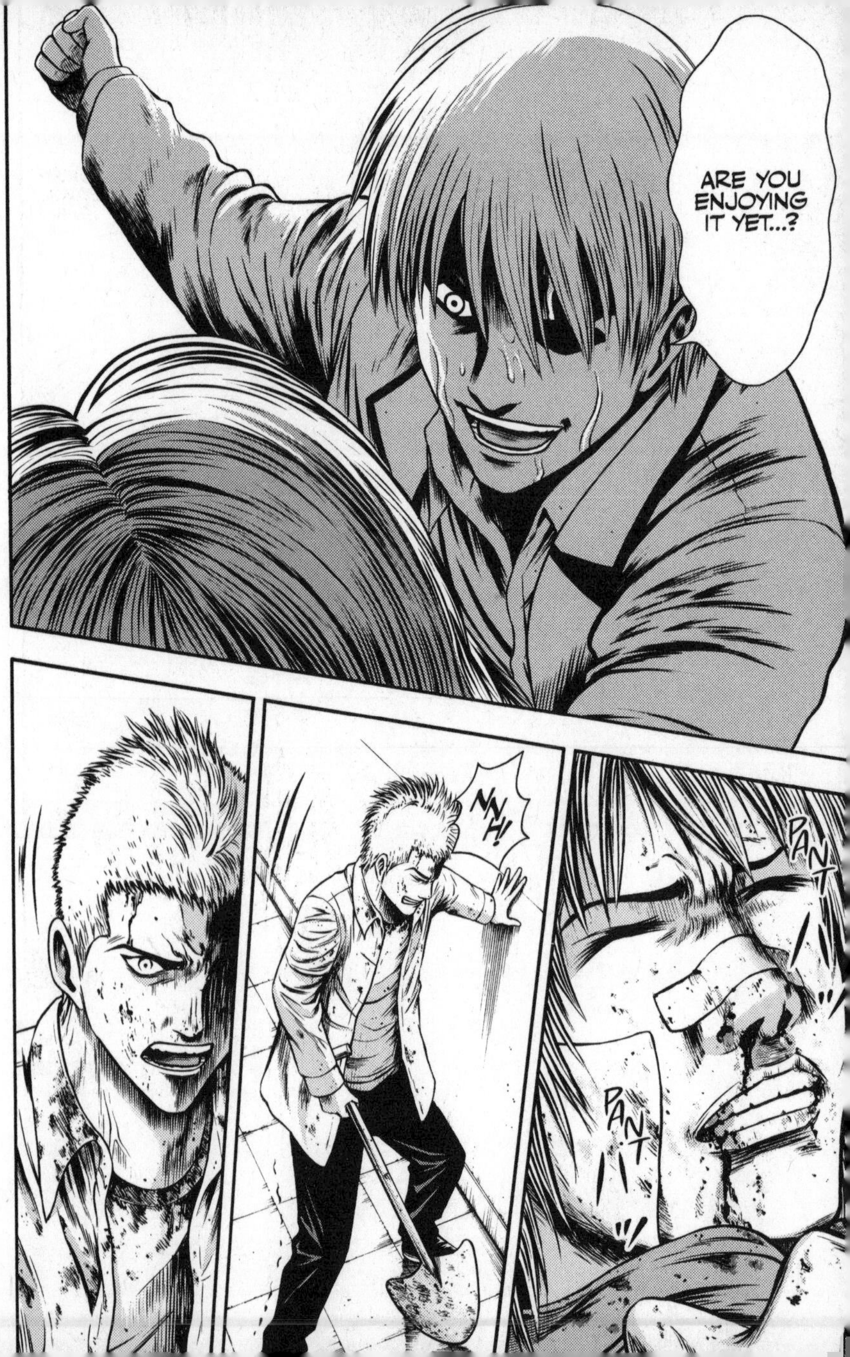
ARE YOU ENJOYING IT YET...?
PANT
PANT
NNH!

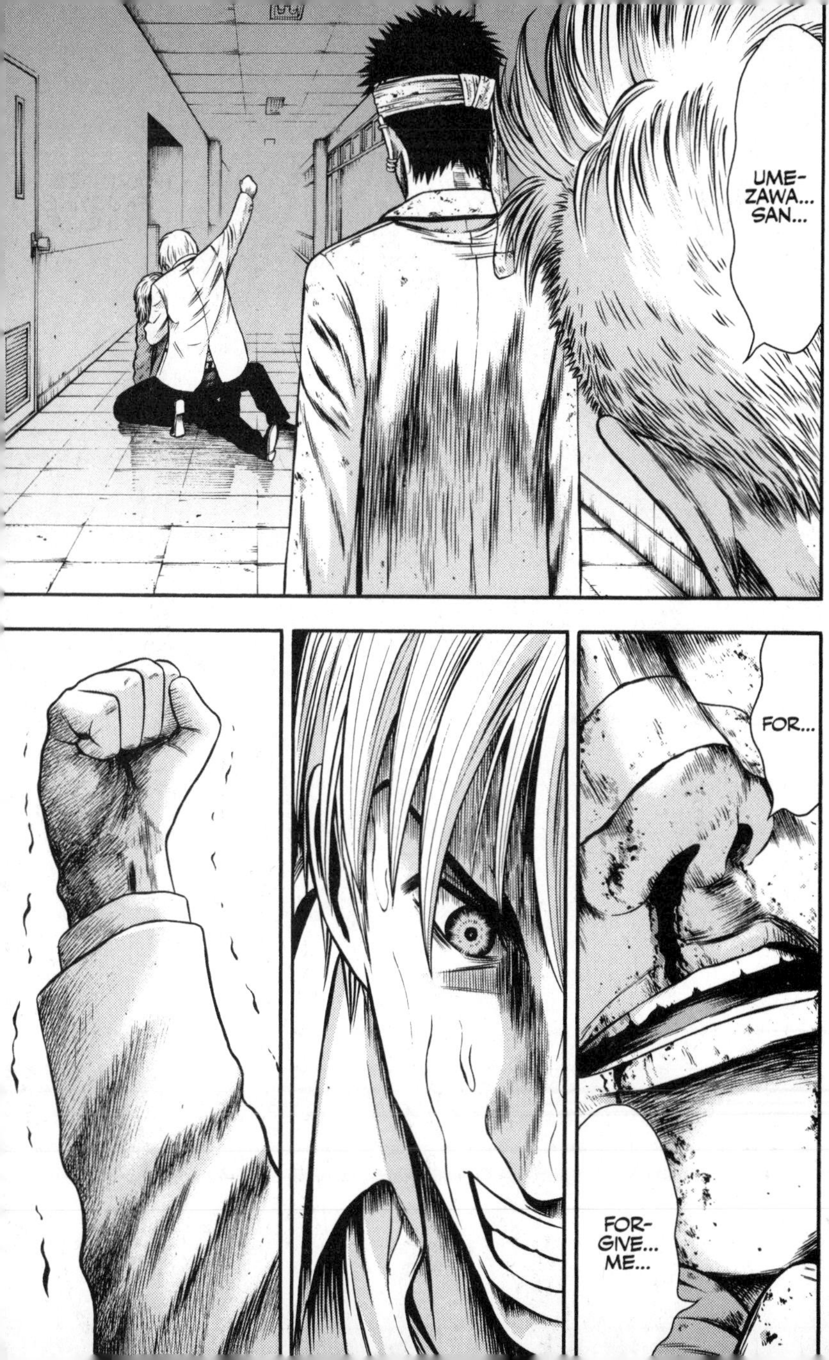
UME-ZAWA... SAN...
FOR...
FOR-GIVE... ME...

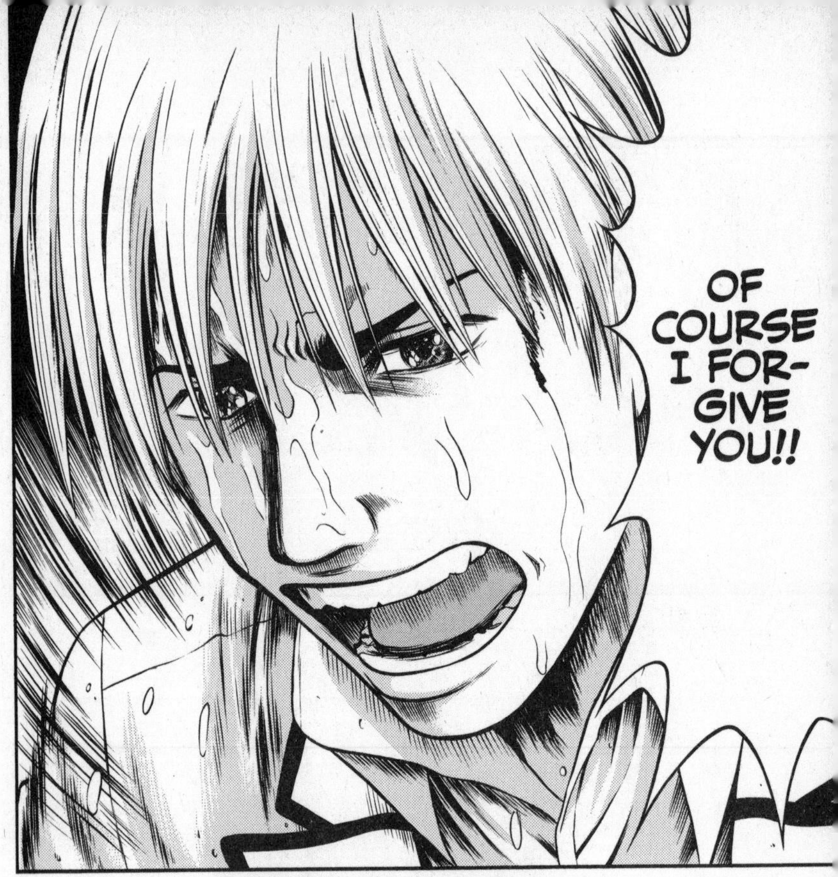
OF COURSE I FOR-GIVE YOU!!
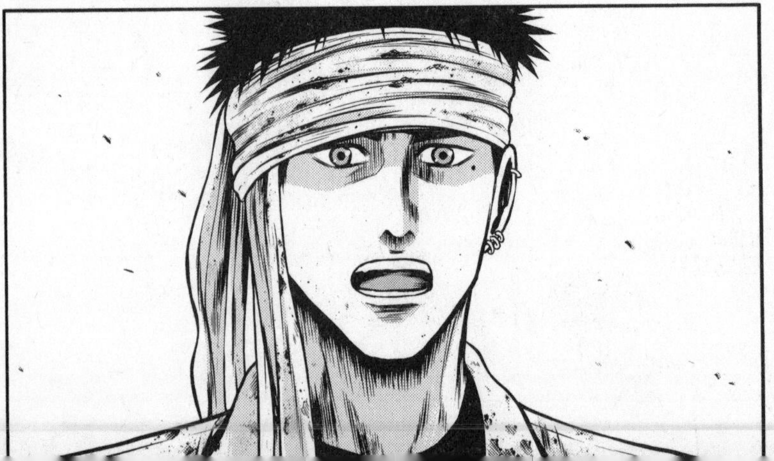

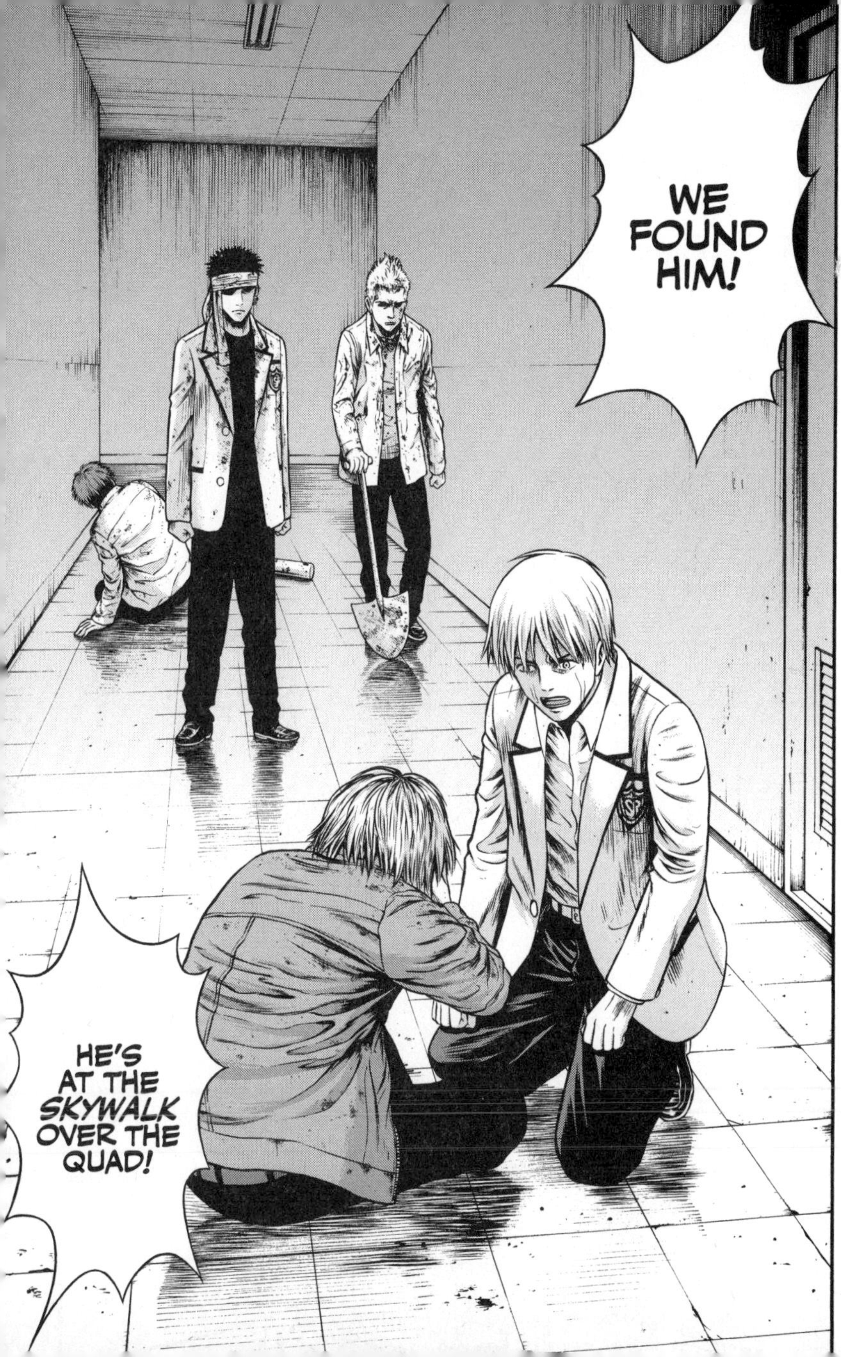
WE FOUND HIM!
HE'S AT THE SKYWALK OVER THE QUAD!

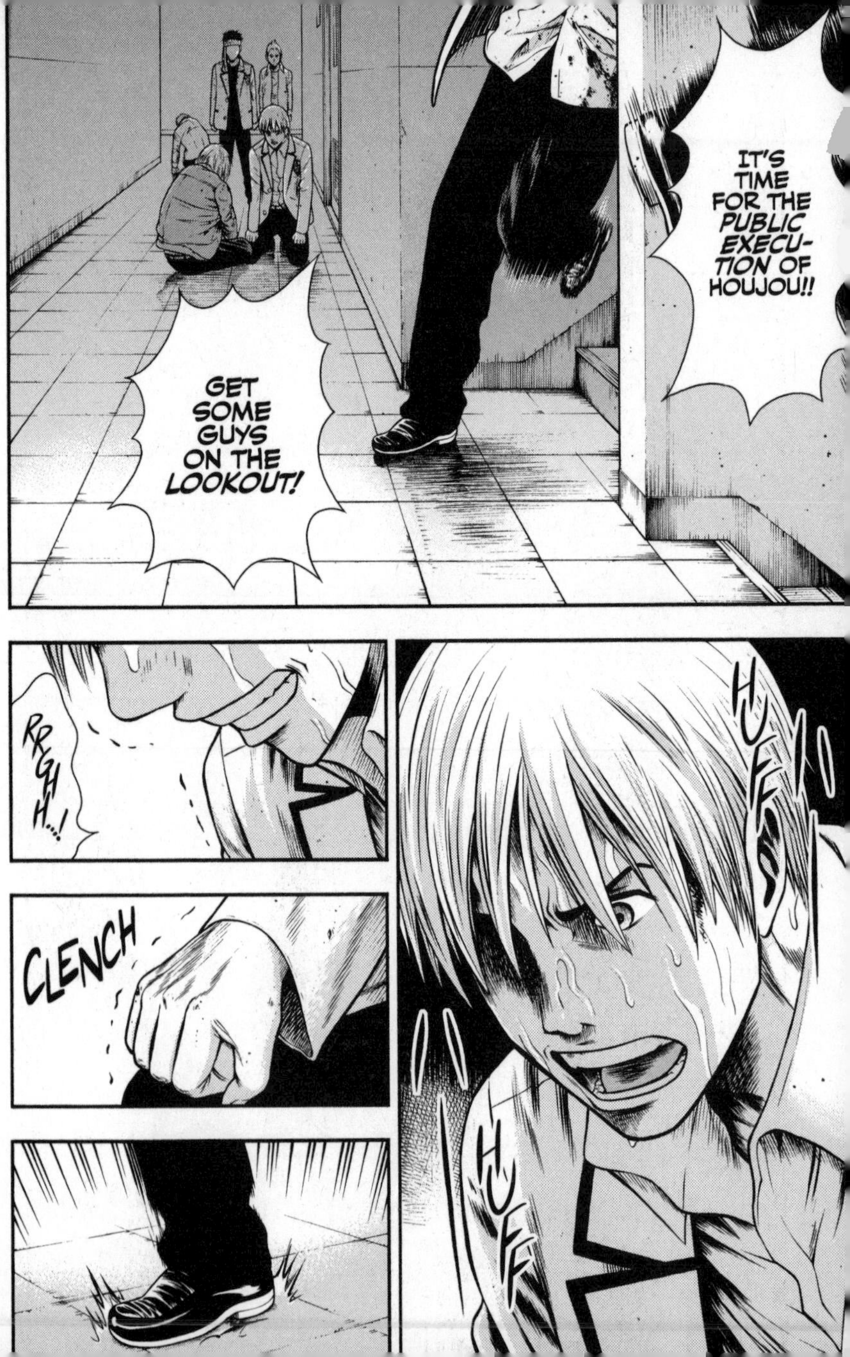
IT'S TIME FOR THE PUBLIC EXECUTION OF HOUJOU!!
GET SOME GUYS ON THE LOOKOUT!
HUFF
HUFF
RRGHH...!
CLENCH

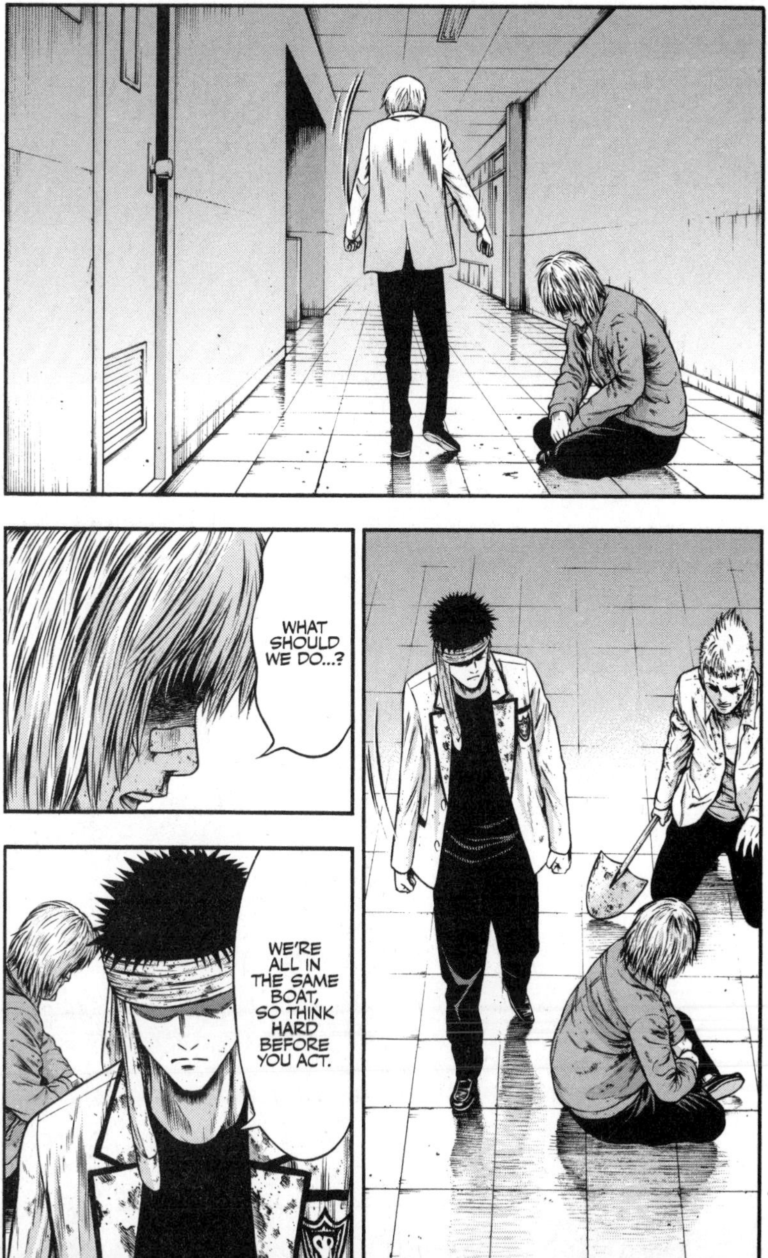
WHAT SHOULD WE DO...?
WE'RE ALL IN THE SAME BOAT, SO THINK HARD BEFORE YOU ACT.

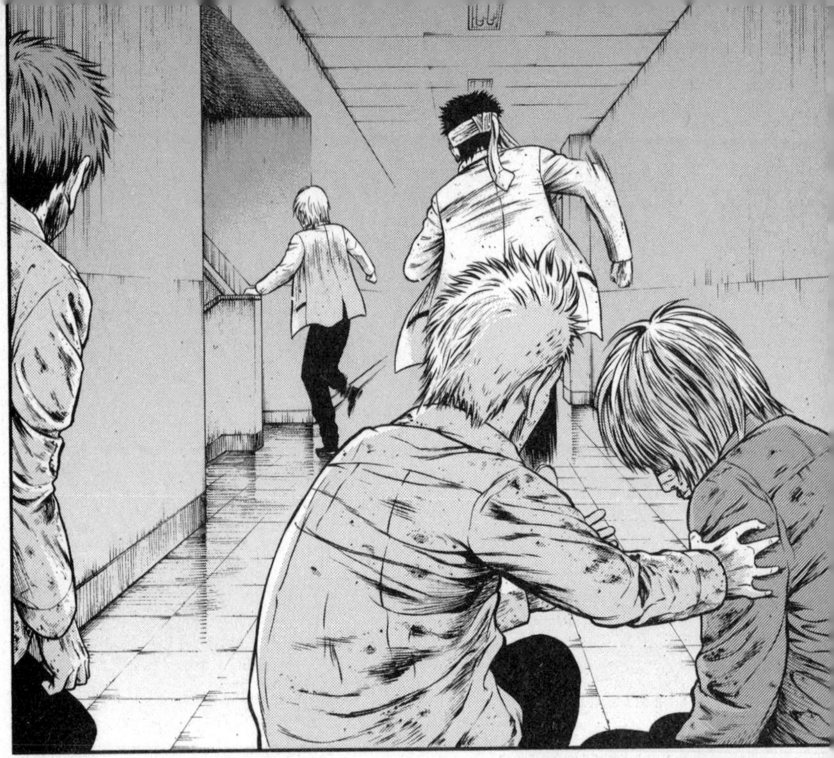
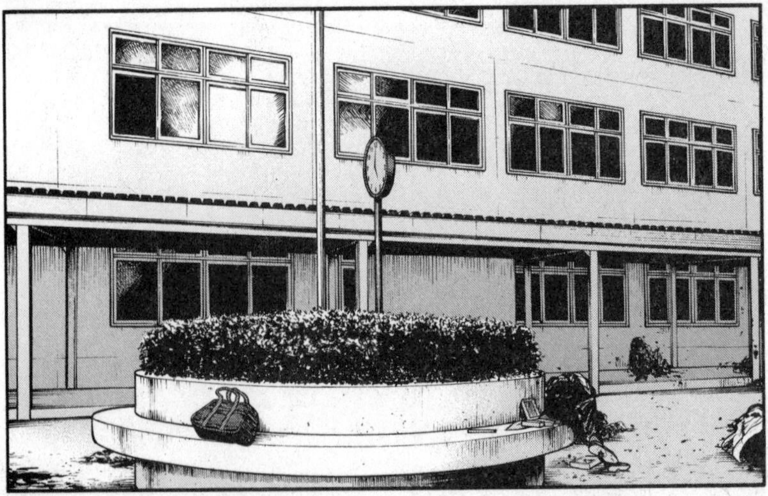

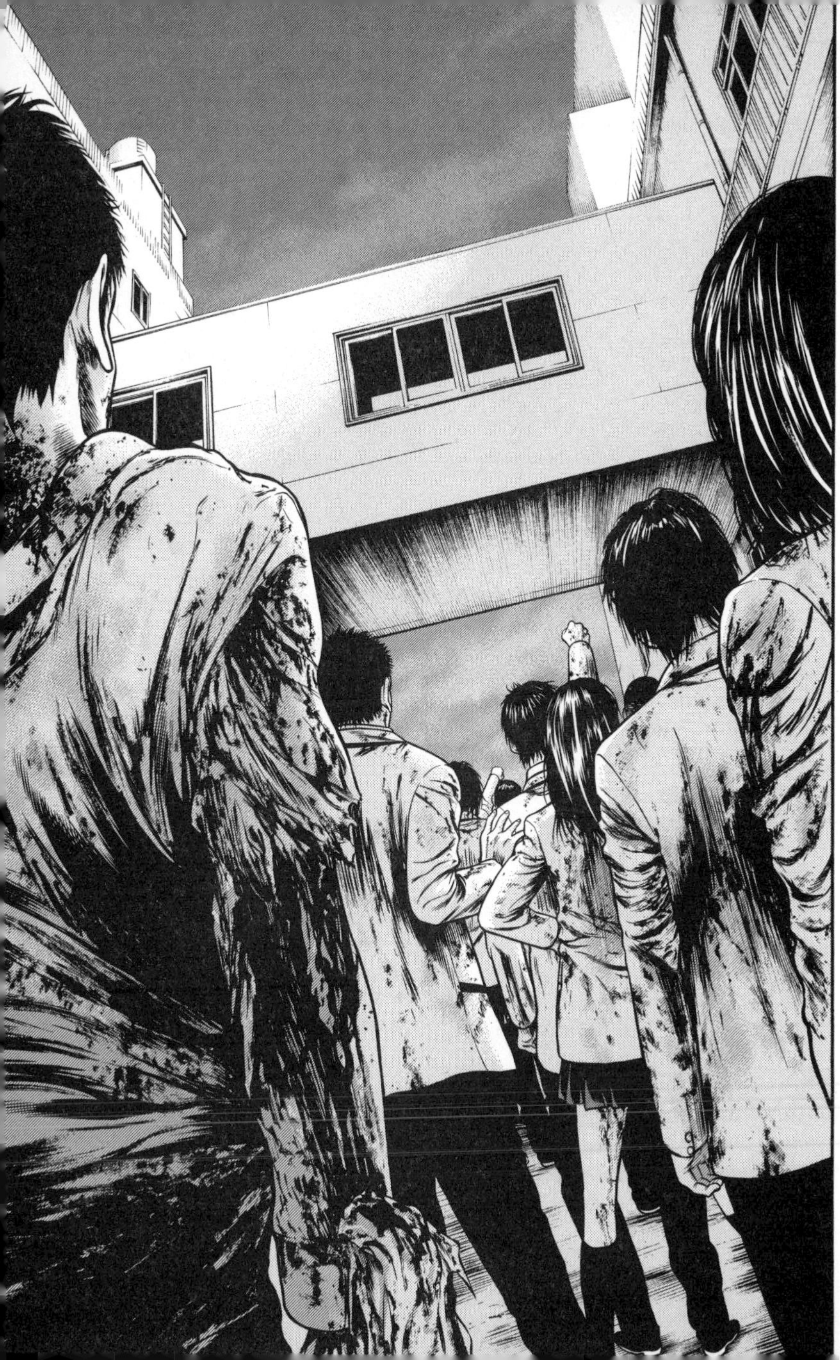

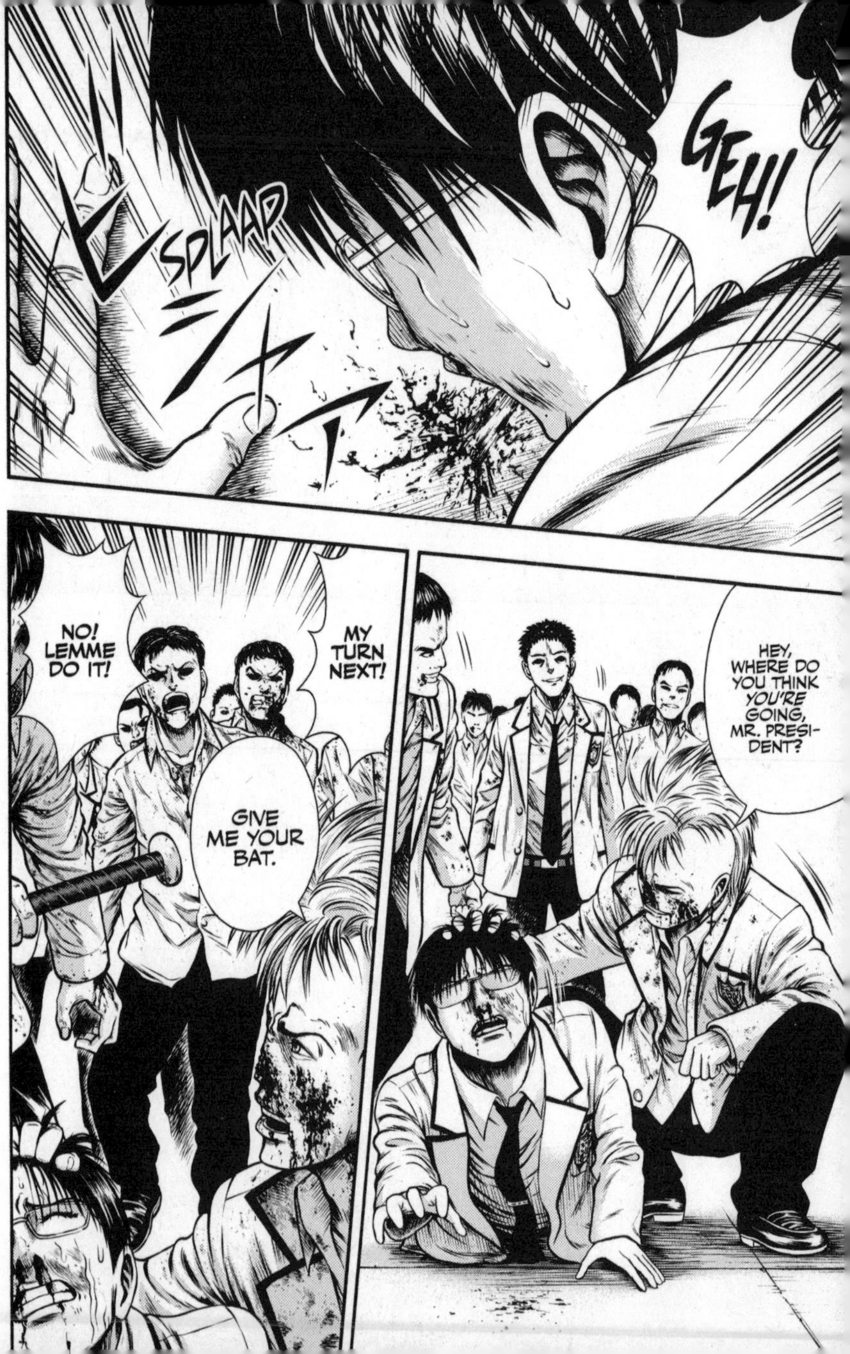
GEH!
SPLAAD
HEY, WHERE DO YOU THINK YOU'RE GOING, MR. PRESIDENT?
MY TURN NEXT!
NO! LEMME DO IT!
GIVE ME YOUR BAT.

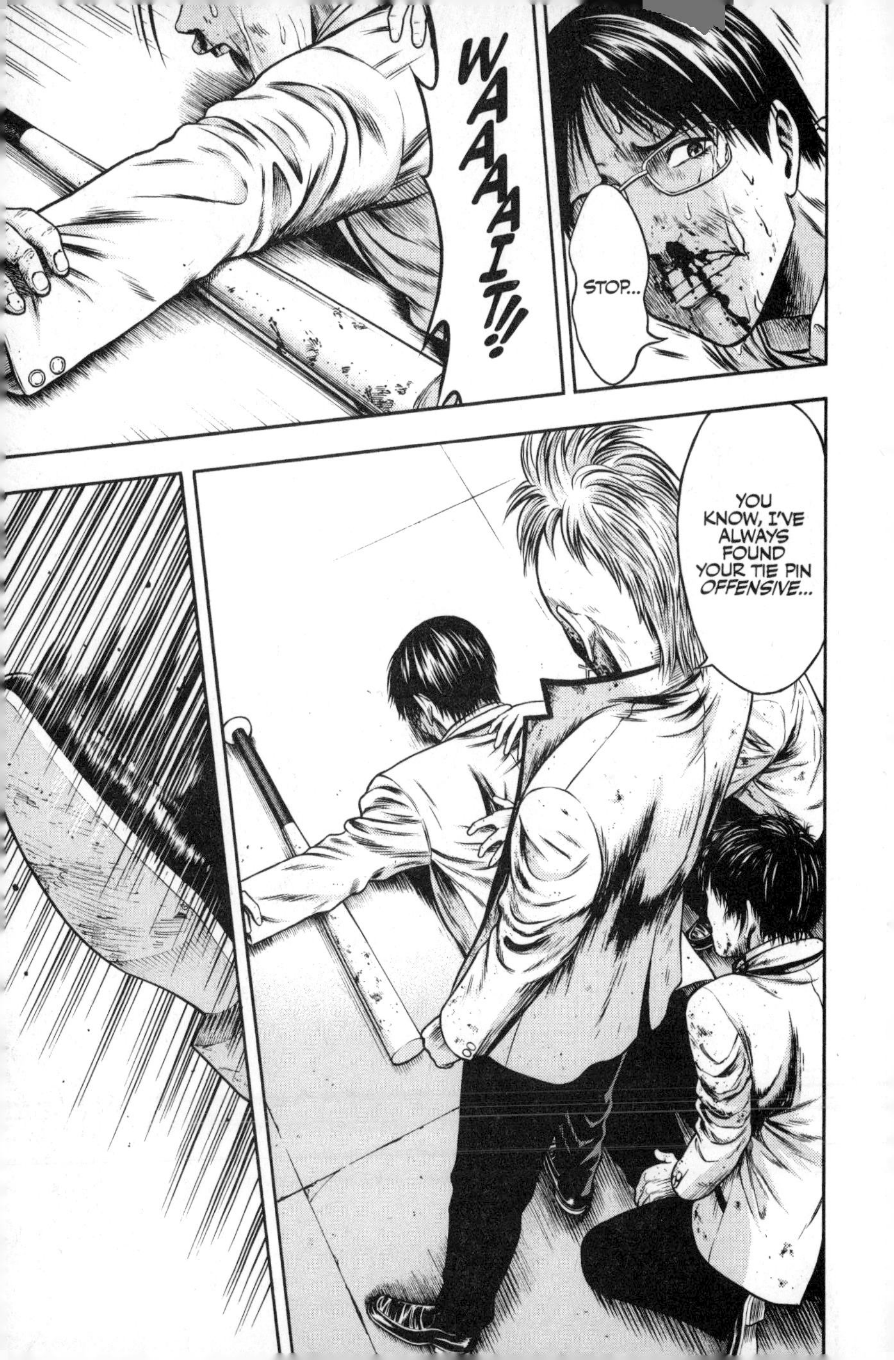
STOP...
WAAAAAIT!!
YOU KNOW, I'VE ALWAYS FOUND YOUR TIE PIN *OFFENSIVE*...

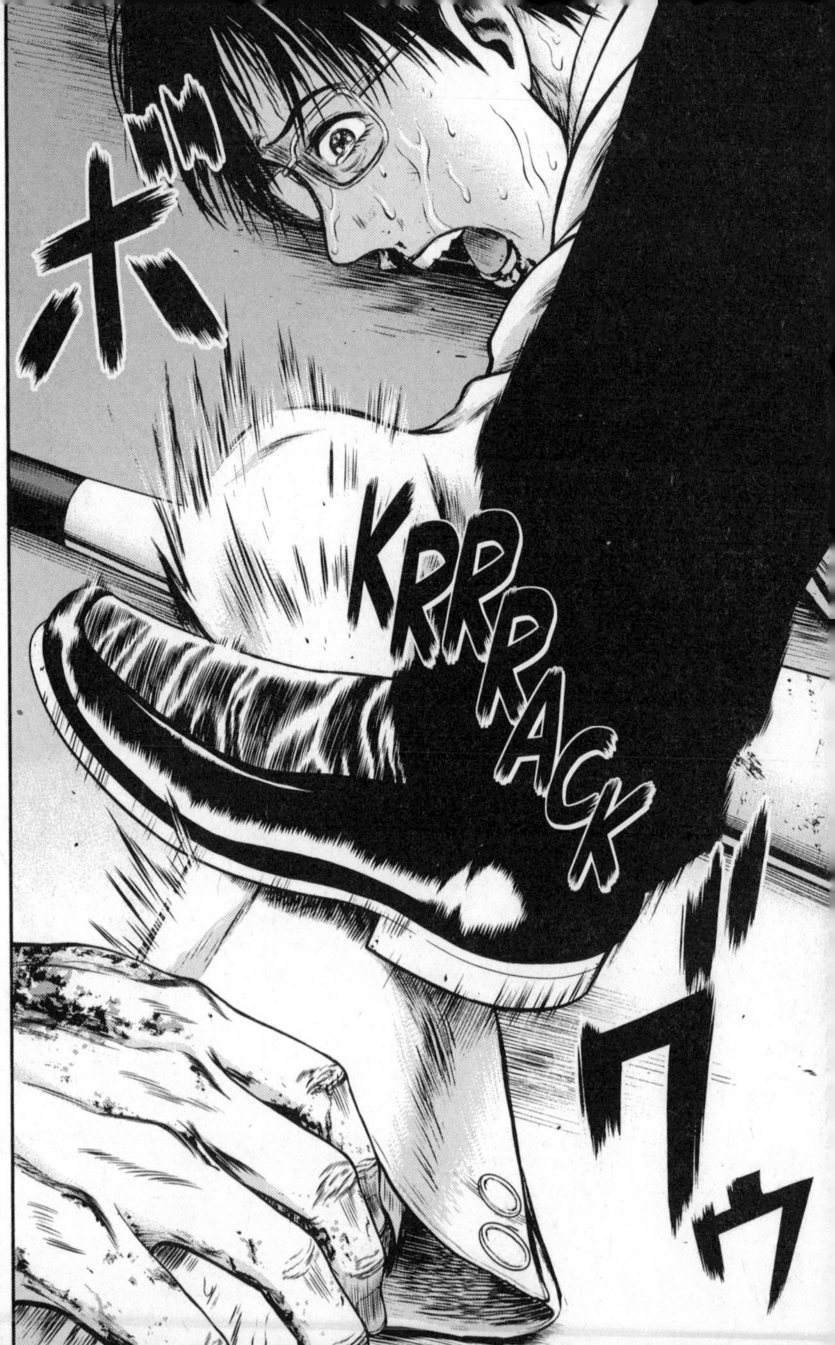
KRRRACK

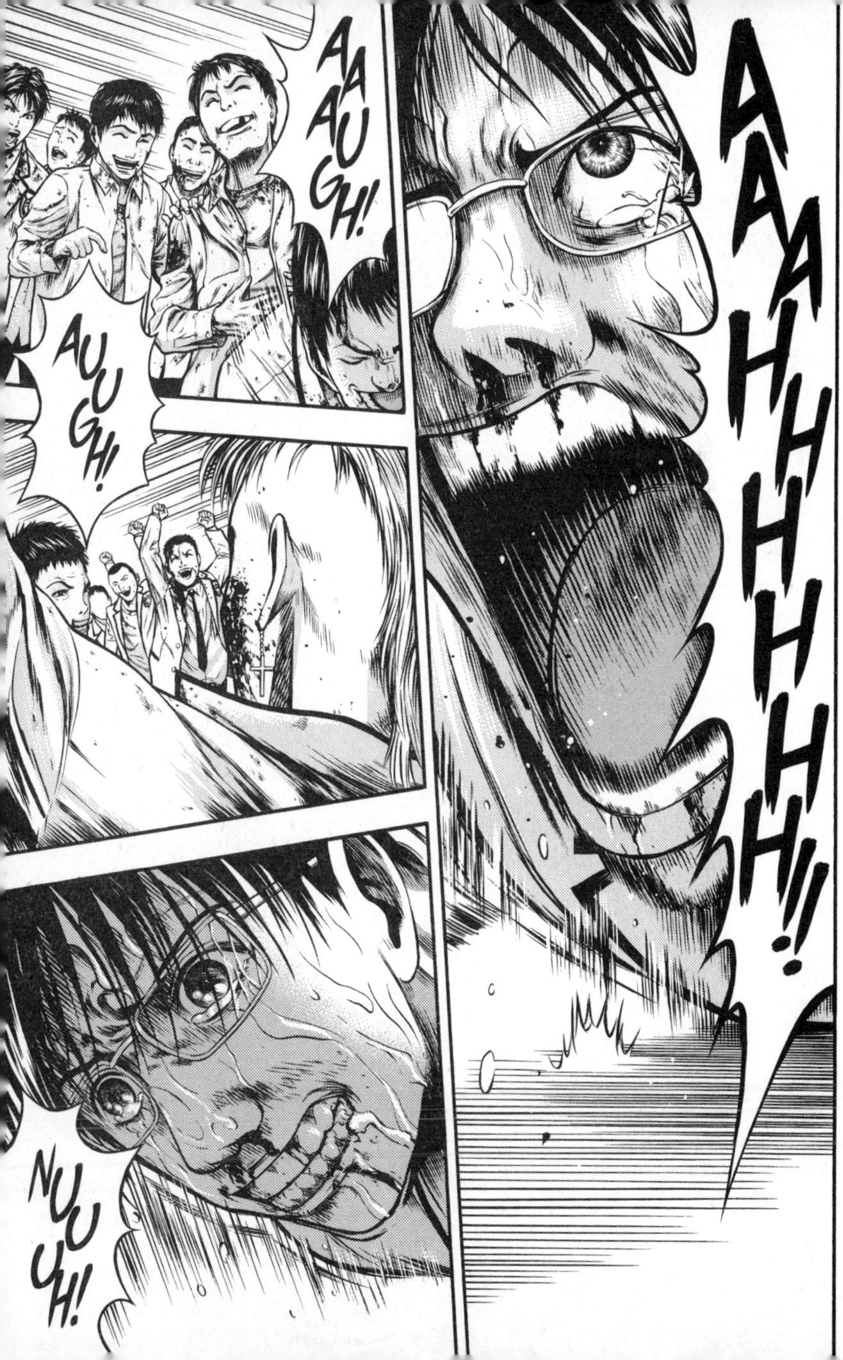
AAAHHHHHHH!!!
AAAAUGH!
AUUUGH!
NUUUUH!

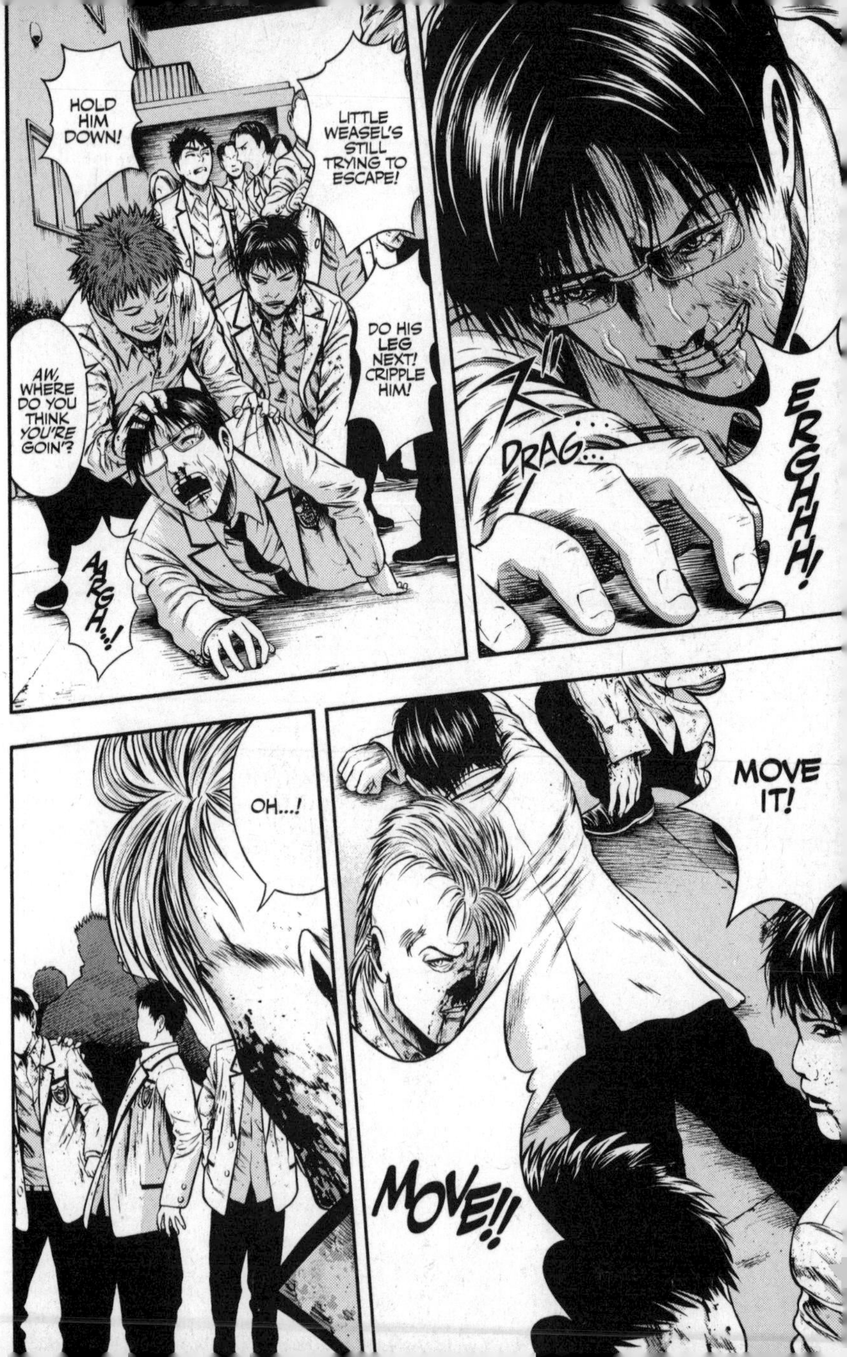
ERGHHH!
DRAG...
LITTLE WEASEL'S STILL TRYING TO ESCAPE!
HOLD HIM DOWN!
DO HIS LEG NEXT! CRIPPLE HIM!
AW, WHERE DO YOU THINK YOU'RE GOIN'?
AARGH...!
MOVE IT!
MOVE!!
OH...!

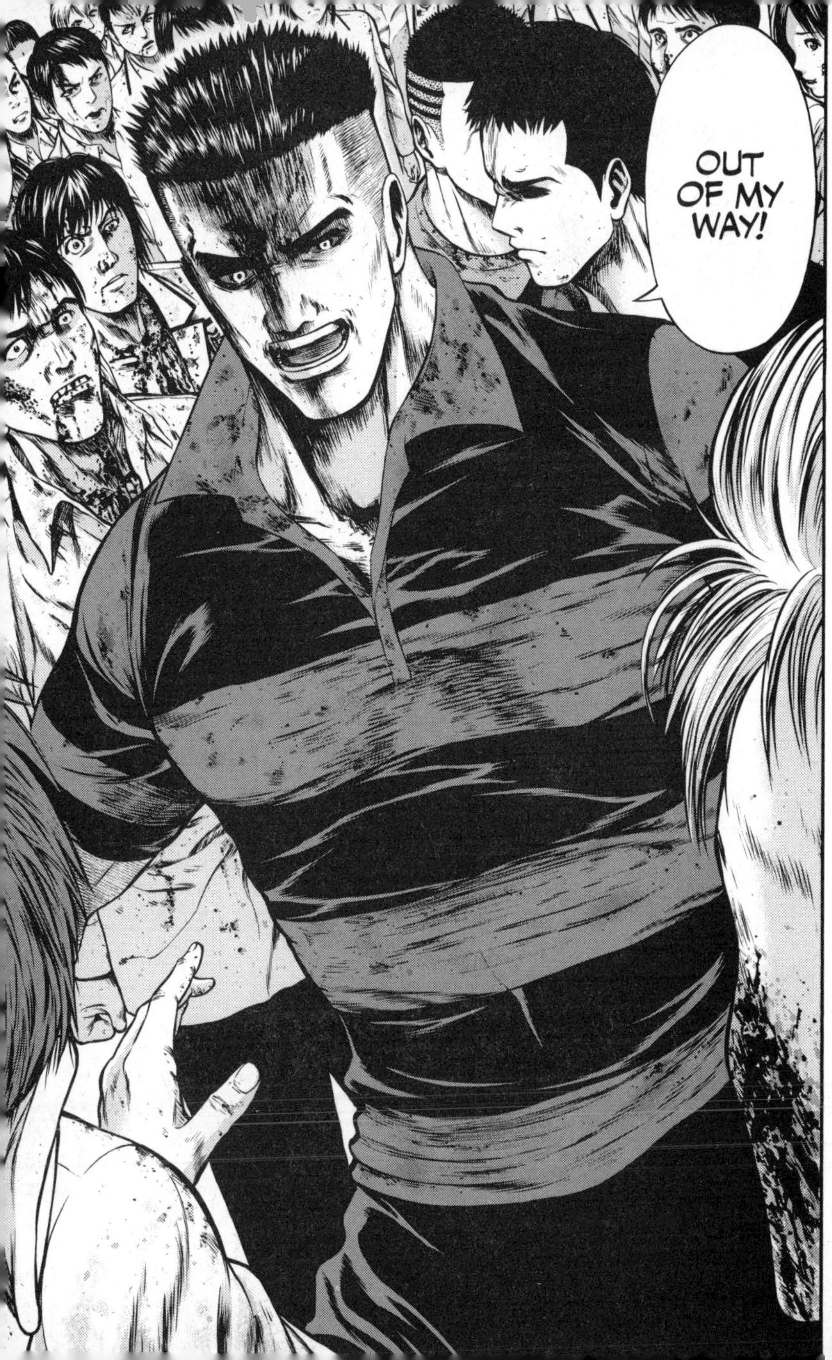
OUT OF MY WAY!

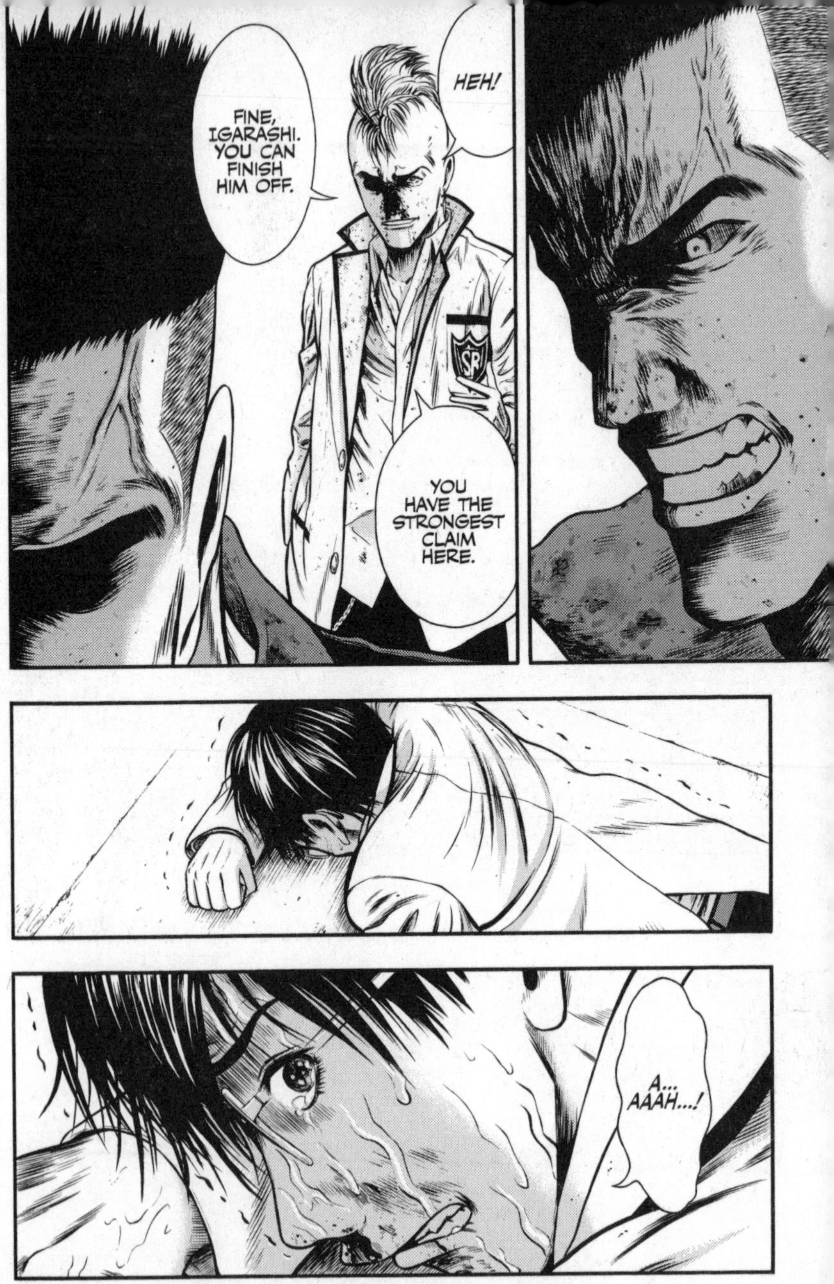
HEH!
FINE, IGARASHI. YOU CAN FINISH HIM OFF.
YOU HAVE THE STRONGEST CLAIM HERE.
A... AAAH...!

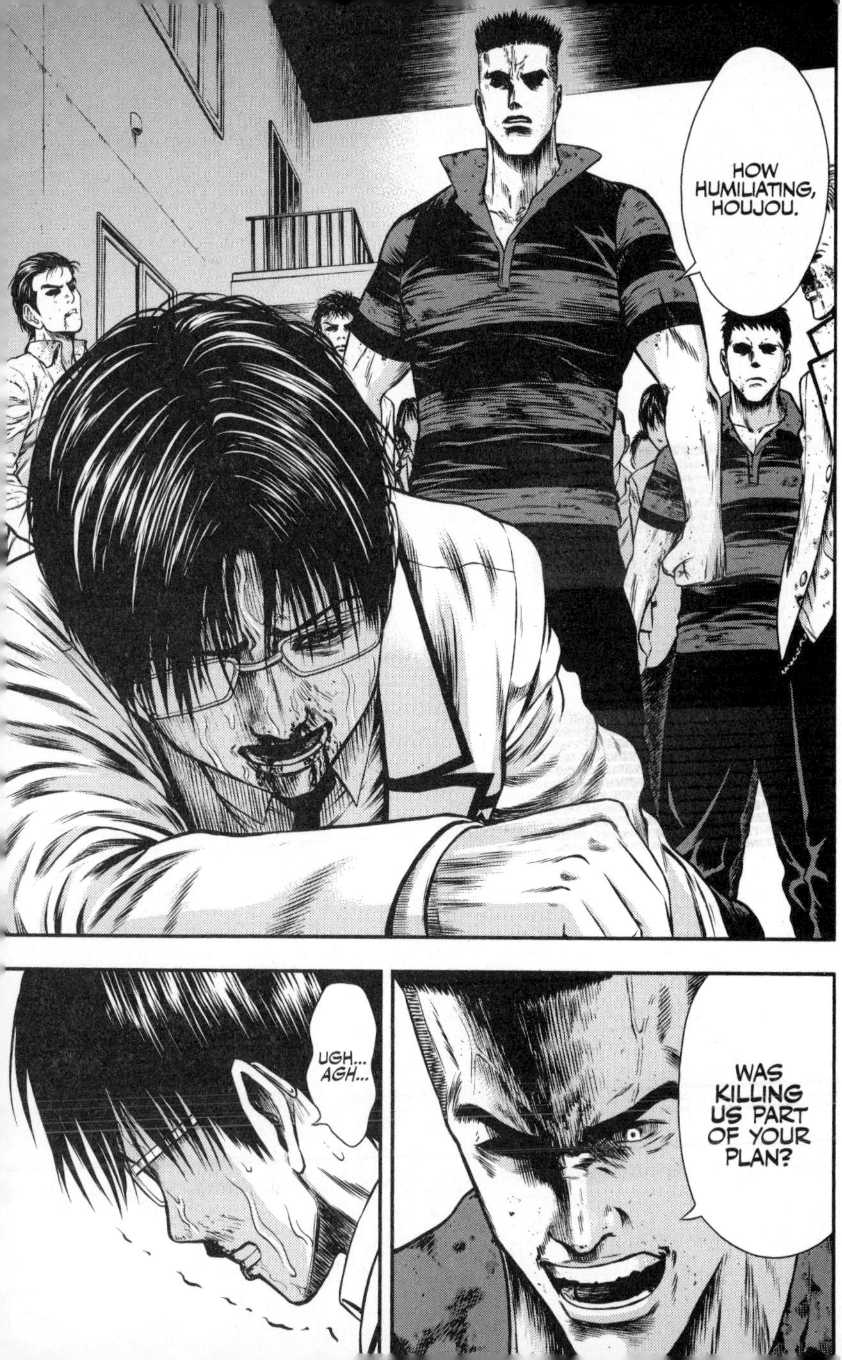
HOW HUMILIATING, HOUJOU.
WAS KILLING US PART OF YOUR PLAN?
UGH... AGH...

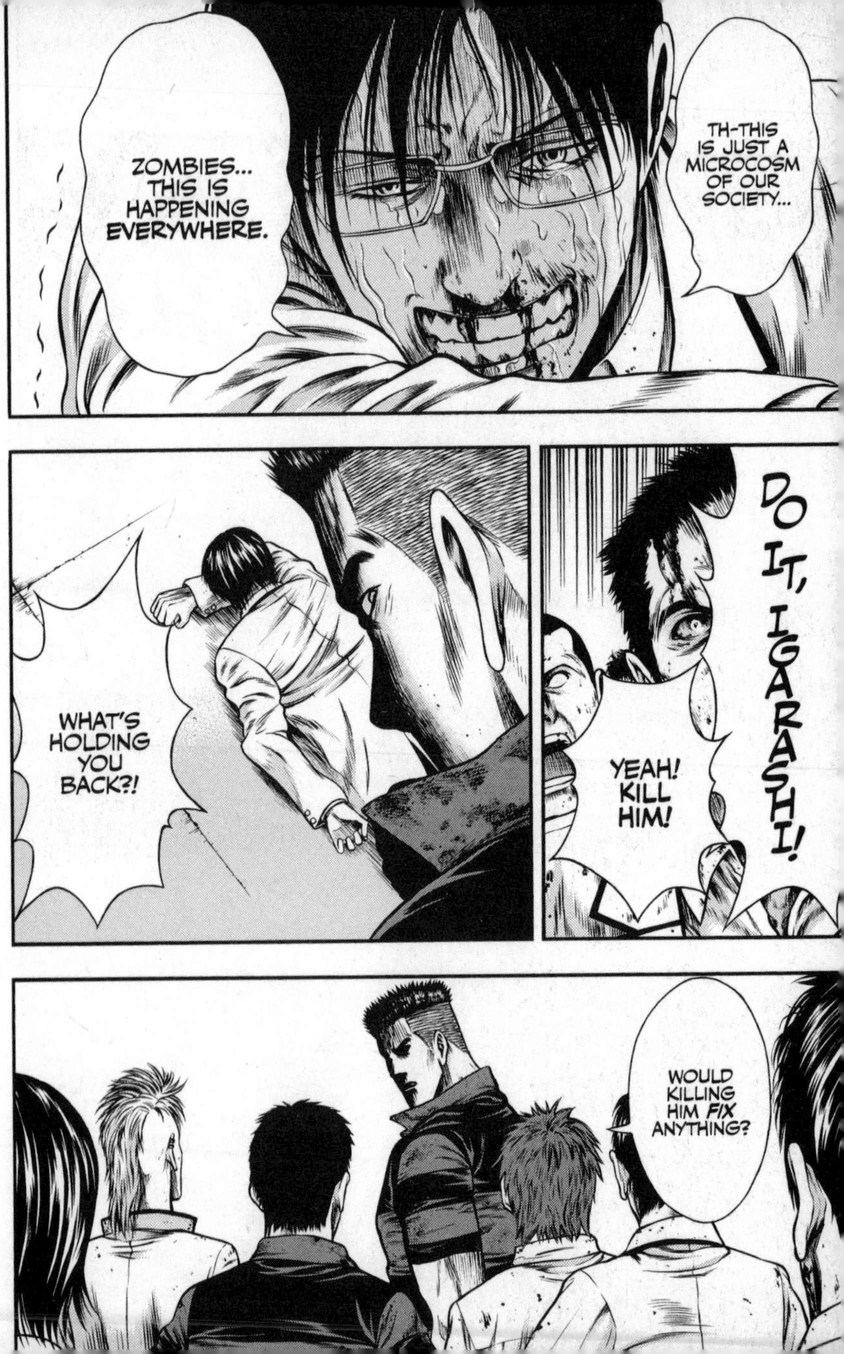
TH-THIS IS JUST A MICROCOSM OF OUR SOCIETY...
ZOMBIES... THIS IS HAPPENING EVERYWHERE.
DO IT, IGARASHI!
YEAH! KILL HIM!
WHAT'S HOLDING YOU BACK?!
WOULD KILLING HIM *FIX* ANYTHING?

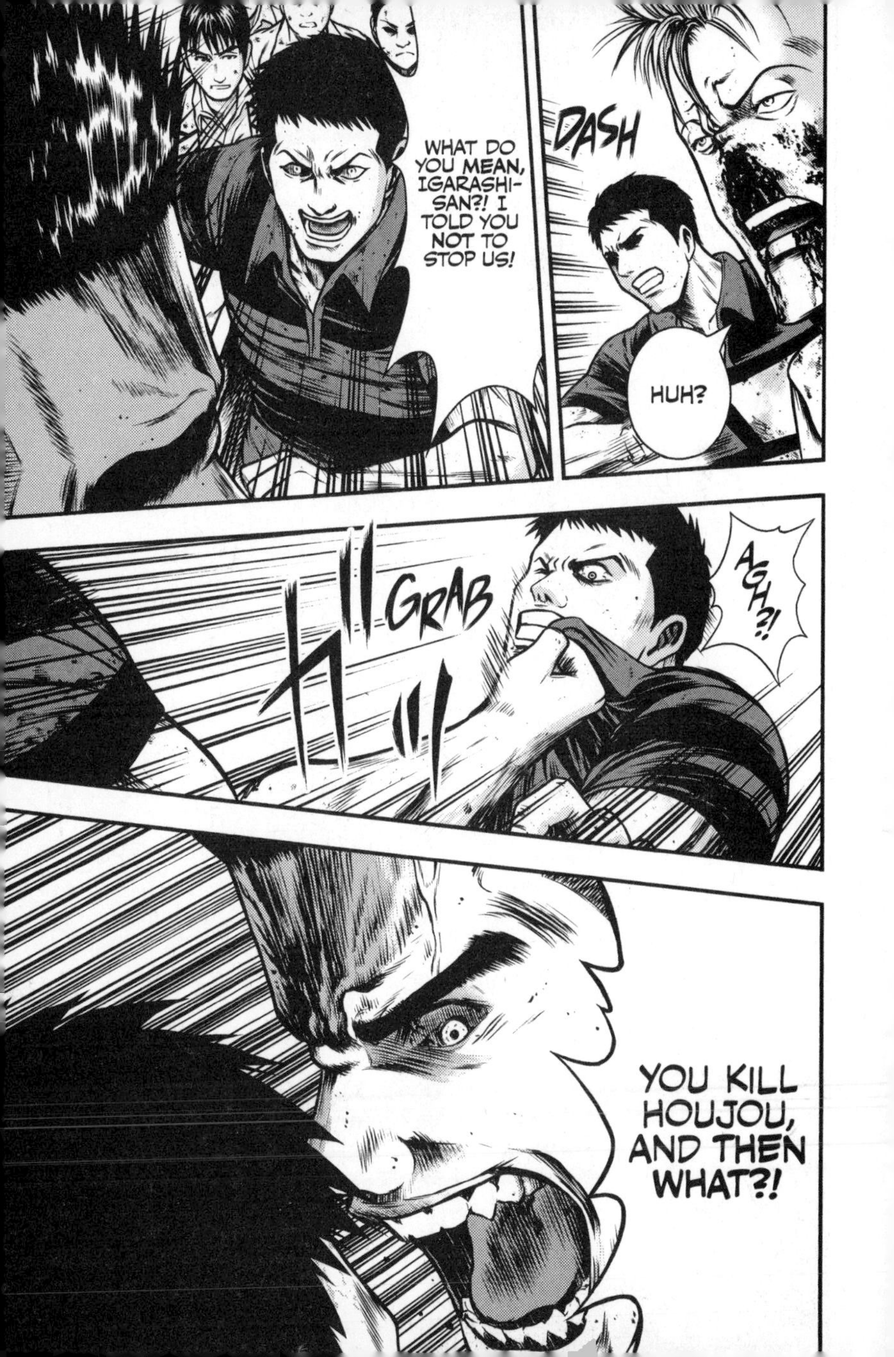
DASH
HUH?
WHAT DO YOU MEAN, IGARASHI-SAN?! I TOLD YOU NOT TO STOP US!
AGH?!
GRAB
YOU KILL HOUJOU, AND THEN WHAT?!

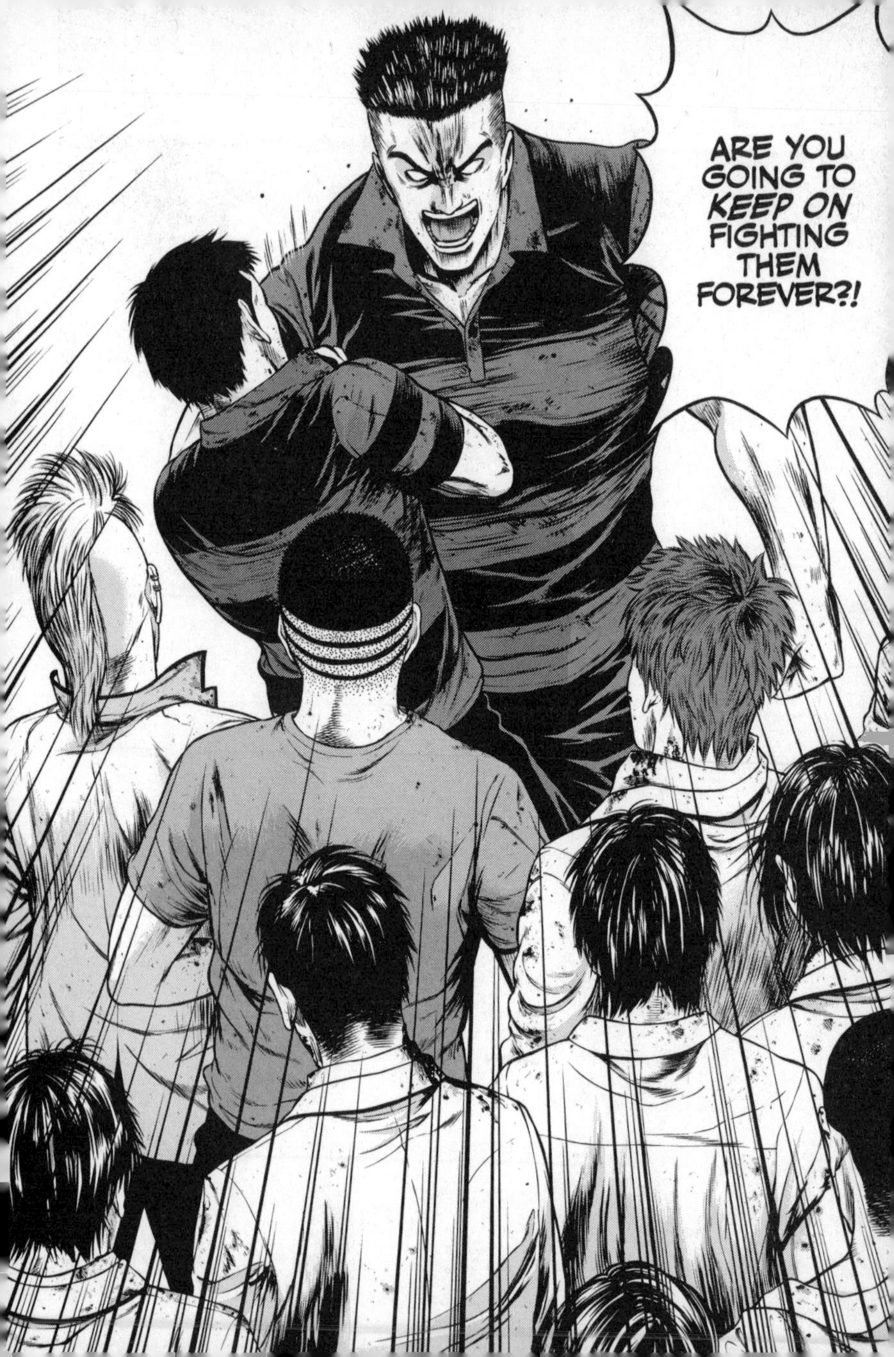
ARE YOU GOING TO *KEEP ON* FIGHTING THEM FOREVER?!

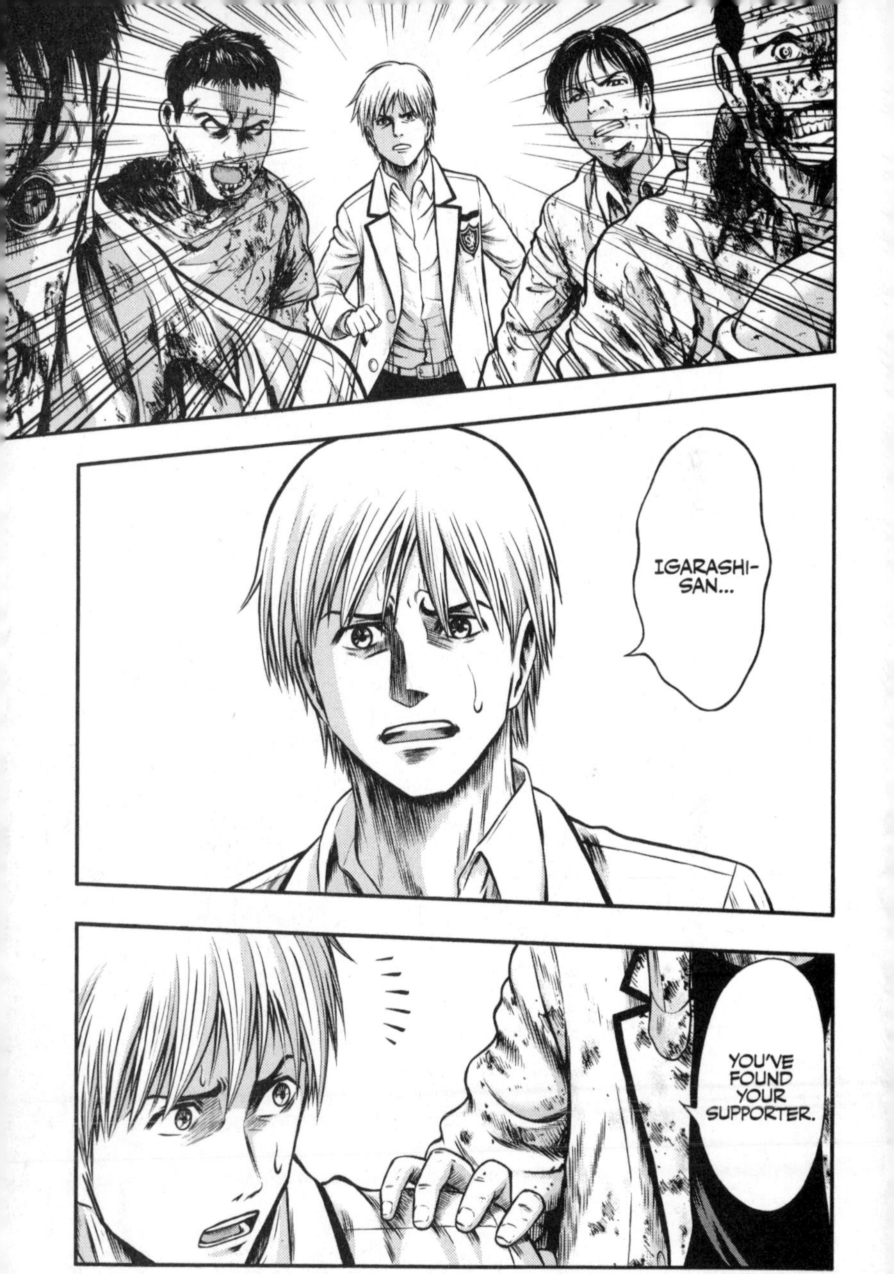
IGARASHI-SAN...
YOU'VE FOUND YOUR SUPPORTER.

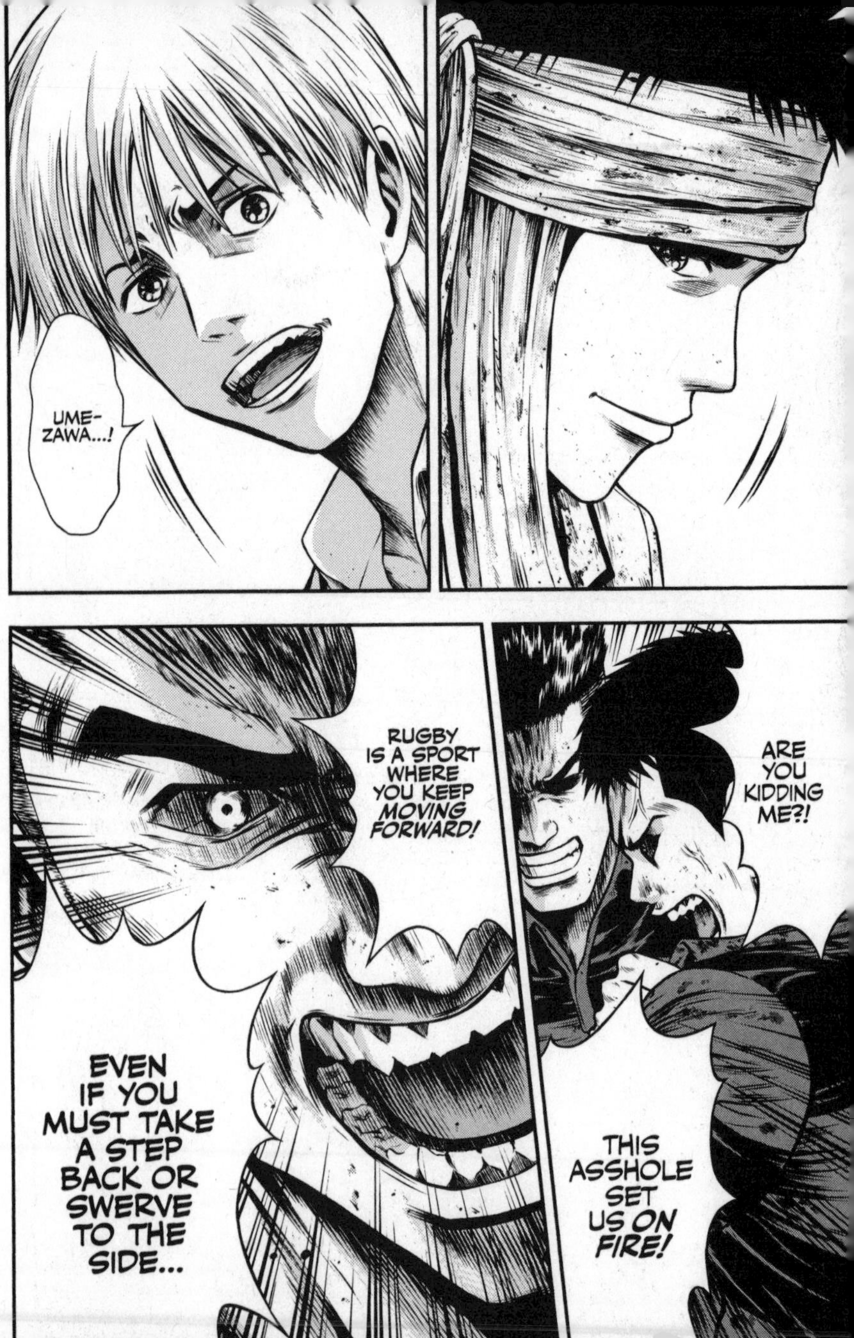
UME-ZAWA...!
ARE YOU KIDDING ME?!
THIS ASSHOLE SET US ON *FIRE!*
RUGBY IS A SPORT WHERE YOU KEEP *MOVING FORWARD!*
EVEN IF YOU MUST TAKE A STEP BACK OR SWERVE TO THE SIDE...

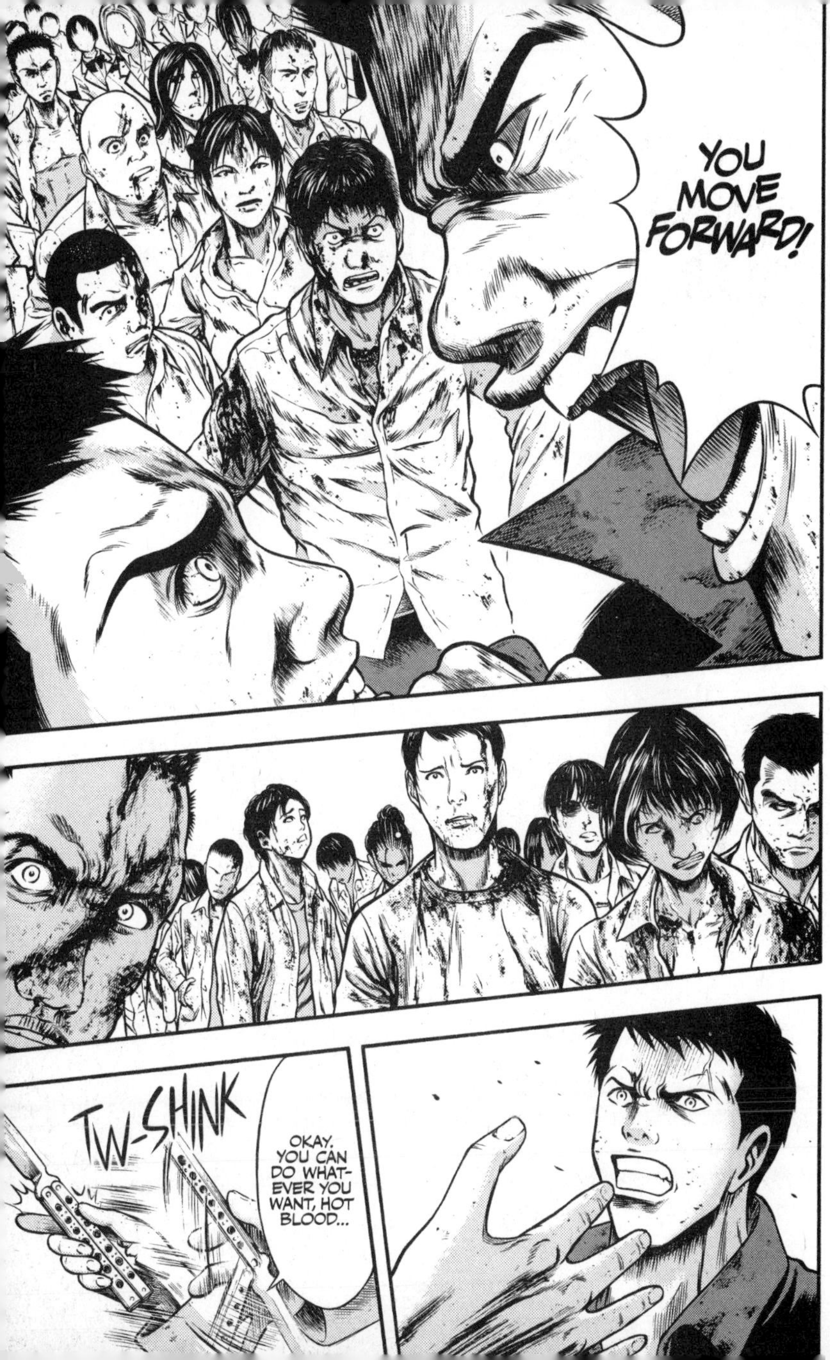
YOU MOVE FORWARD!
TW-SHINK
OKAY. YOU CAN DO WHAT-EVER YOU WANT, HOT BLOOD...

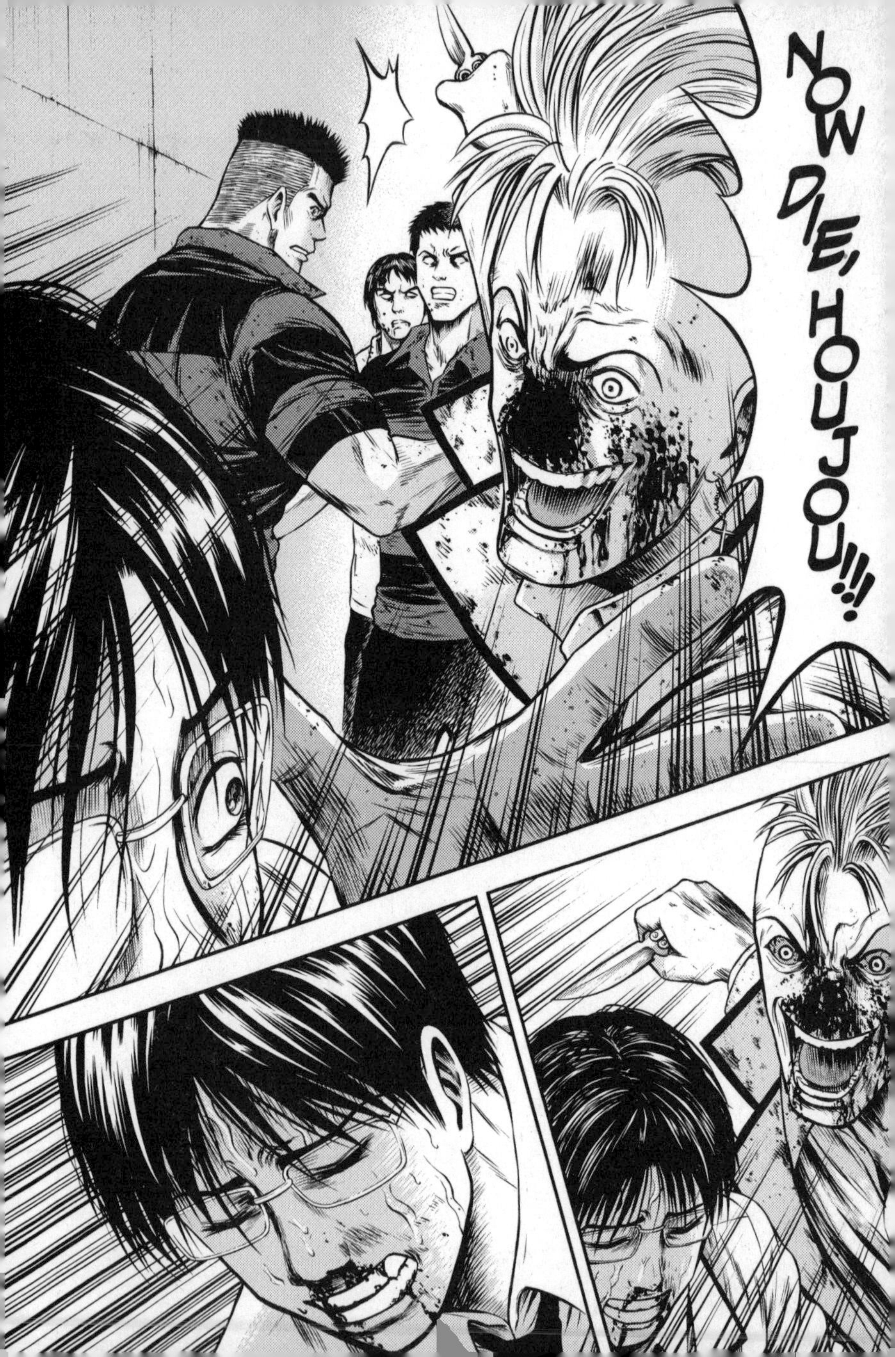
NOW DIE, HOUJOU!!!

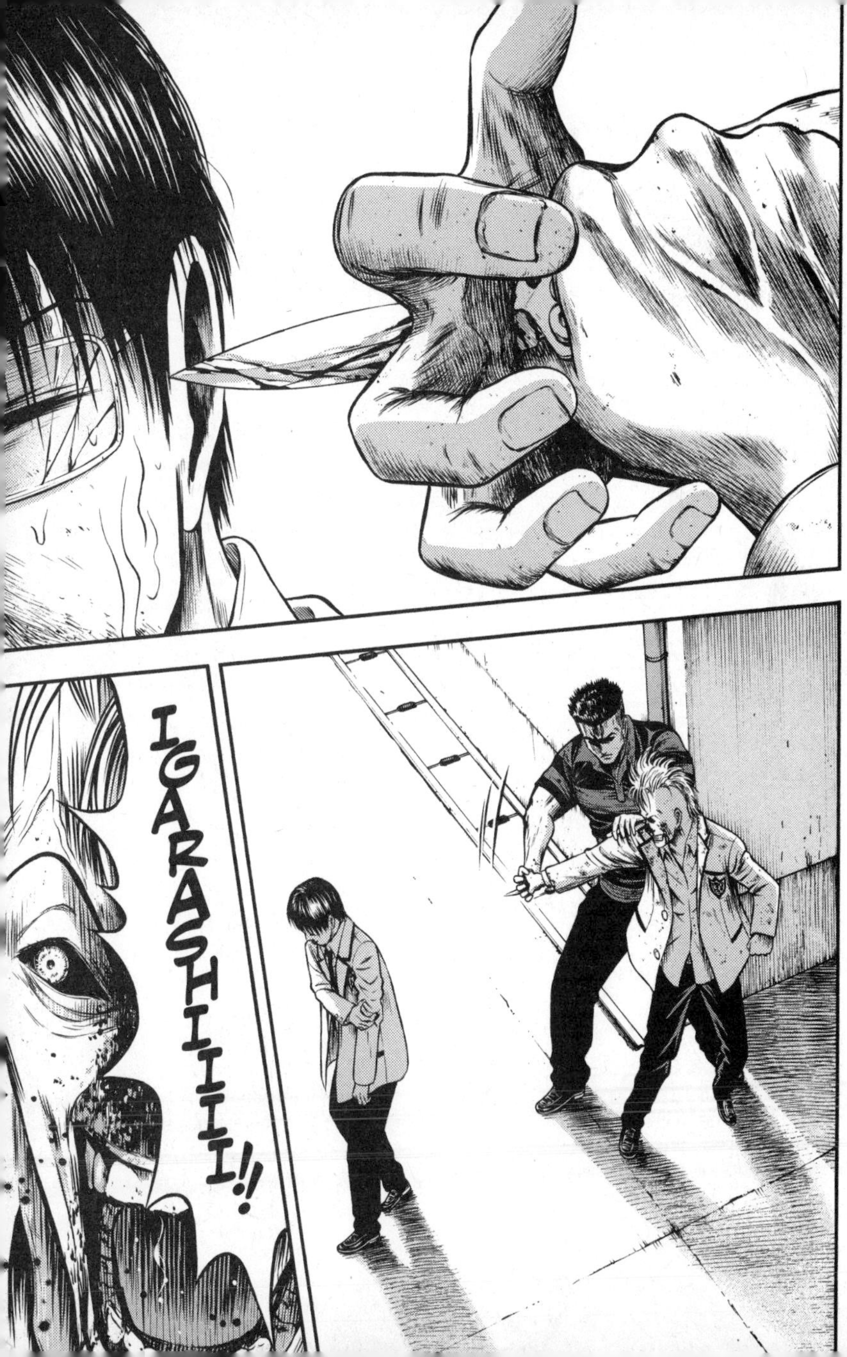
IGARASHIIIII!!

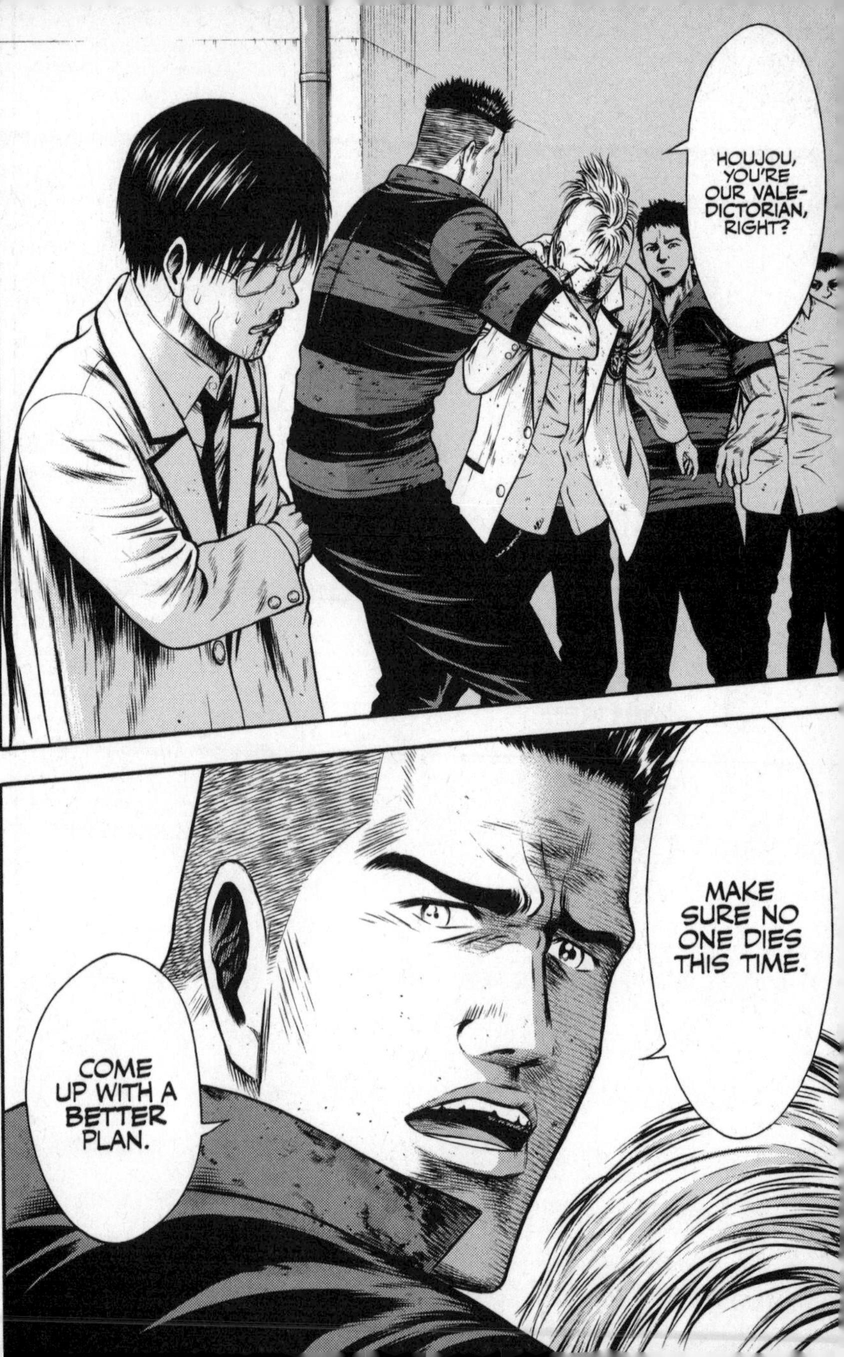
HOUJOU, YOU'RE OUR VALE-DICTORIAN, RIGHT?
MAKE SURE NO ONE DIES THIS TIME.
COME UP WITH A BETTER PLAN.

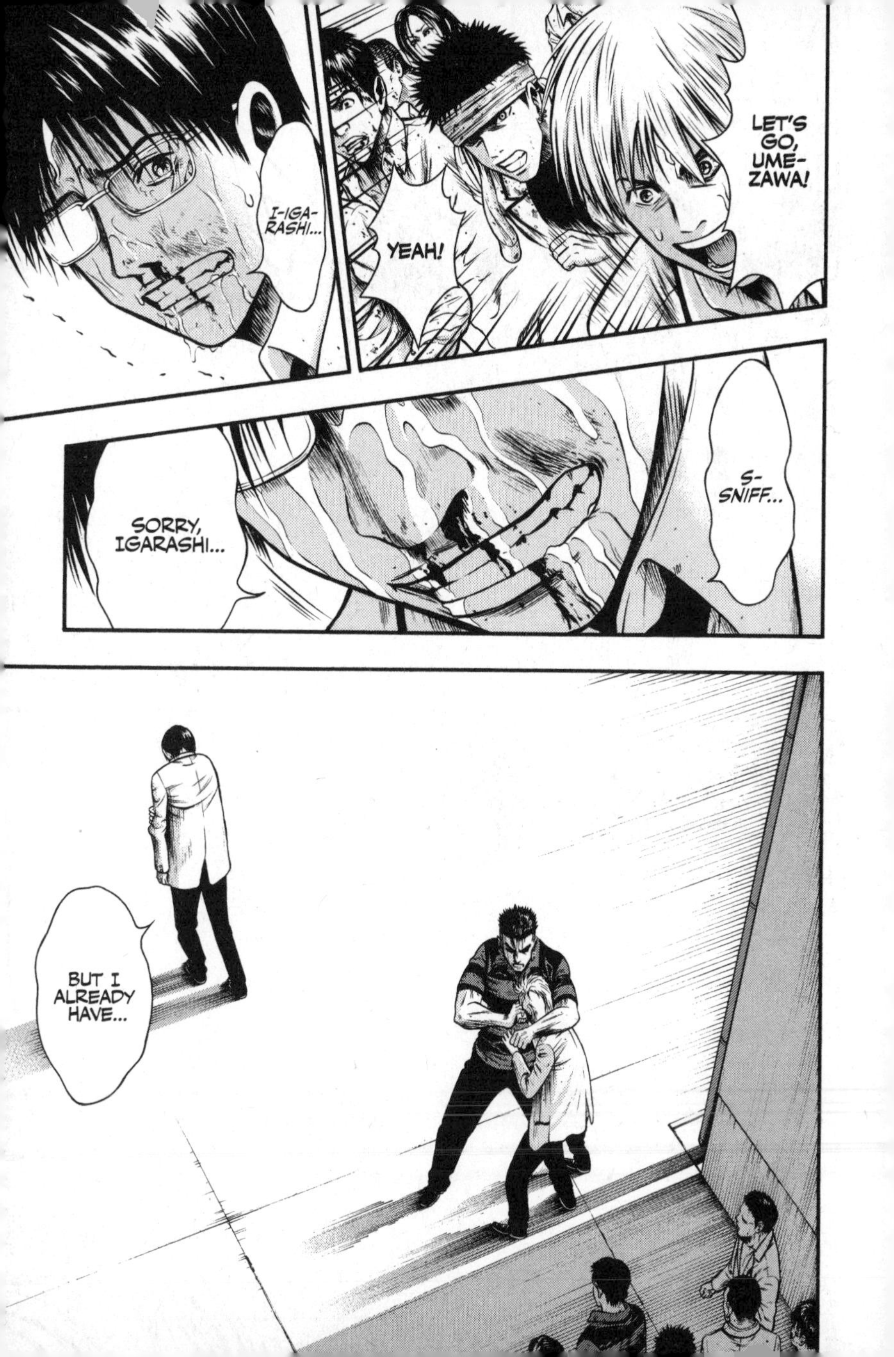

LET'S GO, UME-ZAWA!
YEAH!
I-IGA-RASHI...
S-SNIFF...
SORRY, IGARASHI...
BUT I ALREADY HAVE...

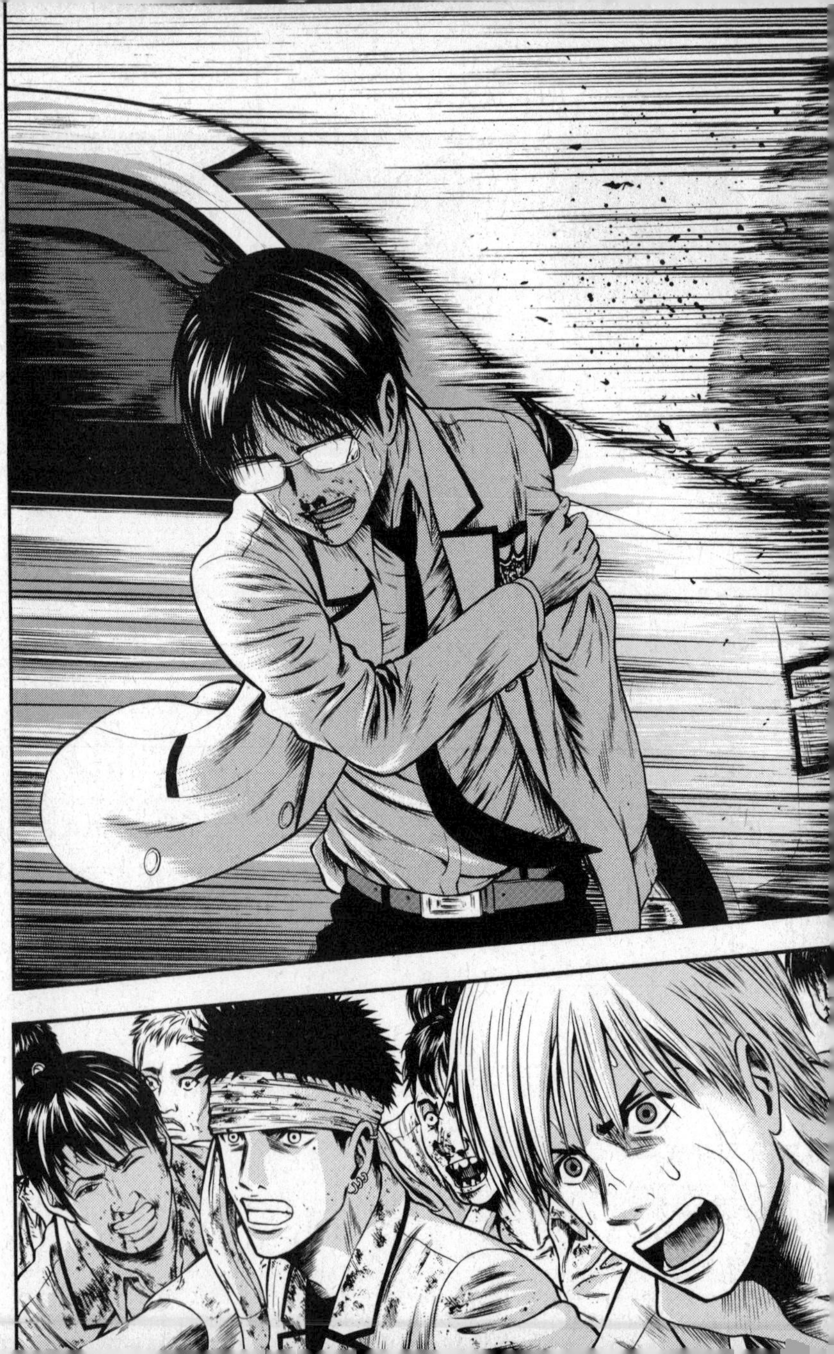

HOUR OF THE ZOMBIE

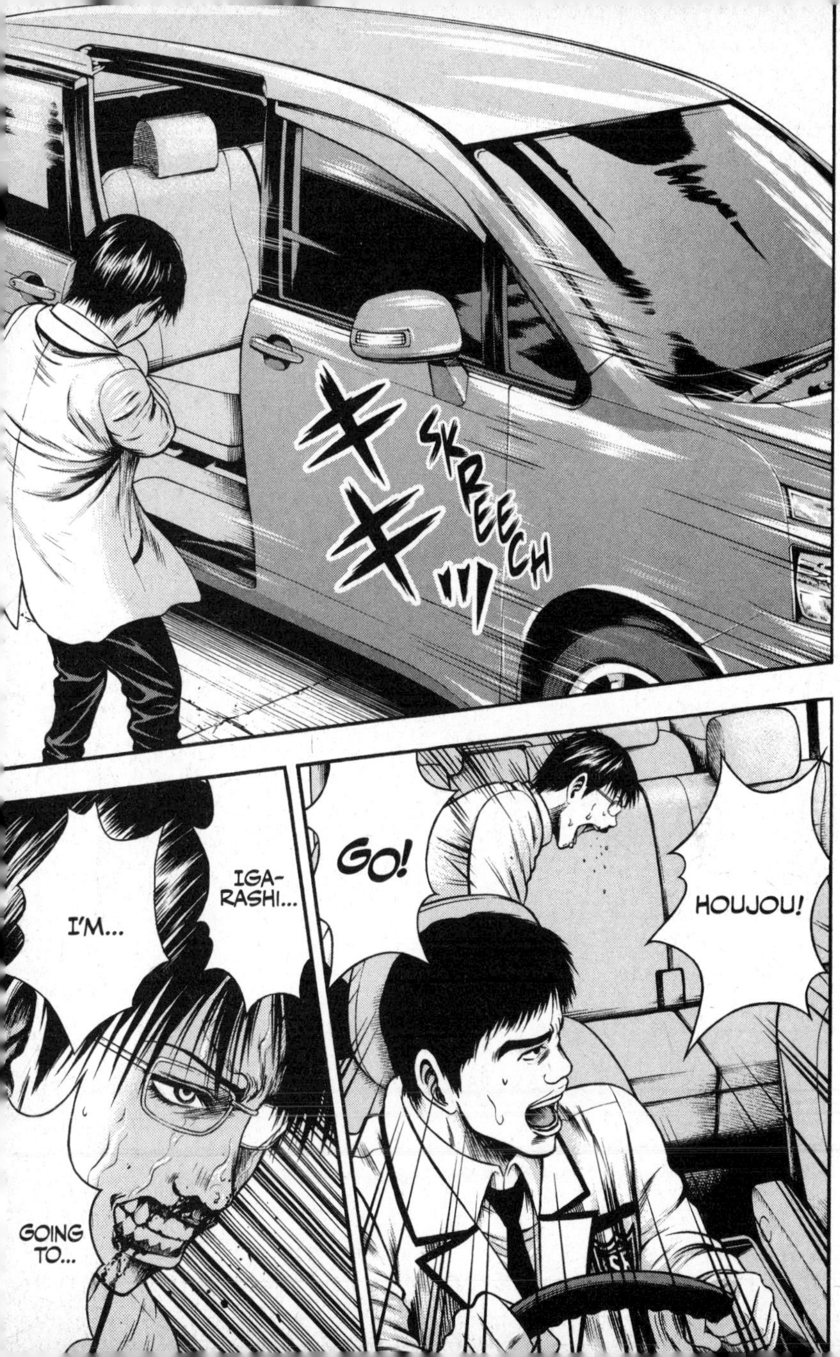
SKREECH
HOUJOU!
GO!
IGA-RASHI...
I'M...
GOING TO...

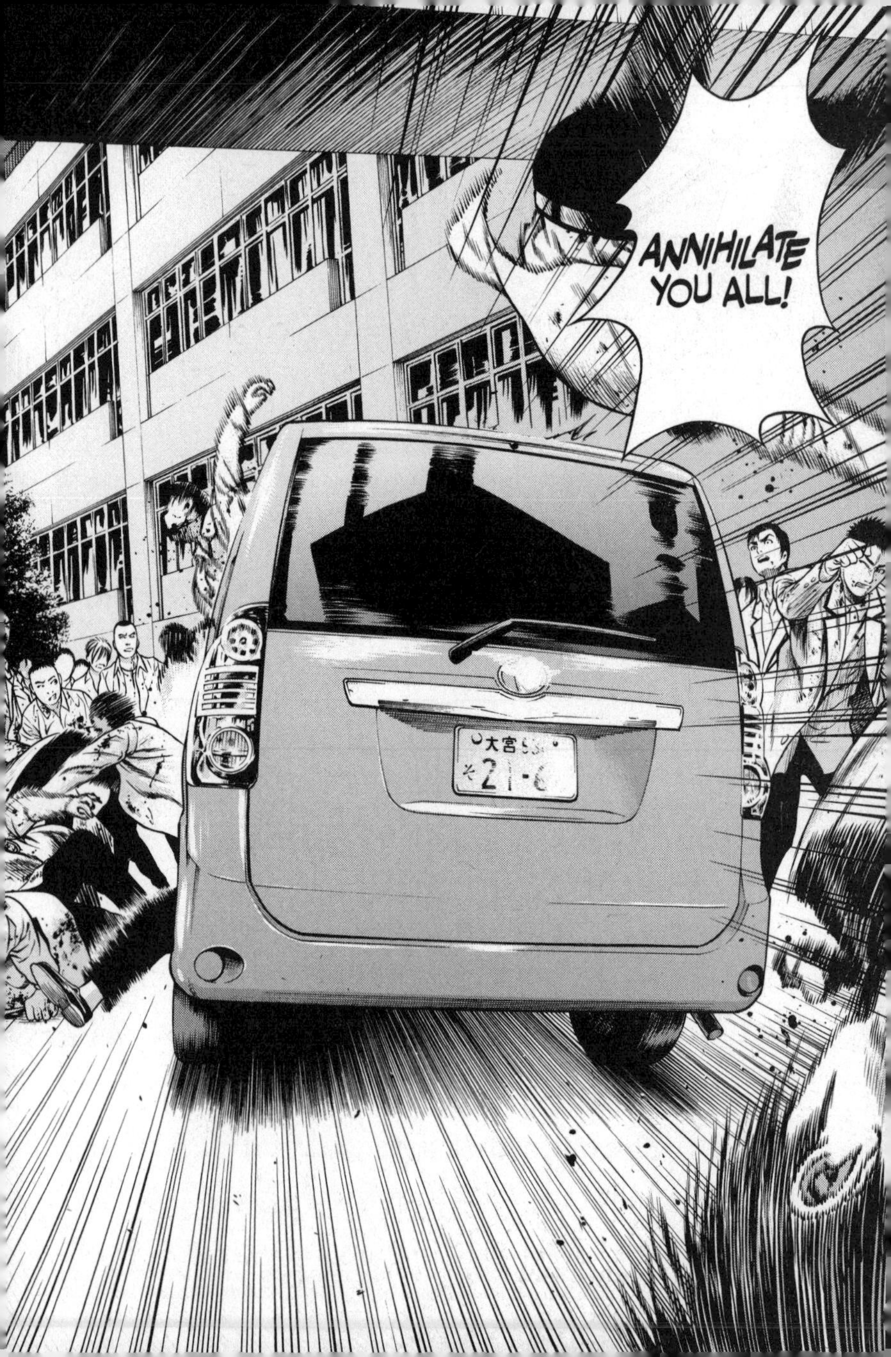
ANNIHILATE YOU ALL!
大宮
21-6

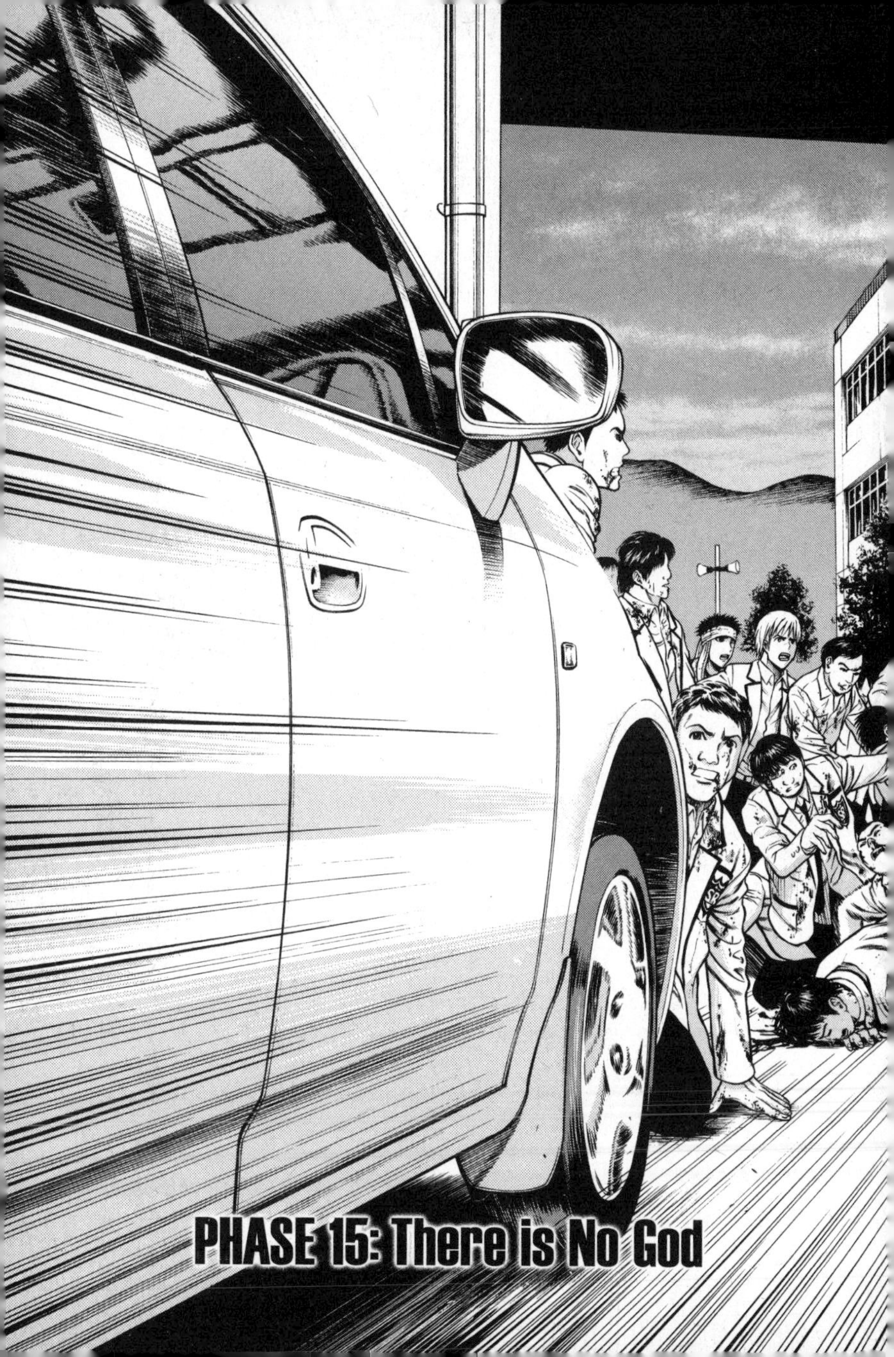
PHASE 15: There is No God

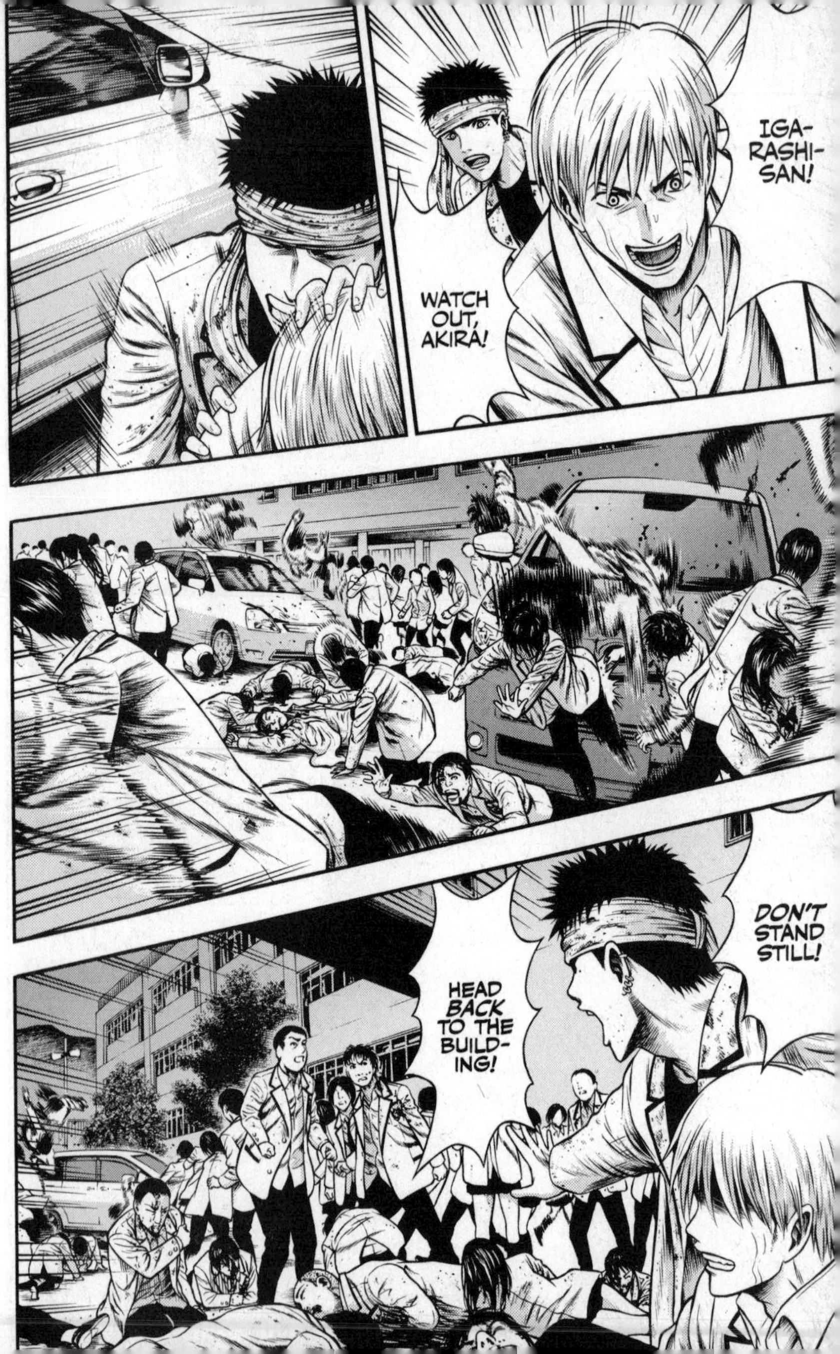
IGA-RASHI-SAN!
WATCH OUT, AKIRA!
DON'T STAND STILL!
HEAD BACK TO THE BUILD-ING!

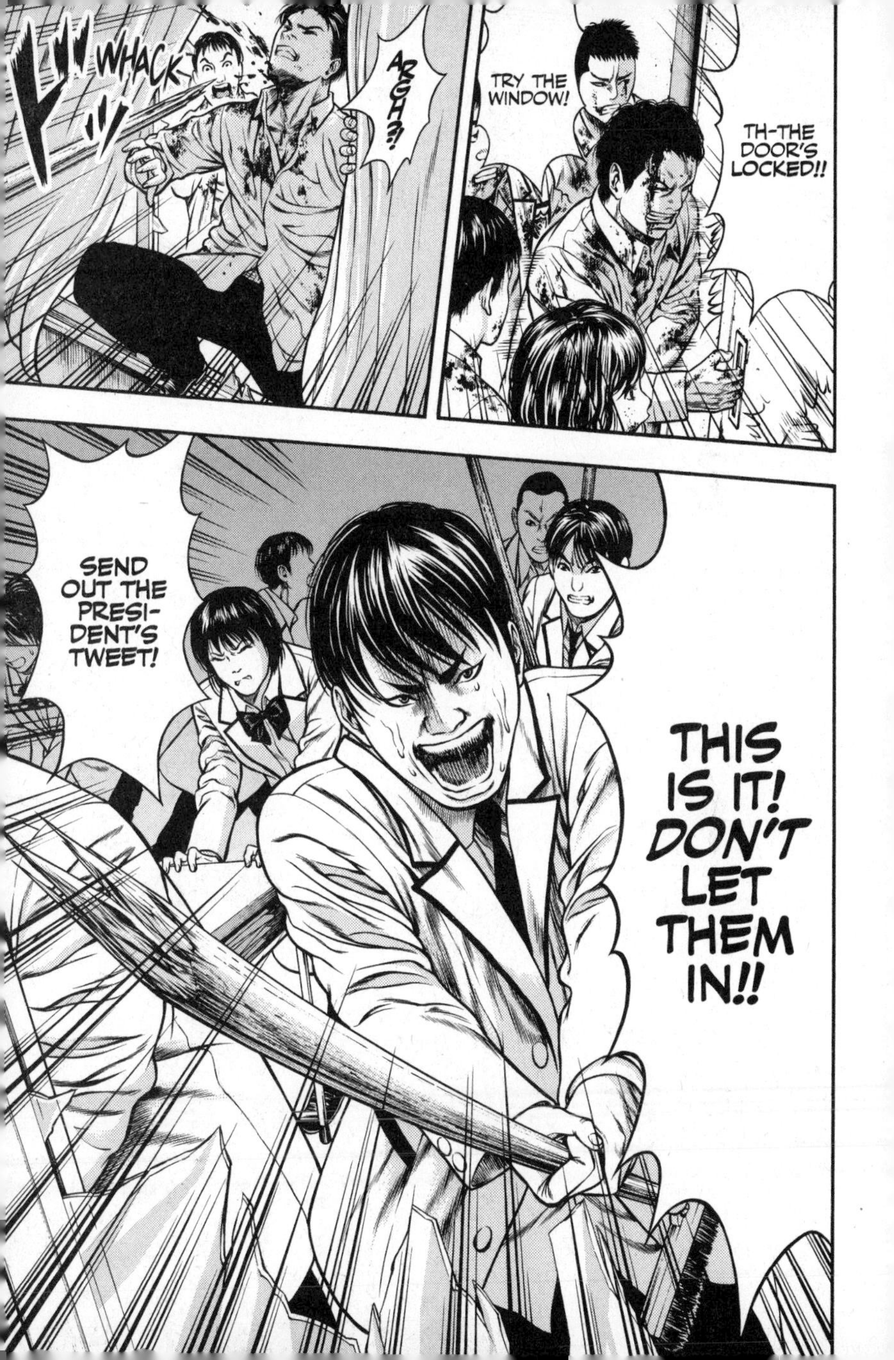
TH-THE DOOR'S LOCKED!!
TRY THE WINDOW!
ARGH?!
WHACK
THIS IS IT! DON'T LET THEM IN!!
SEND OUT THE PRESI-DENT'S TWEET!

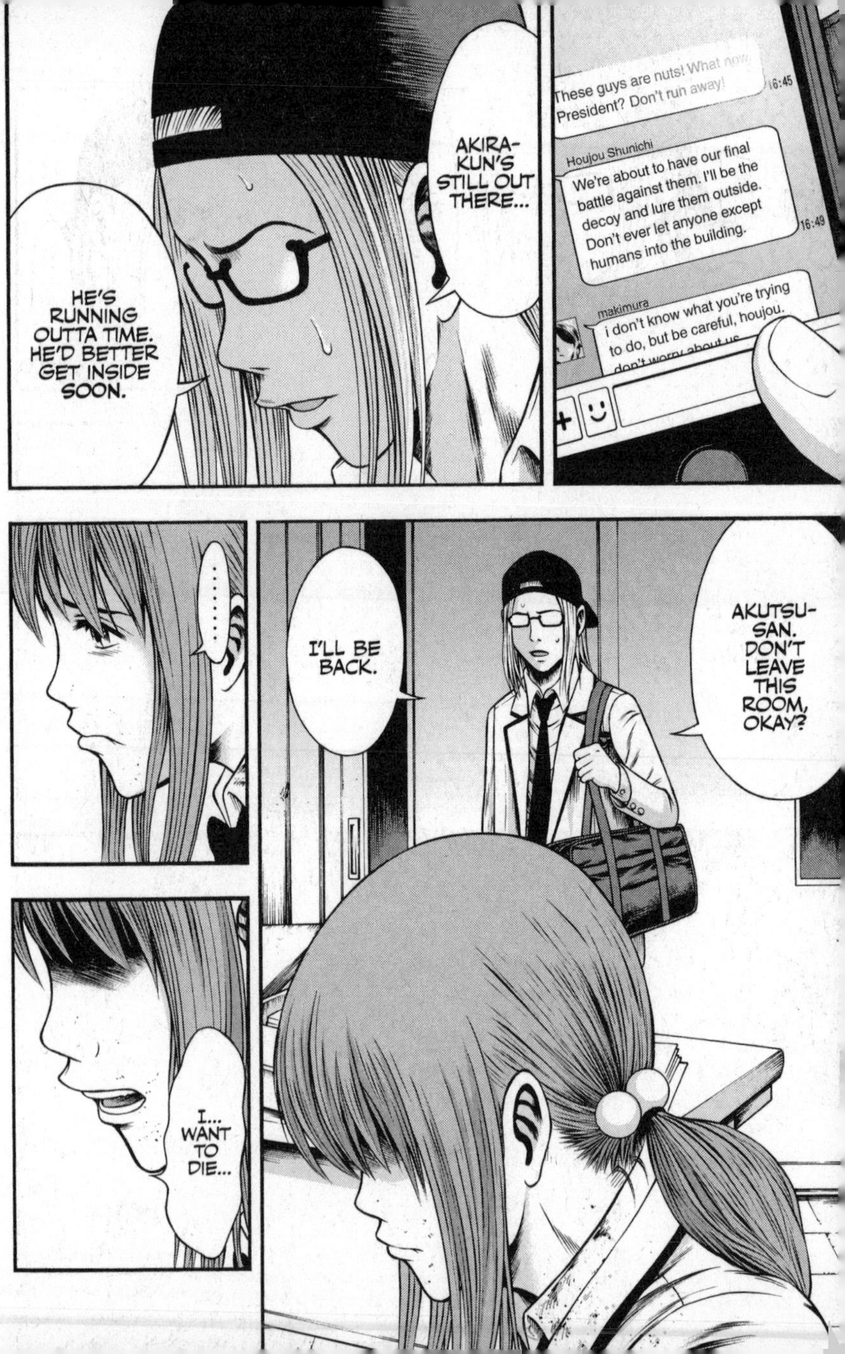
These guys are nuts! What now, President? Don't run away!
16:45
Houjou Shunichi
We're about to have our final battle against them. I'll be the decoy and lure them outside. Don't ever let anyone except humans into the building.
16:49
makimura
i don't know what you're trying to do, but be careful, houjou.
AKIRA-KUN'S STILL OUT THERE...
HE'S RUNNING OUTTA TIME. HE'D BETTER GET INSIDE SOON.
AKUTSU-SAN. DON'T LEAVE THIS ROOM, OKAY?
I'LL BE BACK.
......
I... WANT TO DIE...

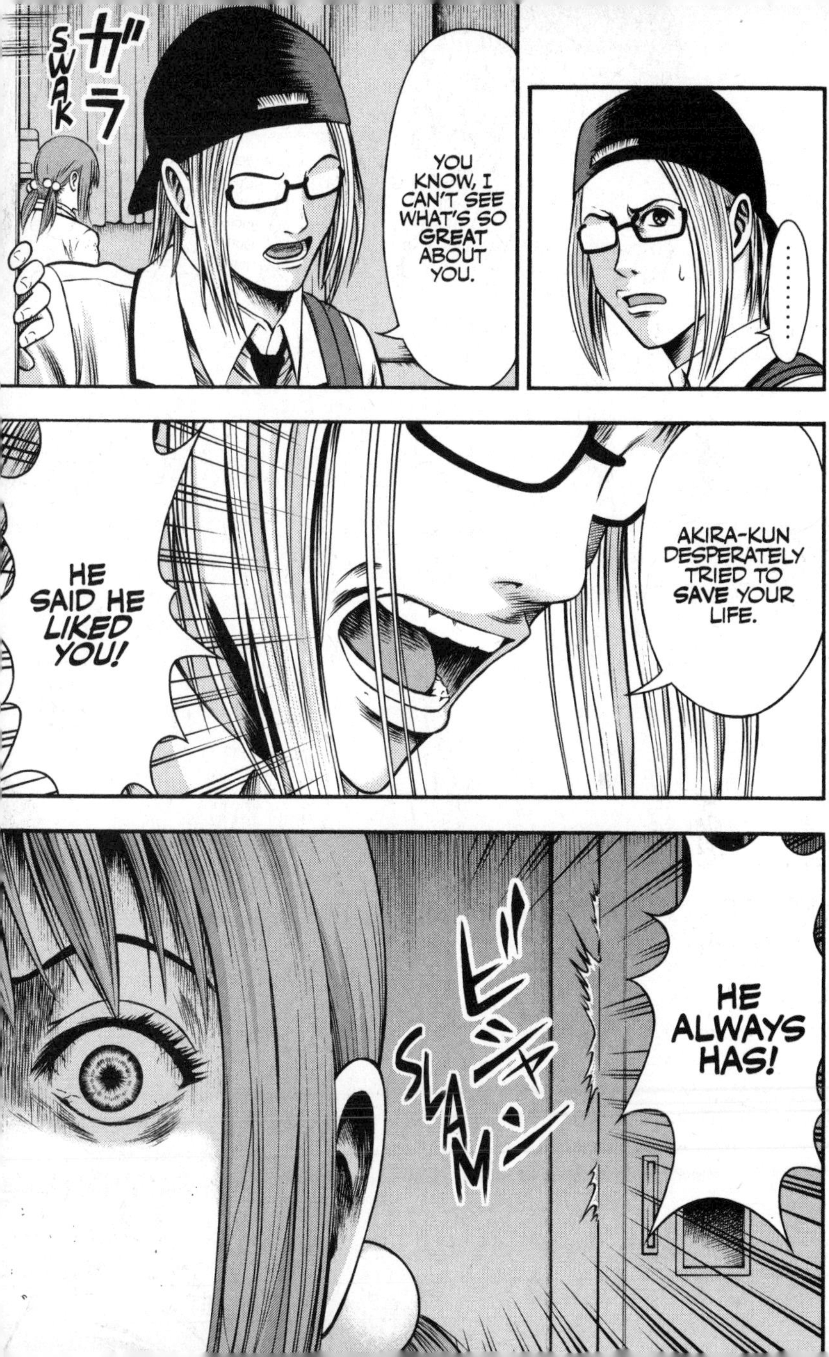

......
ガラ
SWAK
YOU KNOW, I CAN'T SEE WHAT'S SO GREAT ABOUT YOU.
AKIRA-KUN DESPERATELY TRIED TO SAVE YOUR LIFE.
HE SAID HE LIKED YOU!
HE ALWAYS HAS!
ピシャン
SLAM

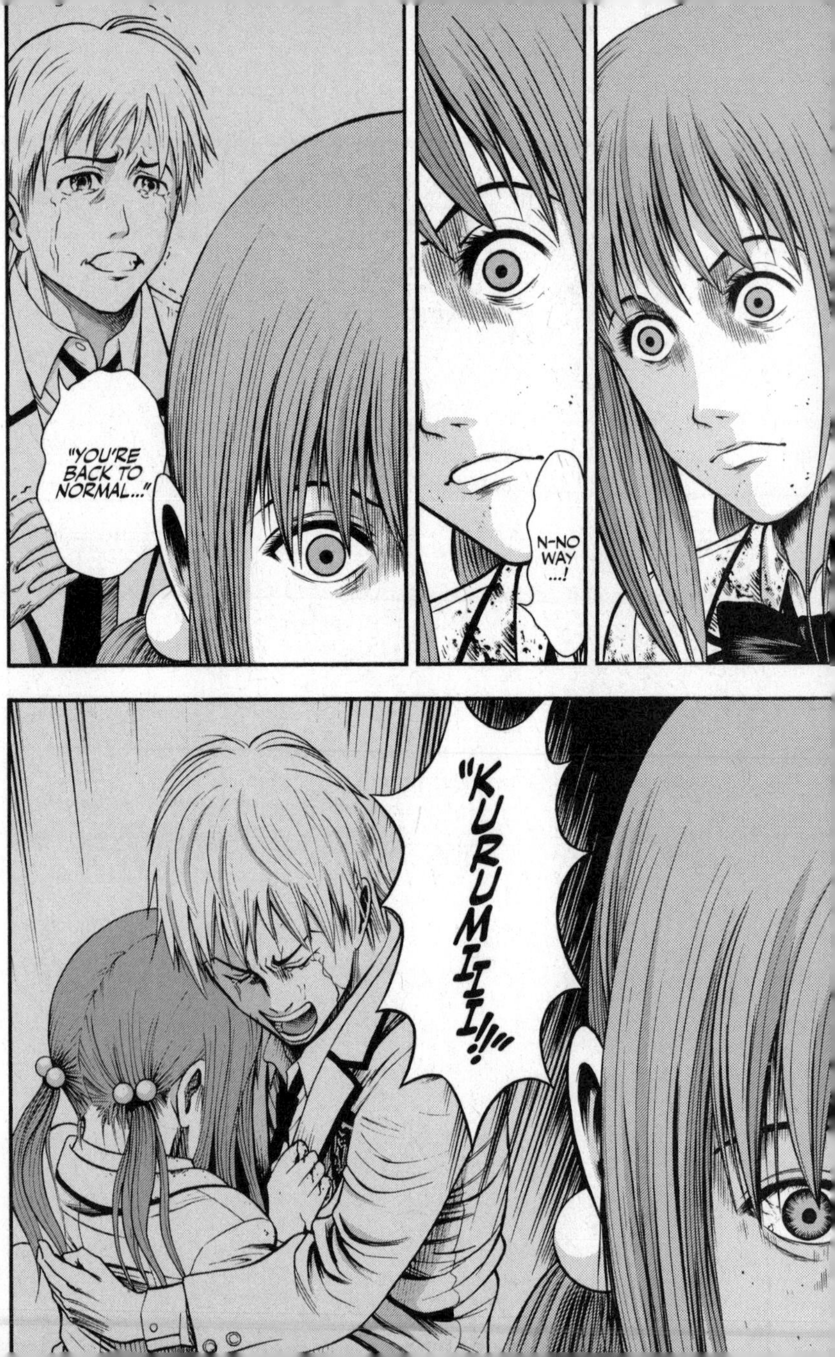
N-NO WAY ...!
"YOU'RE BACK TO NORMAL..."
"KURUMIIII!!"

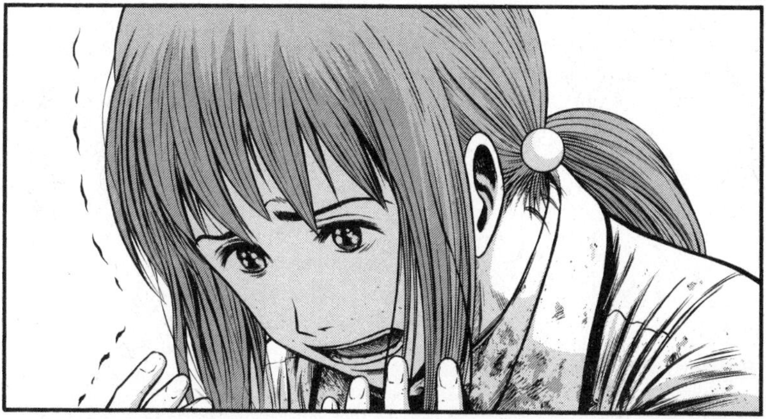

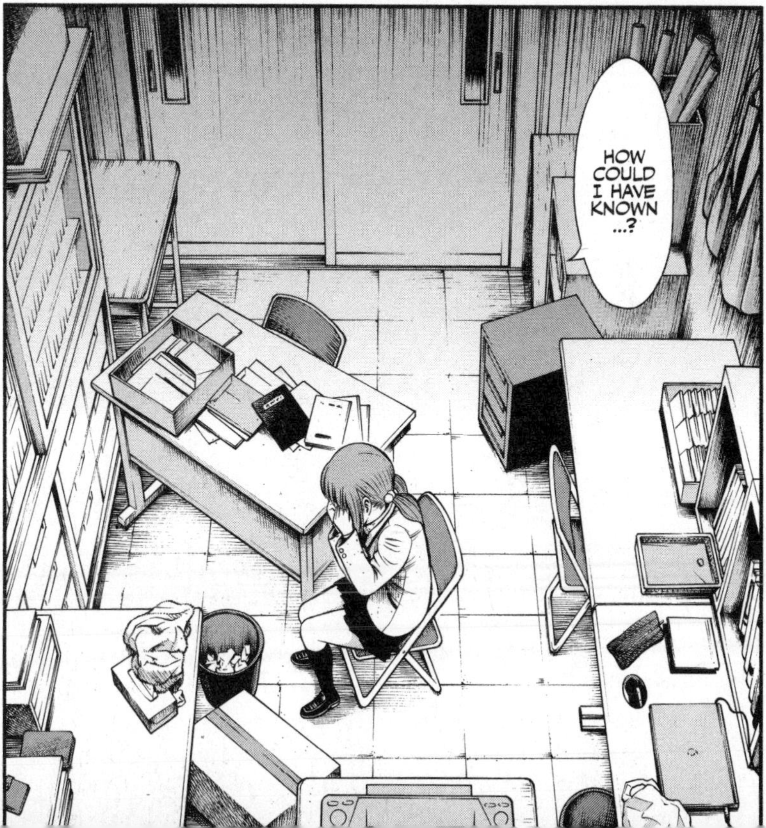
HOW COULD I HAVE KNOWN ...?

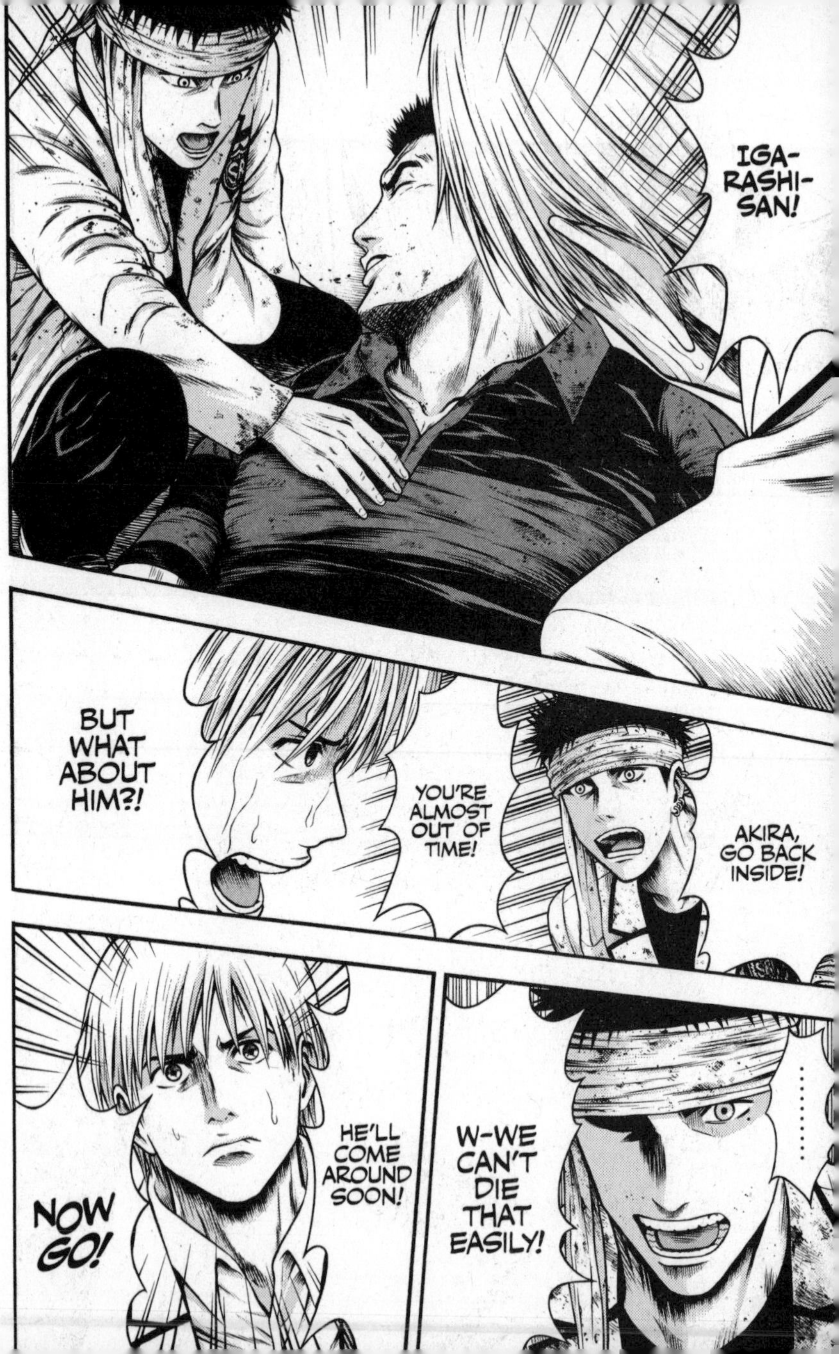
IGA-RASHI-SAN!
AKIRA, GO BACK INSIDE!
YOU'RE ALMOST OUT OF TIME!
BUT WHAT ABOUT HIM?!
W-WE CAN'T DIE THAT EASILY!
HE'LL COME AROUND SOON!
NOW GO!

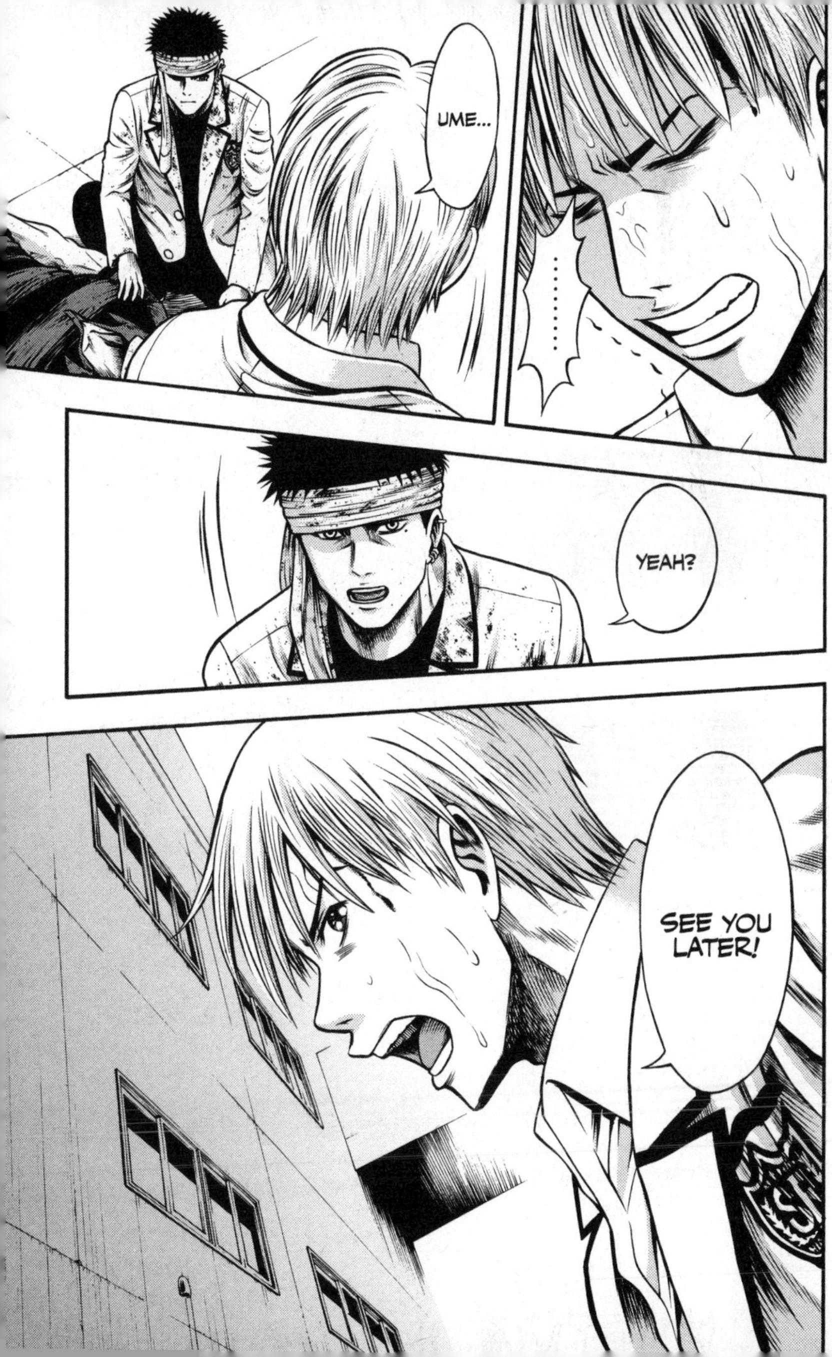
......
UME...
YEAH?
SEE YOU LATER!

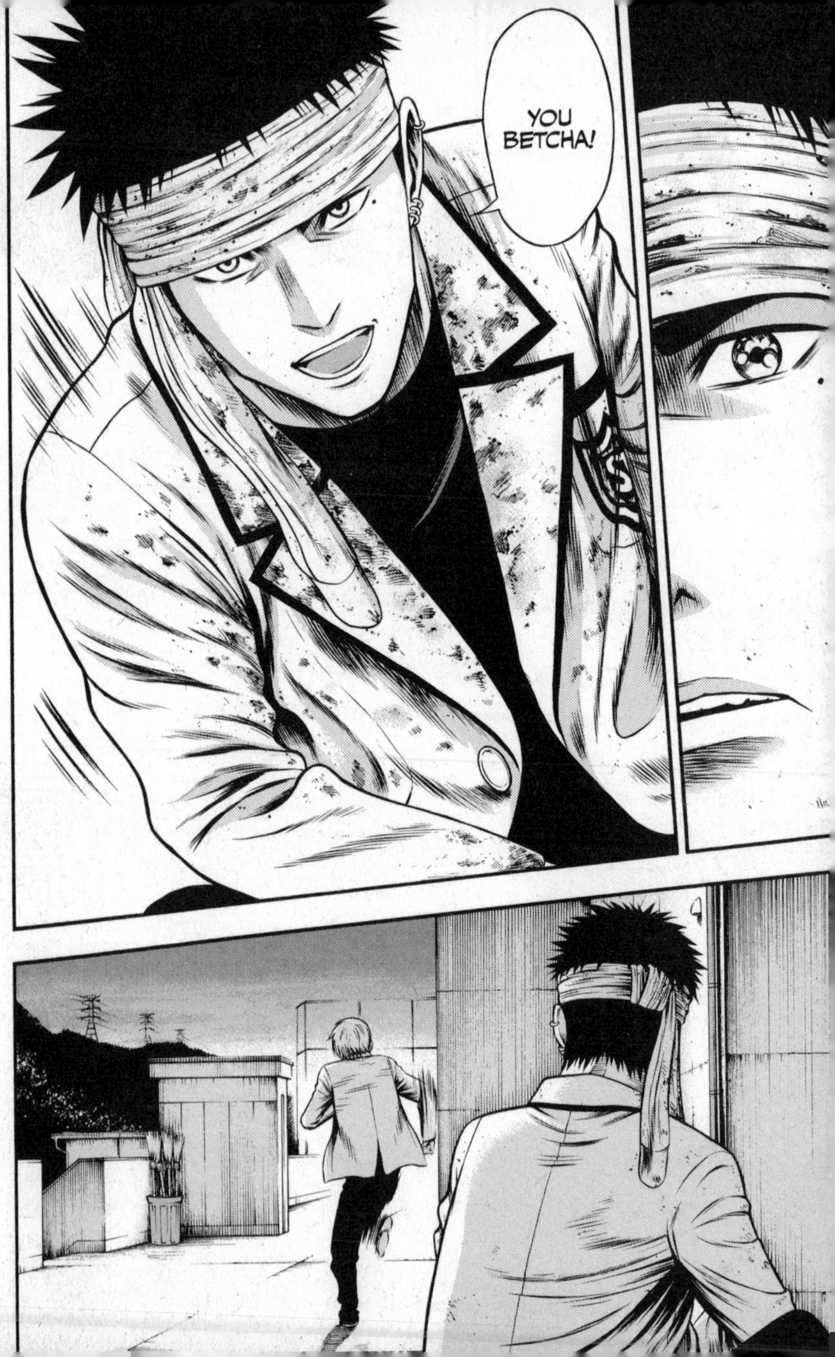
YOU BETCHA!

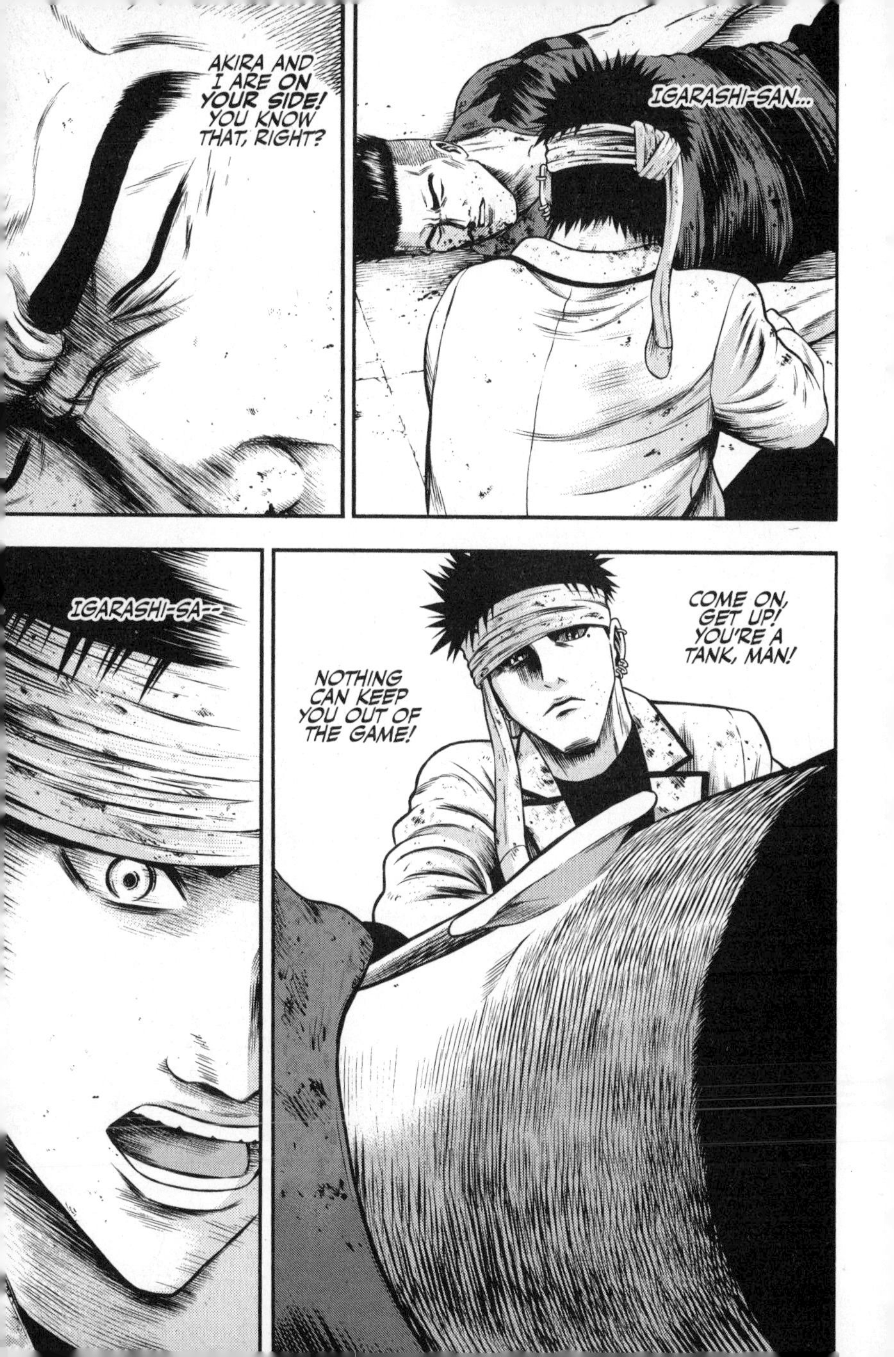
IGARASHI-SAN...
AKIRA AND I ARE ON YOUR SIDE! YOU KNOW THAT, RIGHT?
COME ON, GET UP! YOU'RE A TANK, MAN!
NOTHING CAN KEEP YOU OUT OF THE GAME!
IGARASHI-SA--

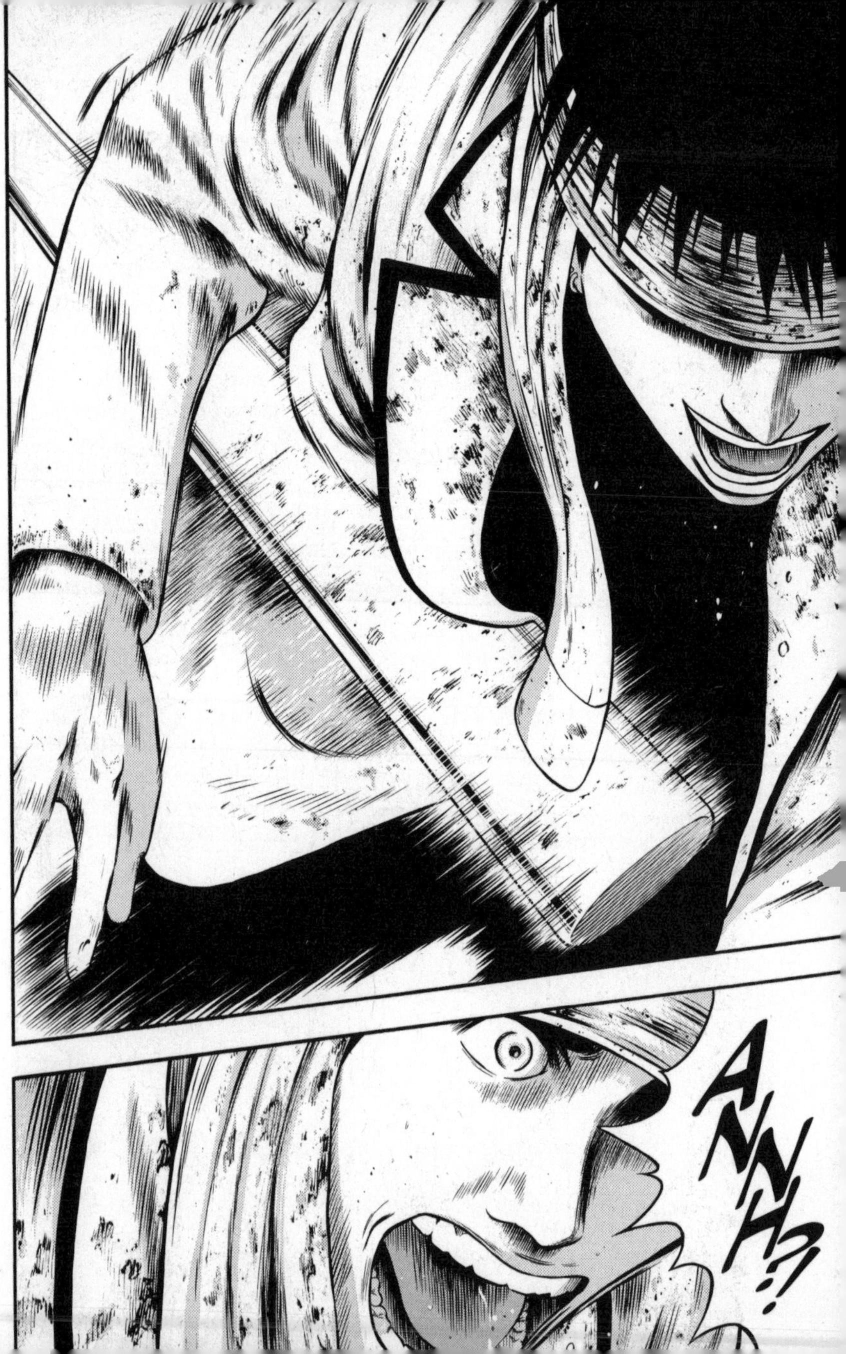
ANH?!

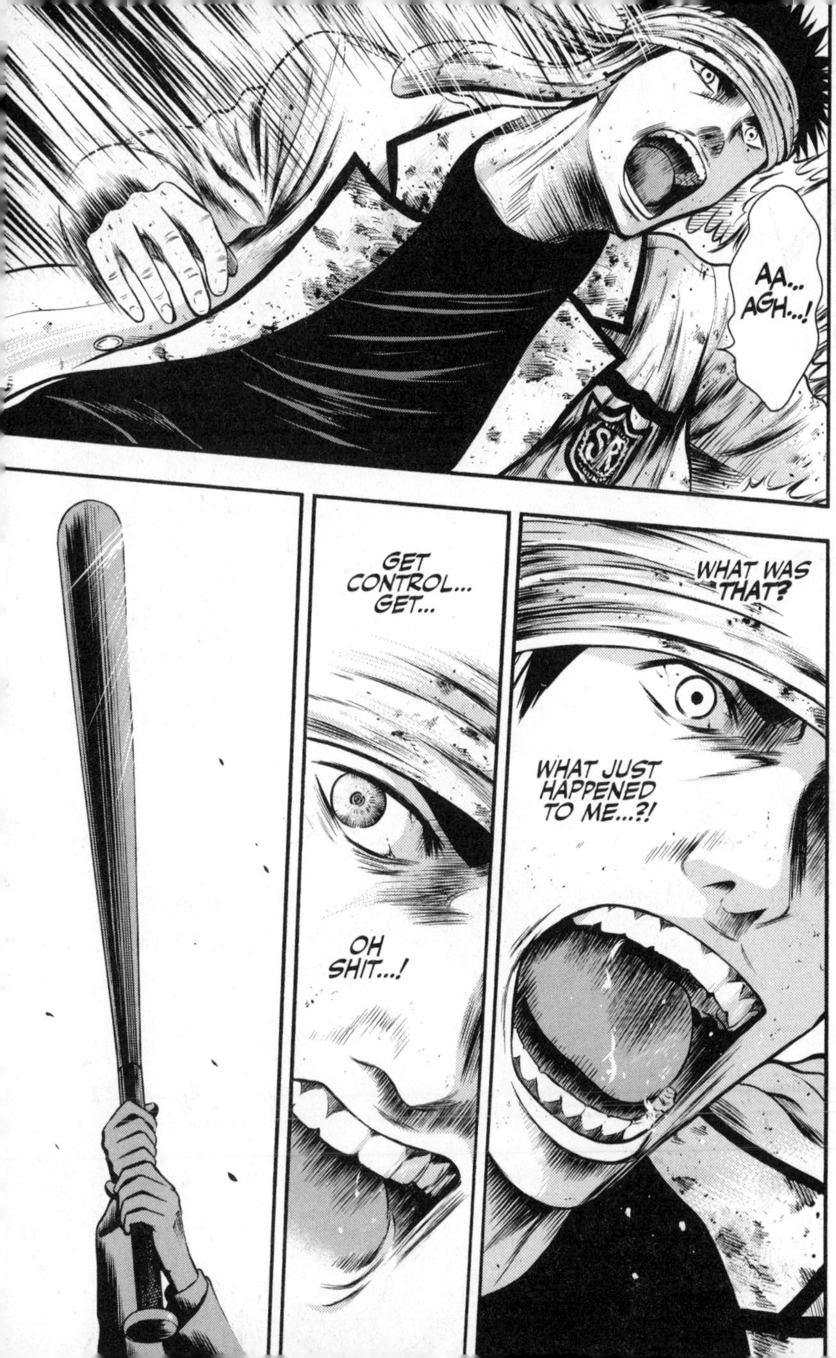
AA... AGH...!
WHAT WAS THAT?
WHAT JUST HAPPENED TO ME...?!
GET CONTROL... GET...
OH SHIT...!

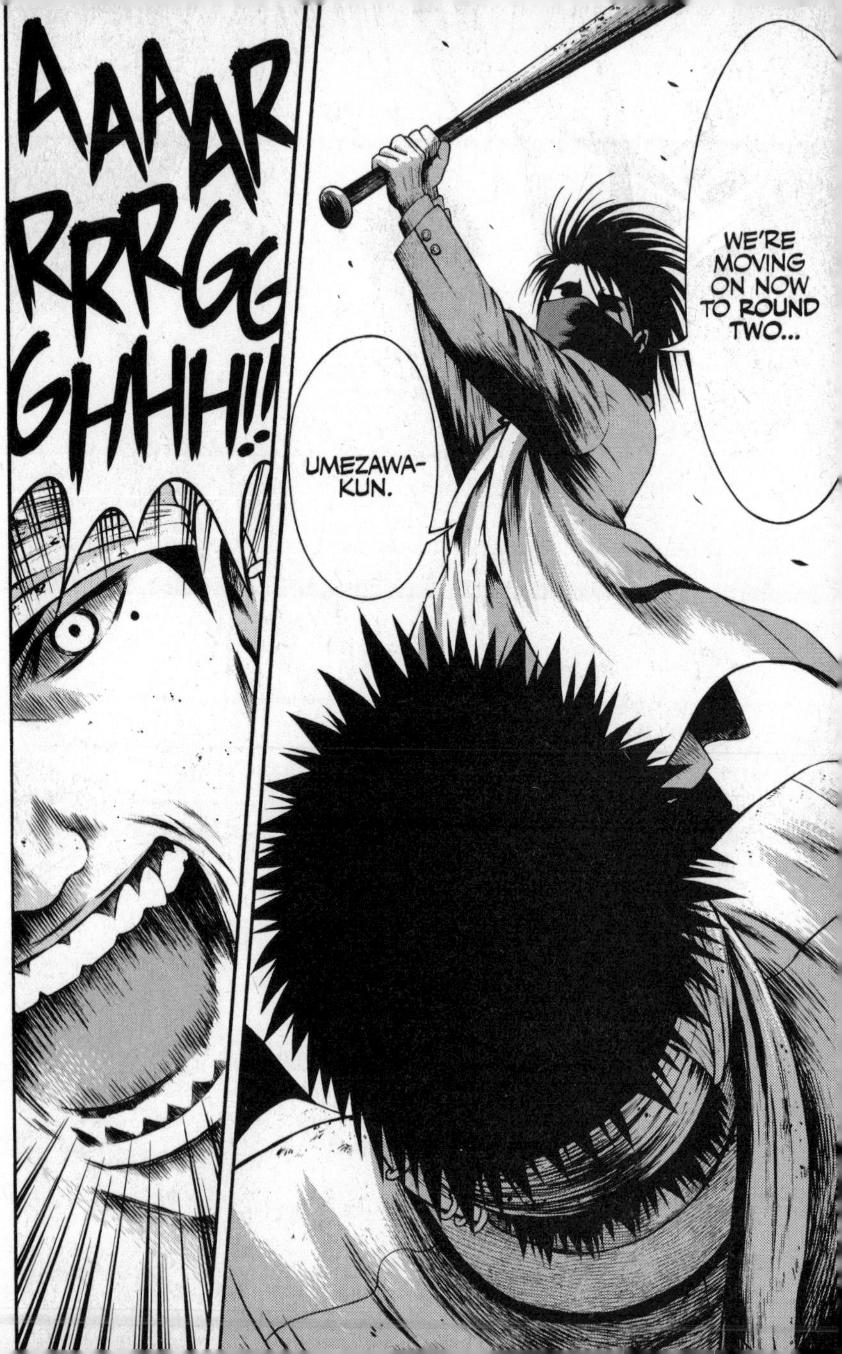
WE'RE MOVING ON NOW TO ROUND TWO...
UMEZAWA-KUN.
AAAARRRRGGGHHH!!!

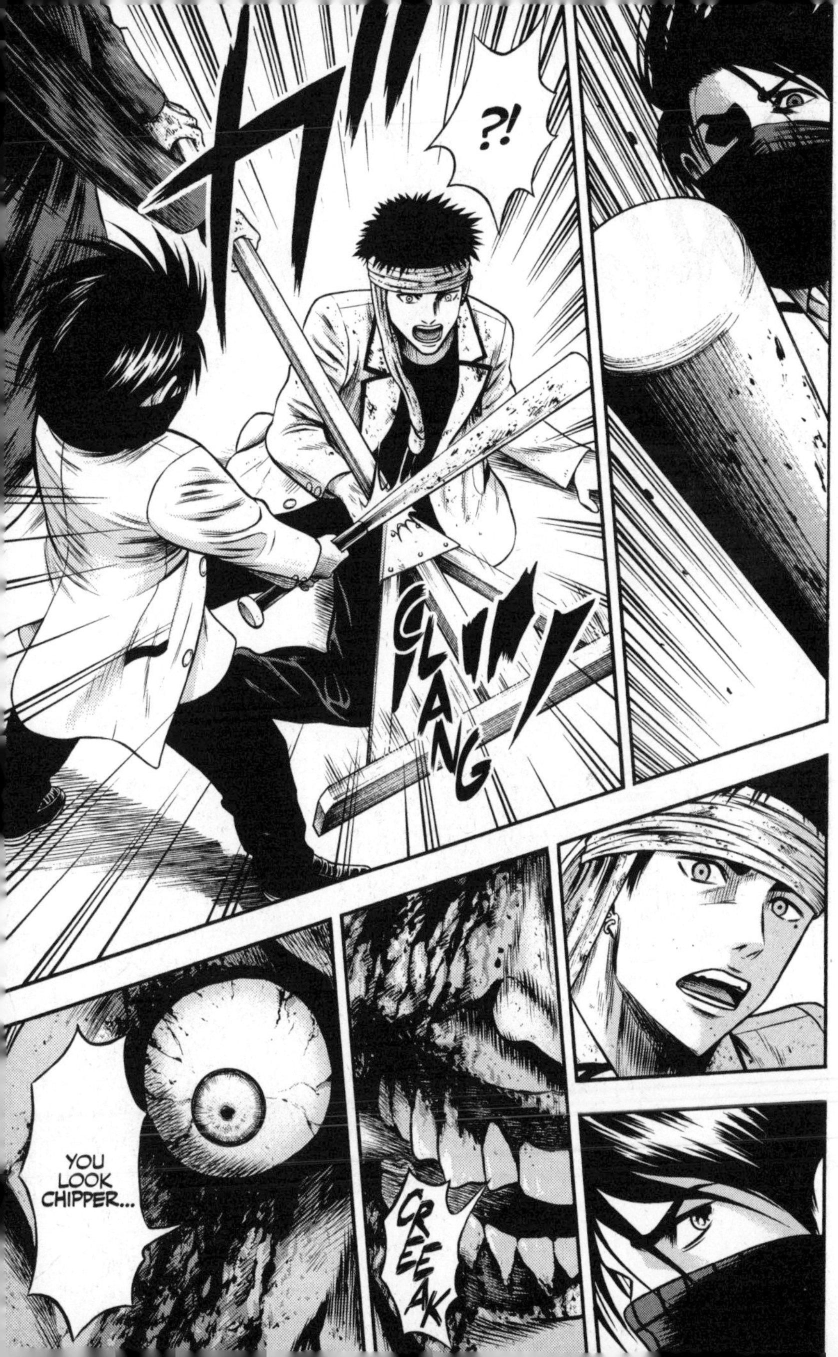
?!
CLANG
CREEAK
YOU LOOK CHIPPER...

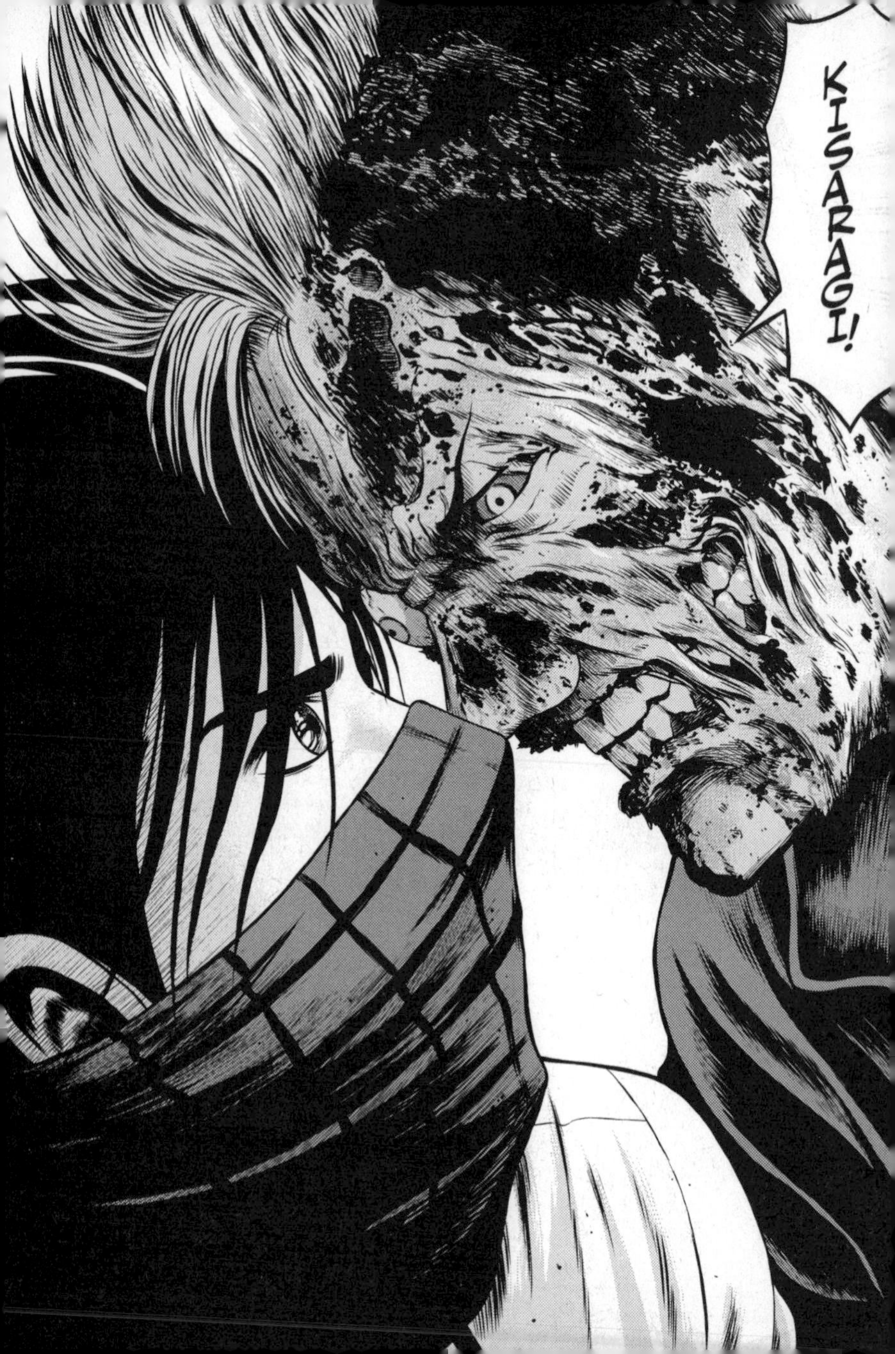
KISARAGI!

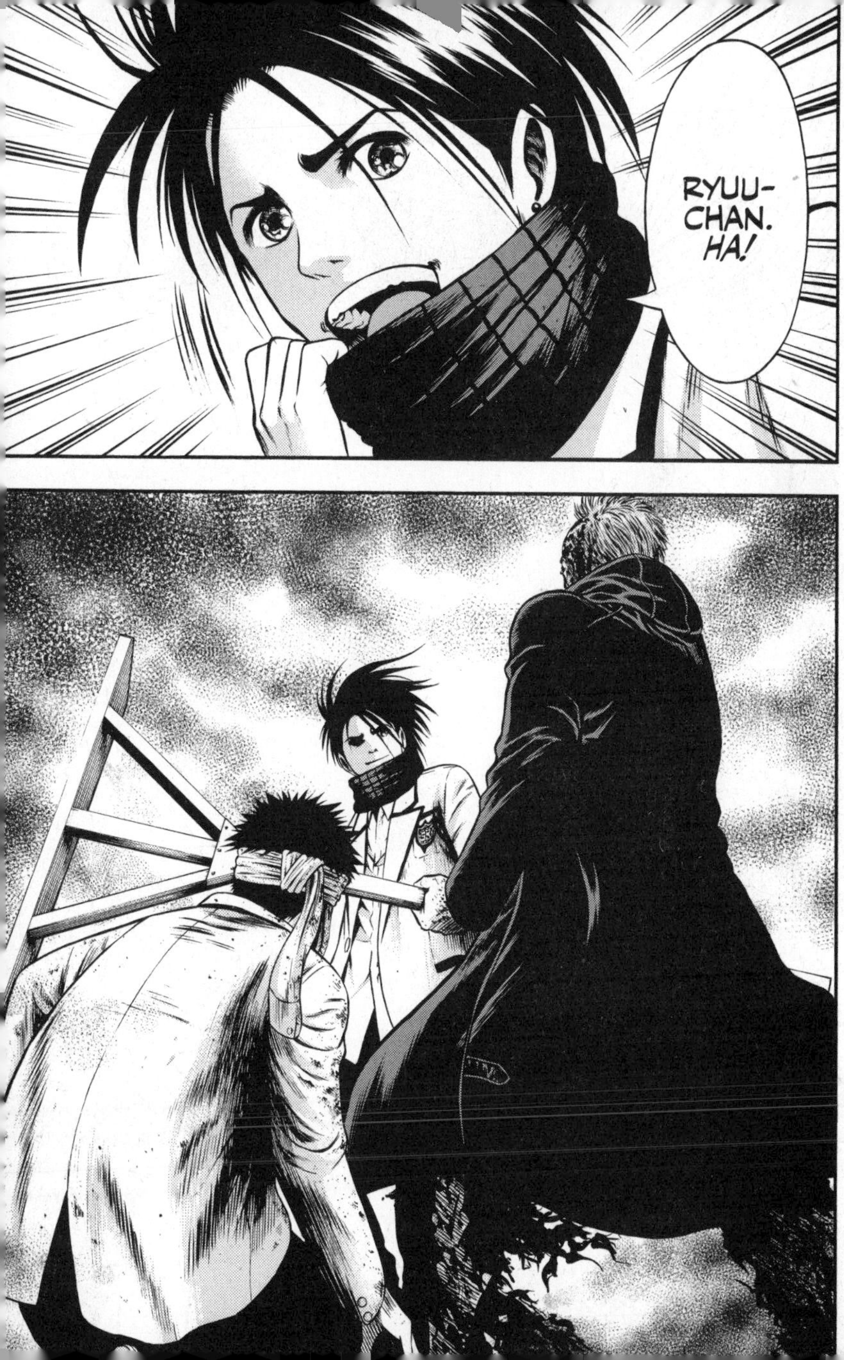
RYUU-CHAN. HA!

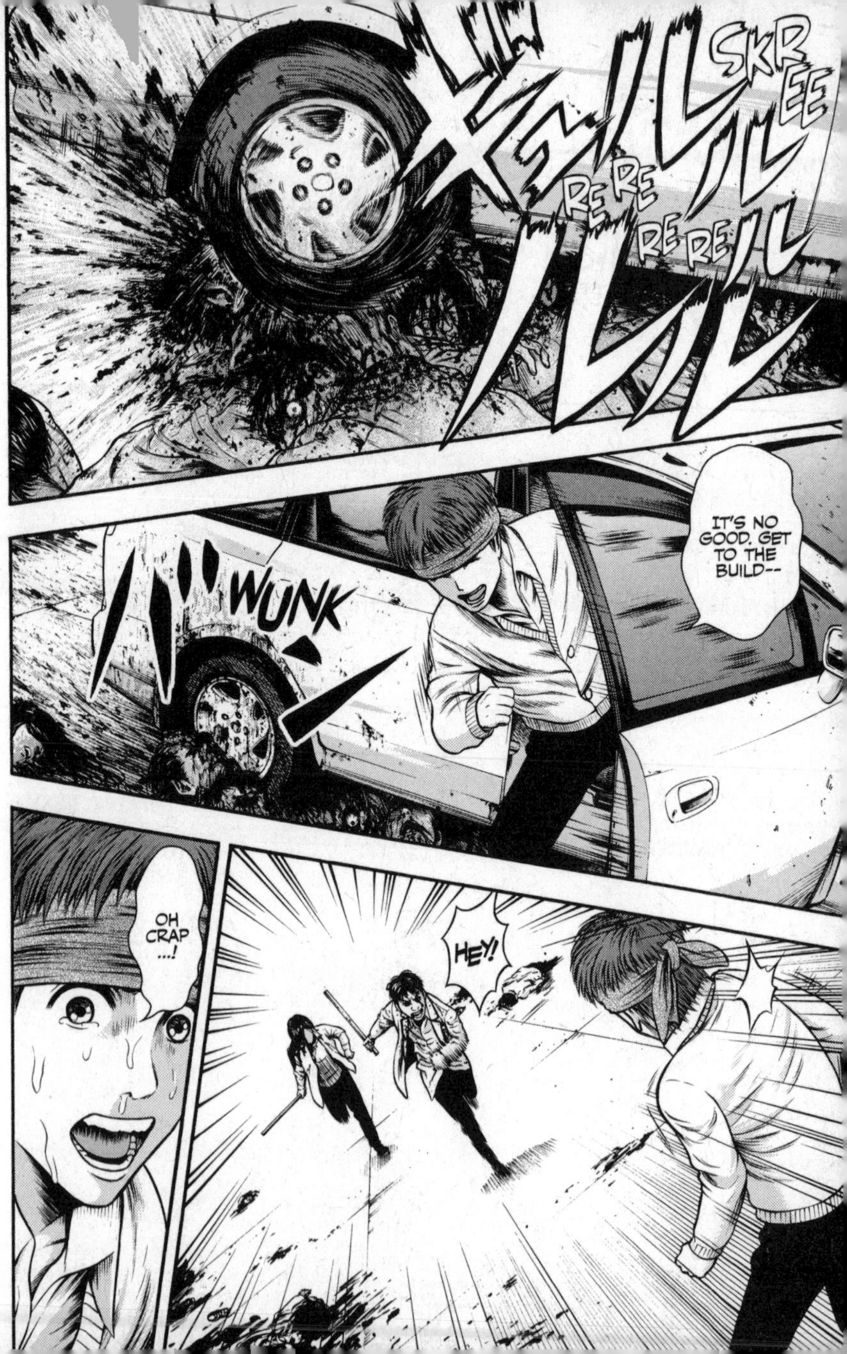
SKREE
REREREREE
IT'S NO GOOD. GET TO THE BUILD--
WUNK
HEY!
OH CRAP ...!

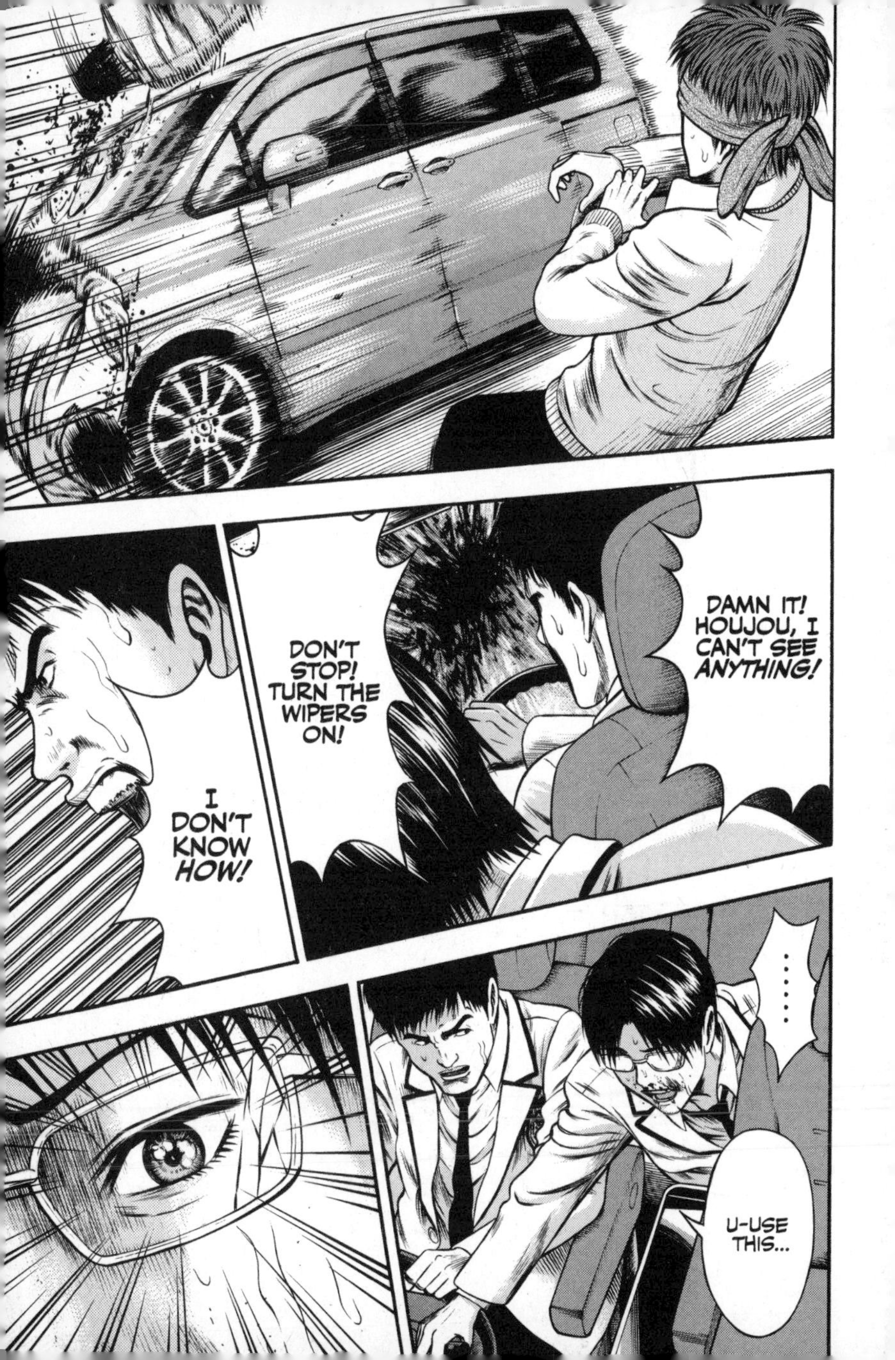
DAMN IT! HOUJOU, I CAN'T SEE ANYTHING!
DON'T STOP! TURN THE WIPERS ON!
I DON'T KNOW HOW!
......
U-USE THIS...

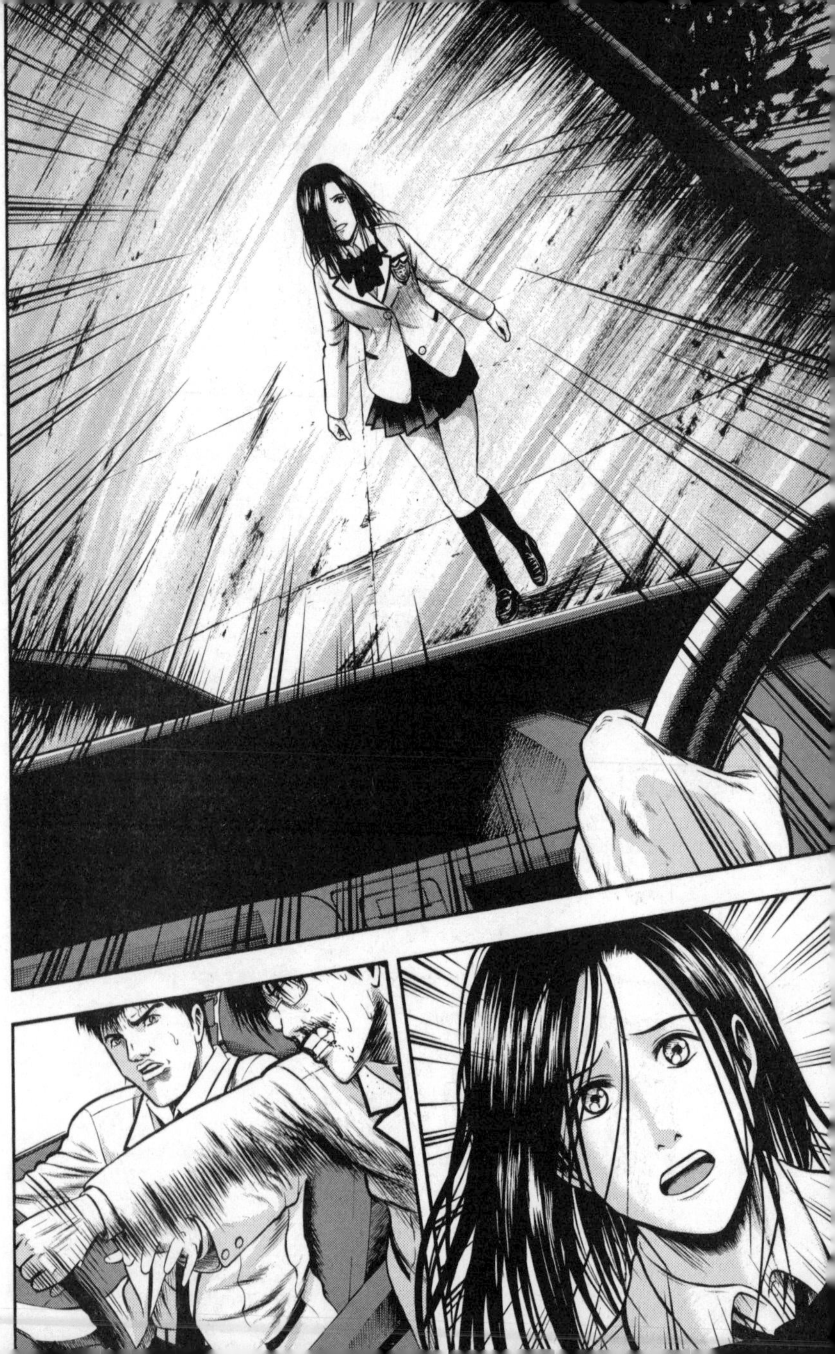

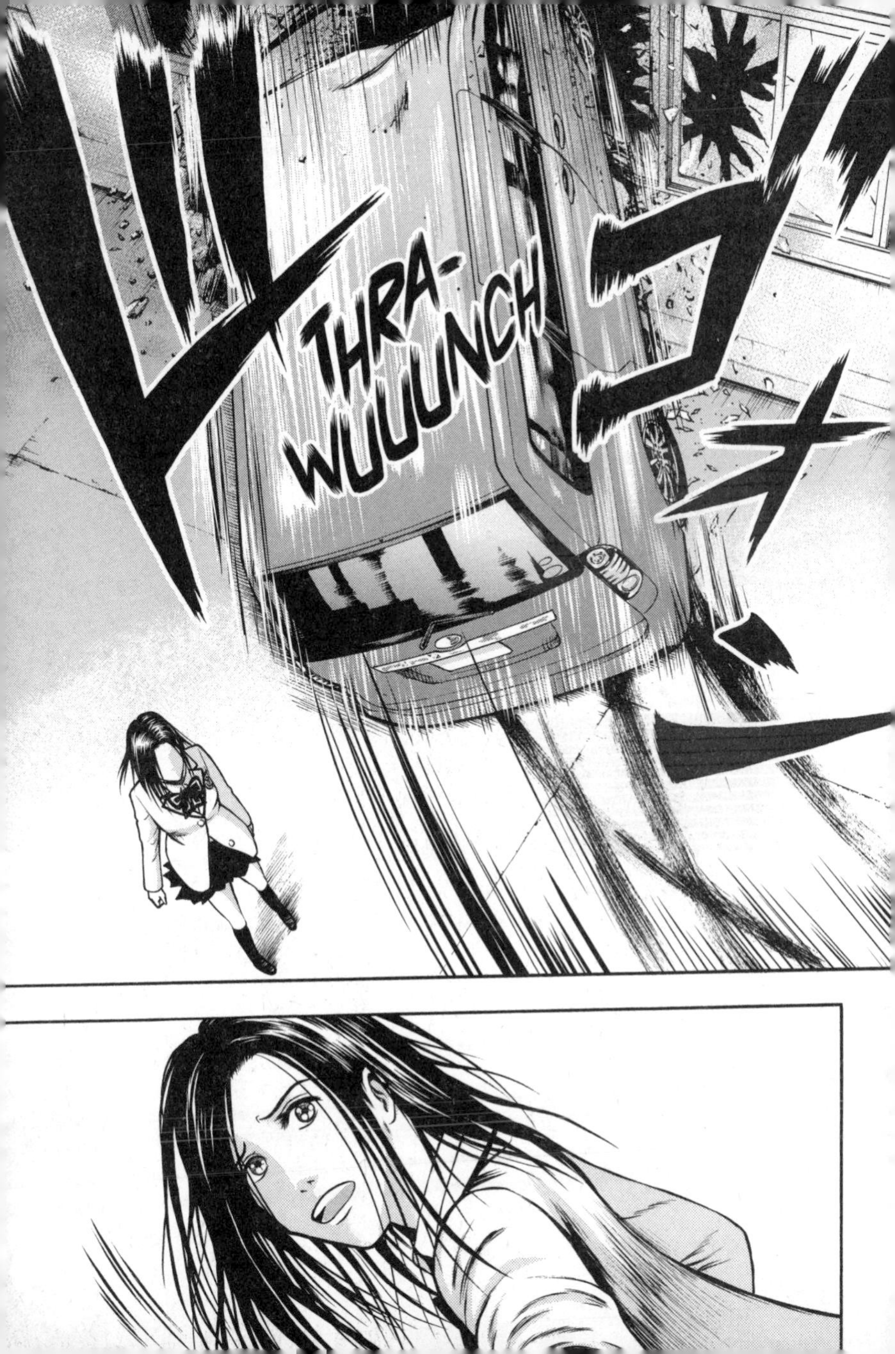
THRA-WUUUNCH

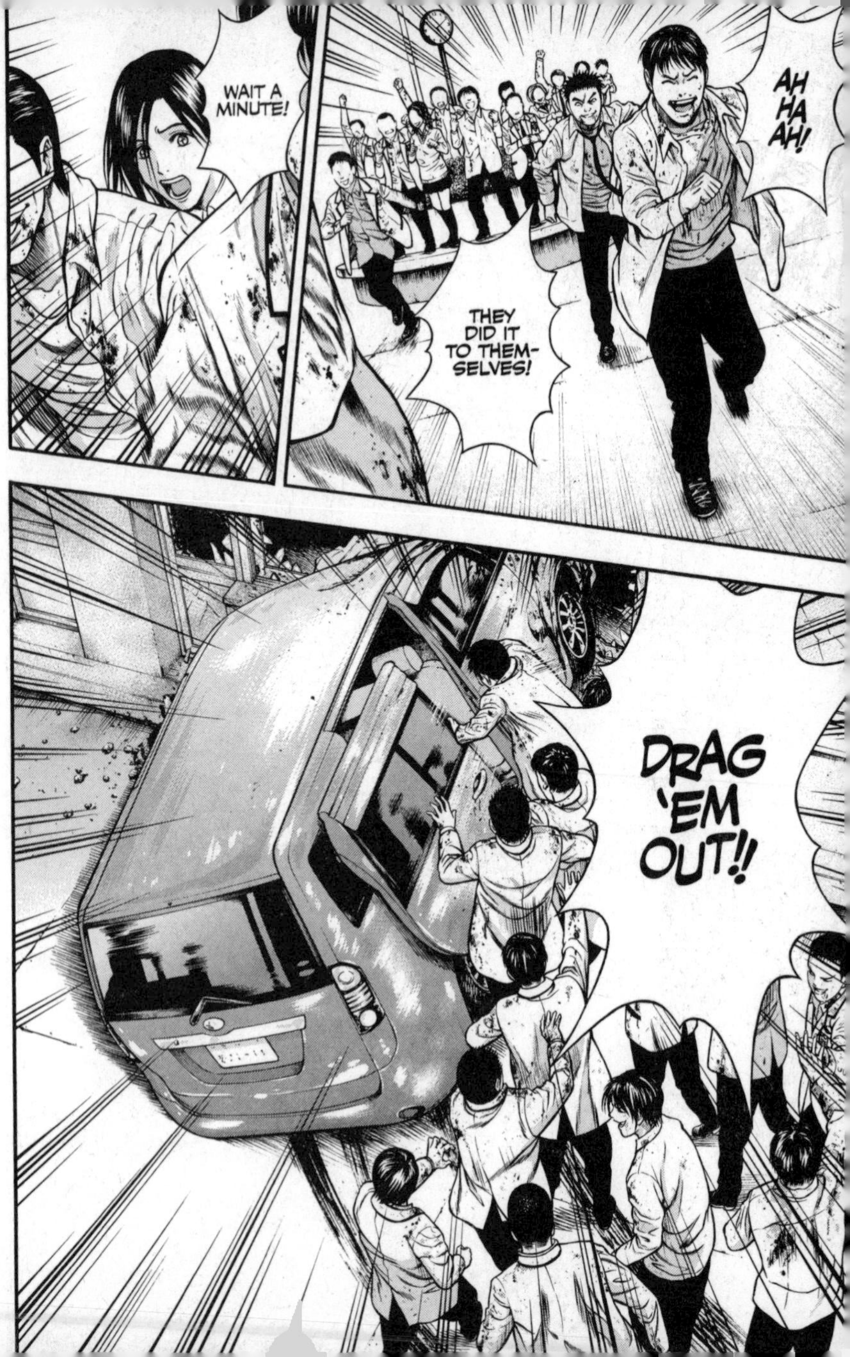
AH HA AH!
THEY DID IT TO THEM-SELVES!
WAIT A MINUTE!
DRAG 'EM OUT!!

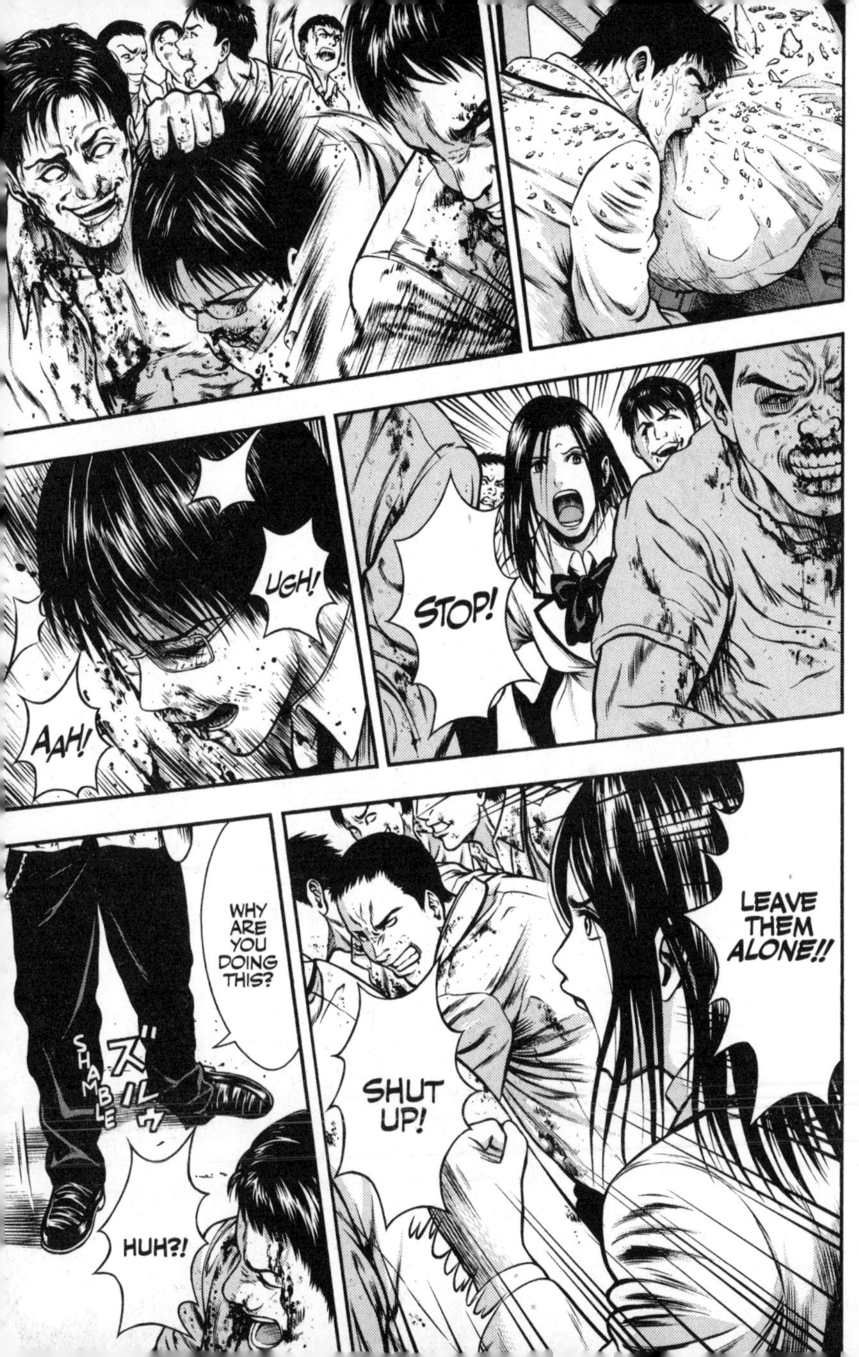
STOP!
UGH!
AAH!
LEAVE THEM ALONE!!
WHY ARE YOU DOING THIS?
SHUT UP!
HUH?!
SHAMBLE

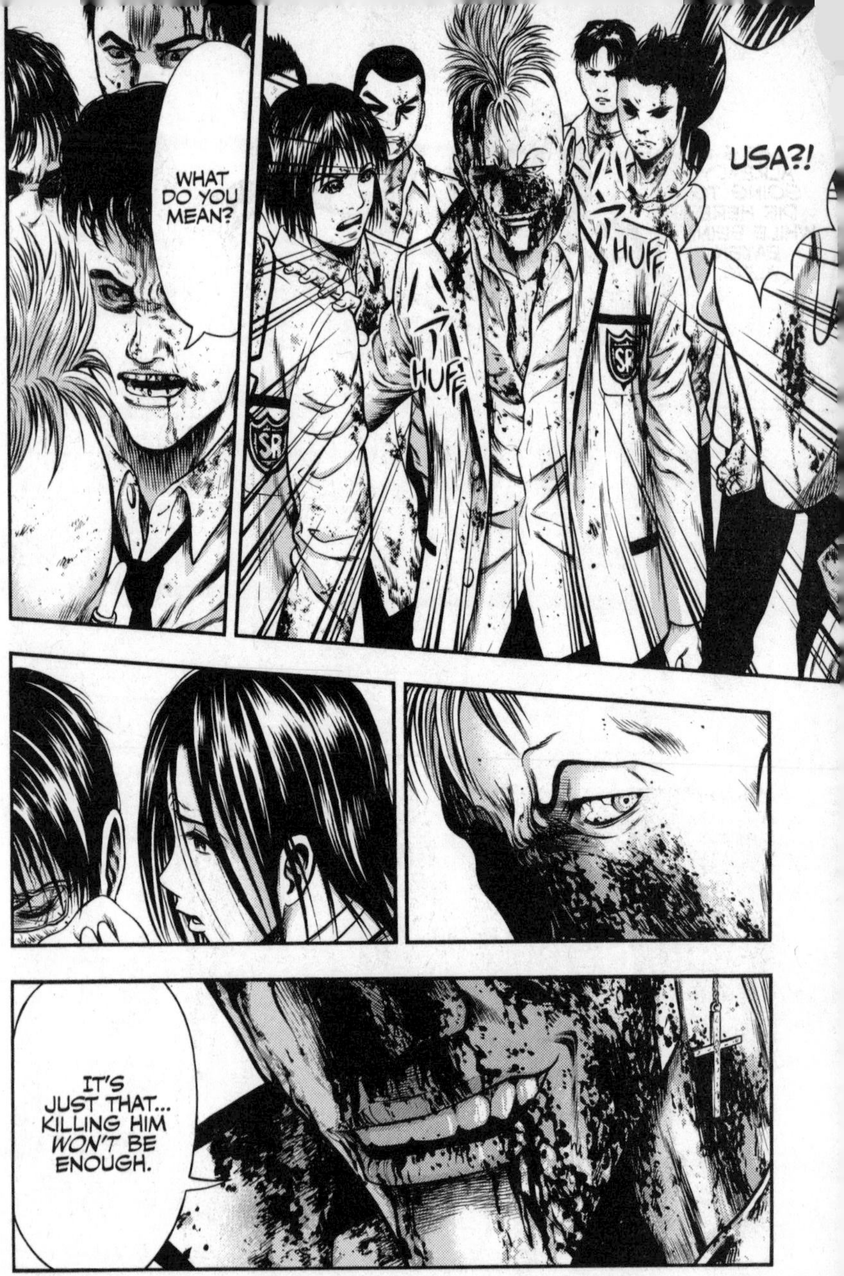
USA?!
HUFF
HUFF
WHAT DO YOU MEAN?
IT'S JUST THAT... KILLING HIM *WON'T* BE ENOUGH.

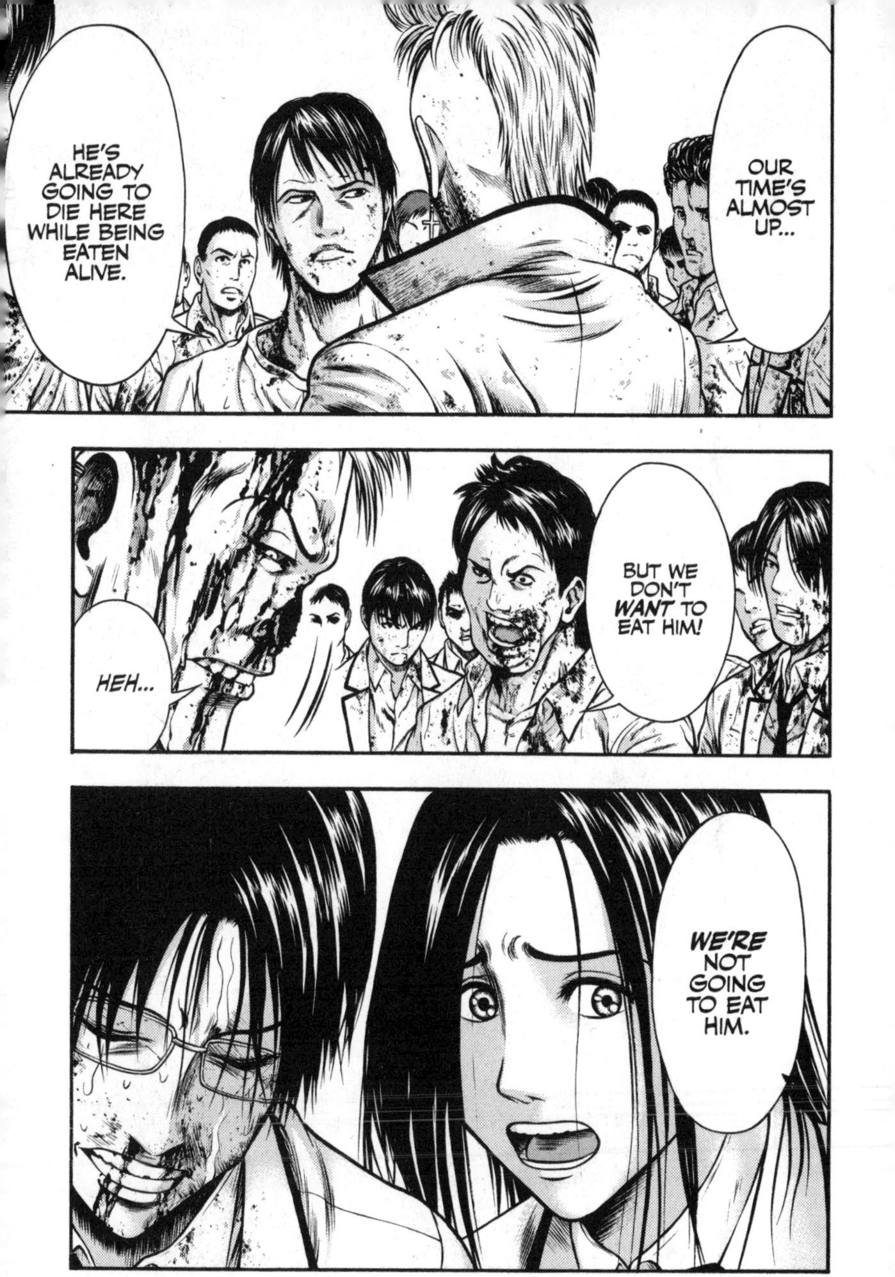
OUR TIME'S ALMOST UP...
HE'S ALREADY GOING TO DIE HERE WHILE BEING EATEN ALIVE.
BUT WE DON'T *WANT* TO EAT HIM!
HEH...
WE'RE NOT GOING TO EAT HIM.

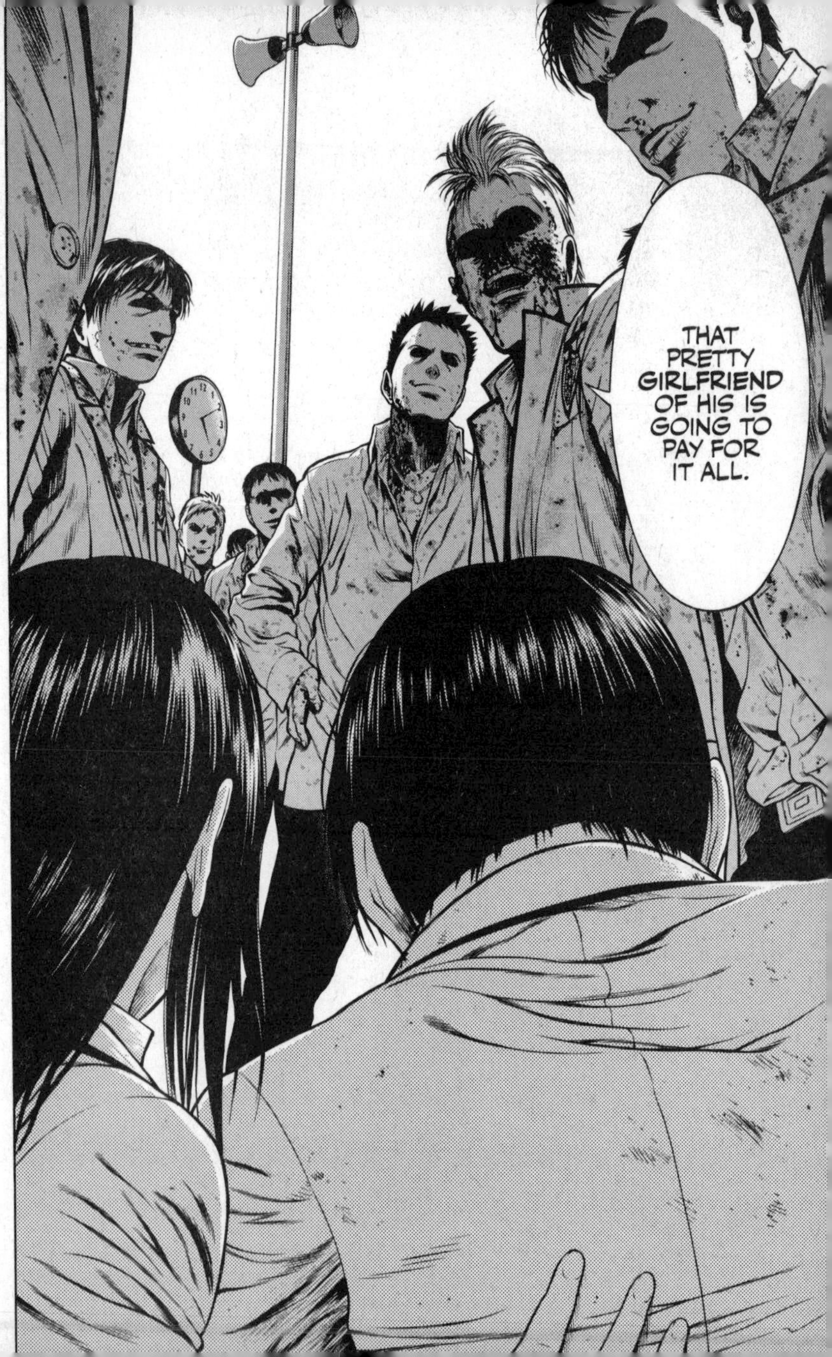
THAT PRETTY GIRLFRIEND OF HIS IS GOING TO PAY FOR IT ALL.

HOUR OF THE ZOMBIE

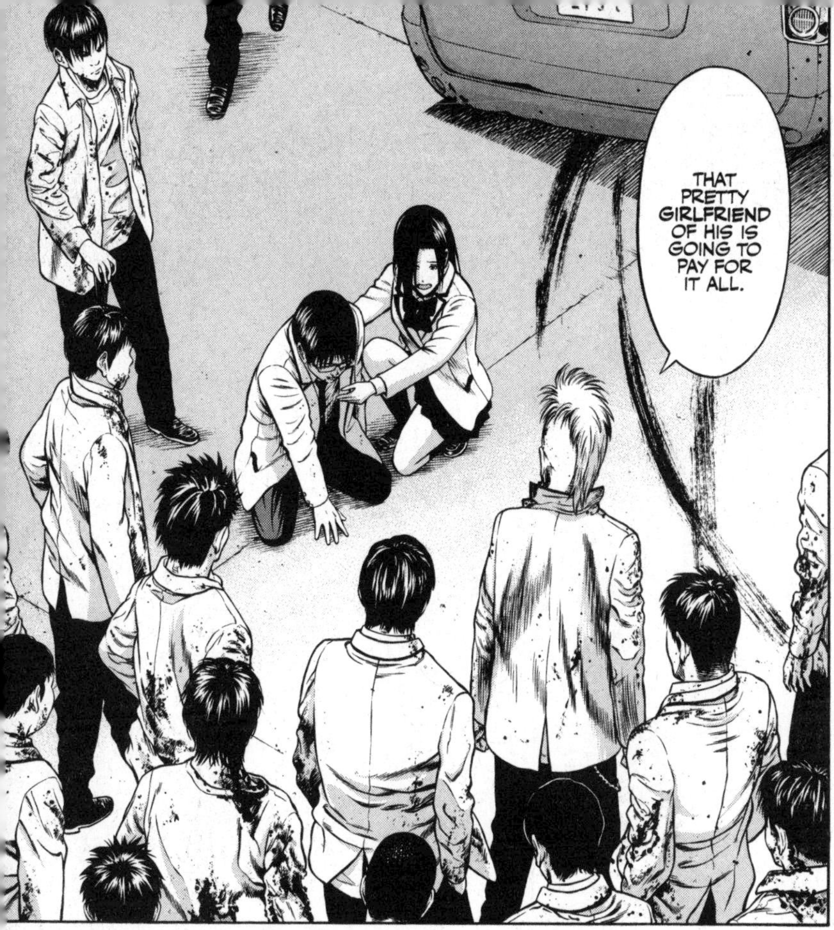
THAT PRETTY GIRLFRIEND OF HIS IS GOING TO PAY FOR IT ALL.

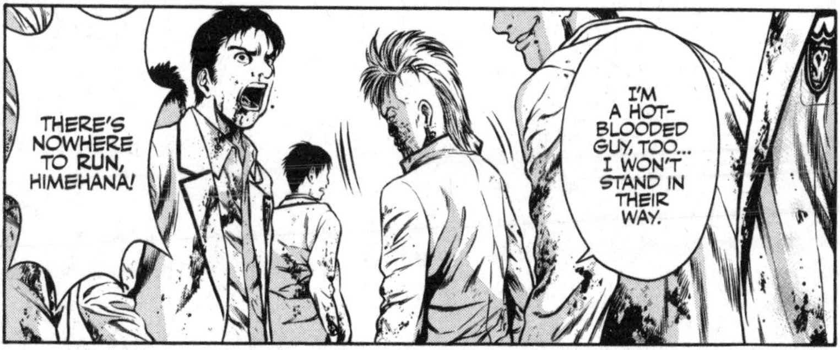
I'M A HOT-BLOODED GUY, TOO... I WON'T STAND IN THEIR WAY.
THERE'S NOWHERE TO RUN, HIMEHANA!

PHASE 16: The Immortal Man

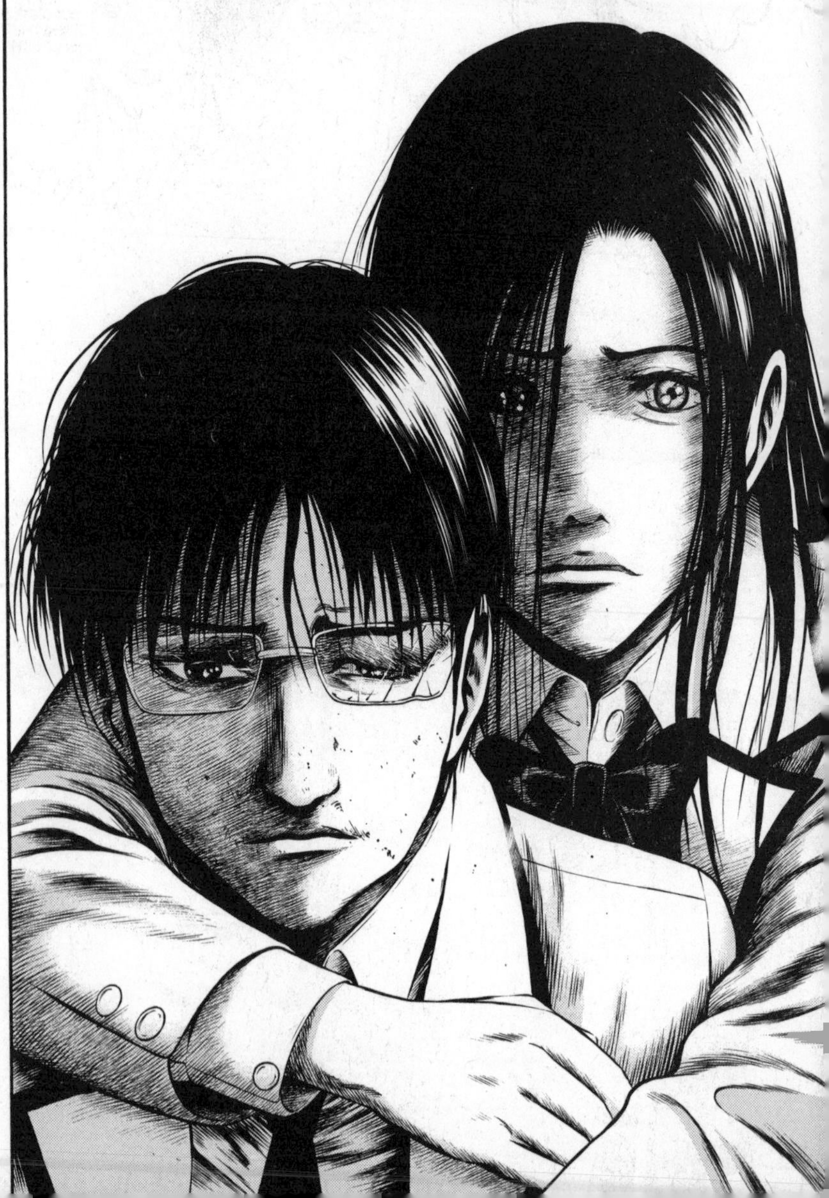

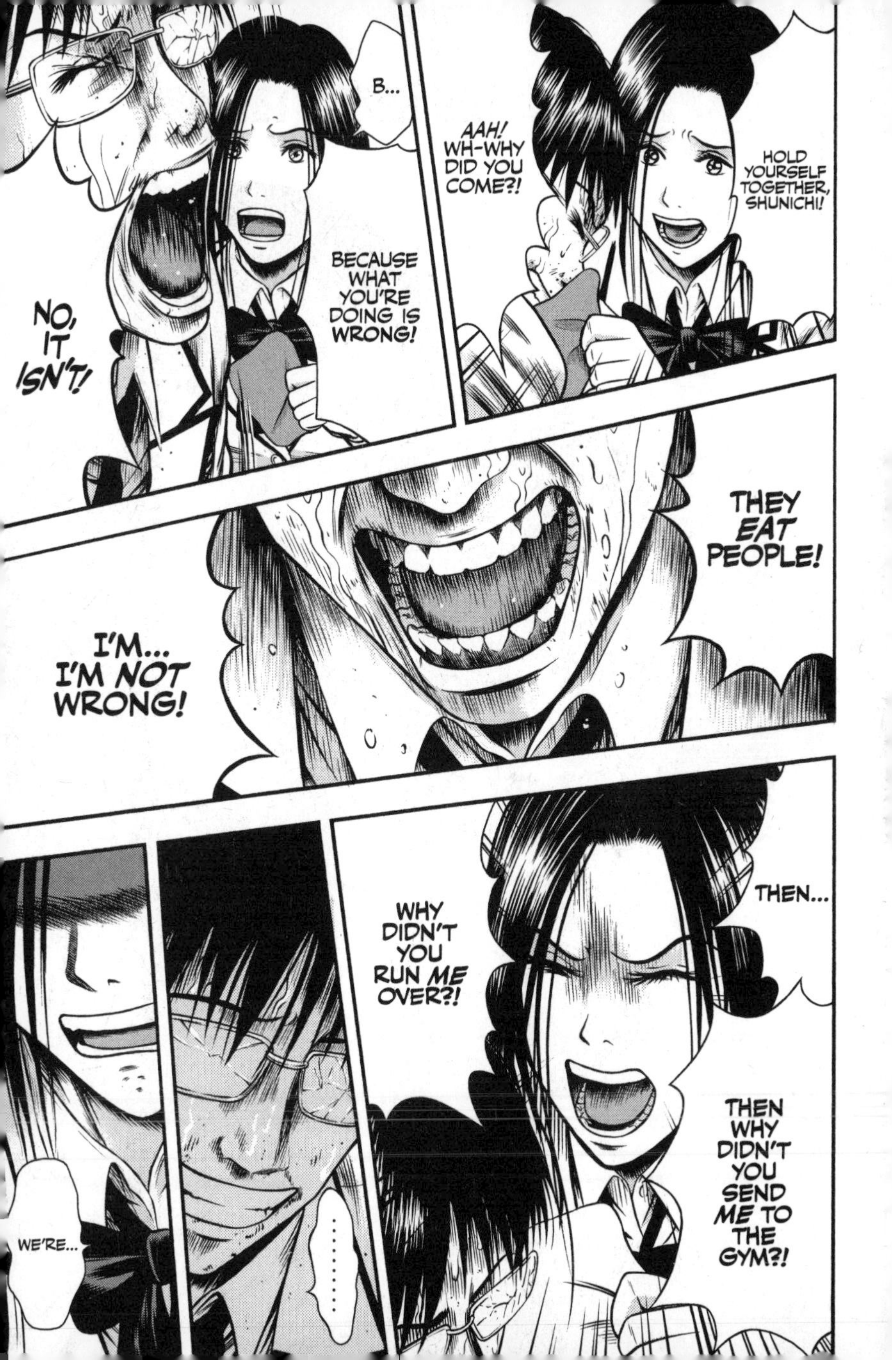
HOLD YOURSELF TOGETHER, SHUNICHI!
AAH! WH-WHY DID YOU COME?!
B...
BECAUSE WHAT YOU'RE DOING IS WRONG!
NO, IT ISN'T!
THEY EAT PEOPLE!
I'M... I'M NOT WRONG!
THEN...
WHY DIDN'T YOU RUN ME OVER?!
THEN WHY DIDN'T YOU SEND ME TO THE GYM?!
......
WE'RE...

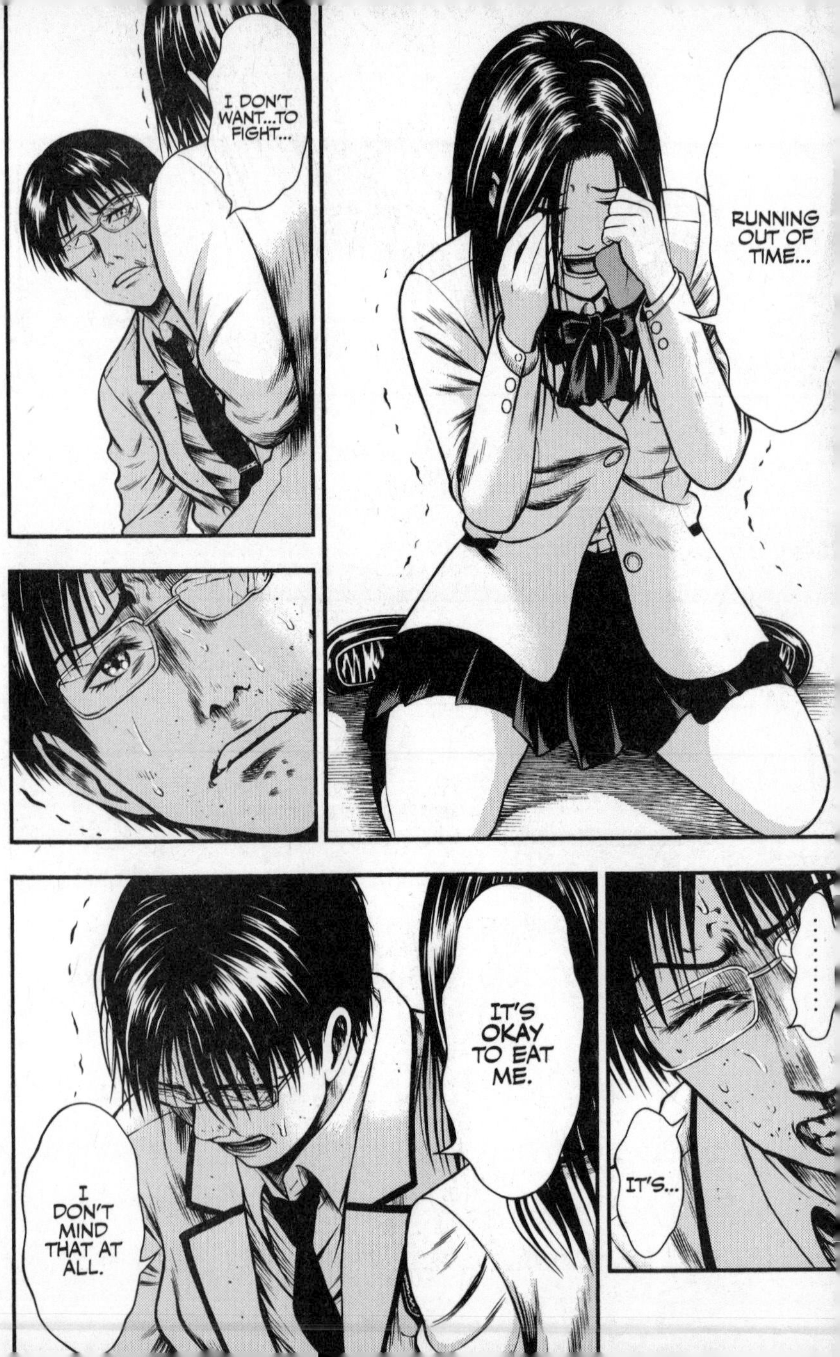
RUNNING OUT OF TIME...
I DON'T WANT...TO FIGHT...
......
IT'S...
IT'S OKAY TO EAT ME.
I DON'T MIND THAT AT ALL.

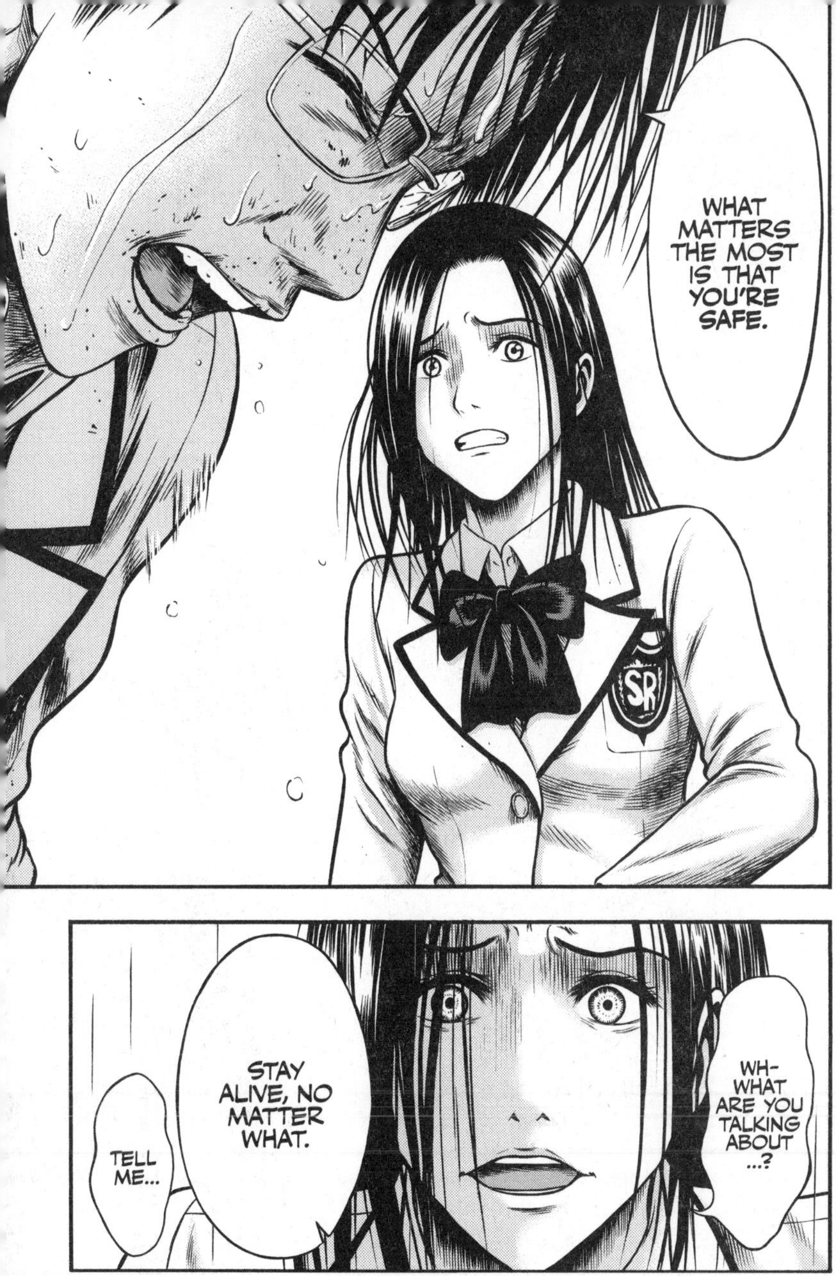
WHAT MATTERS THE MOST IS THAT YOU'RE SAFE.
WH- WHAT ARE YOU TALKING ABOUT ...?
STAY ALIVE, NO MATTER WHAT.
TELL ME...

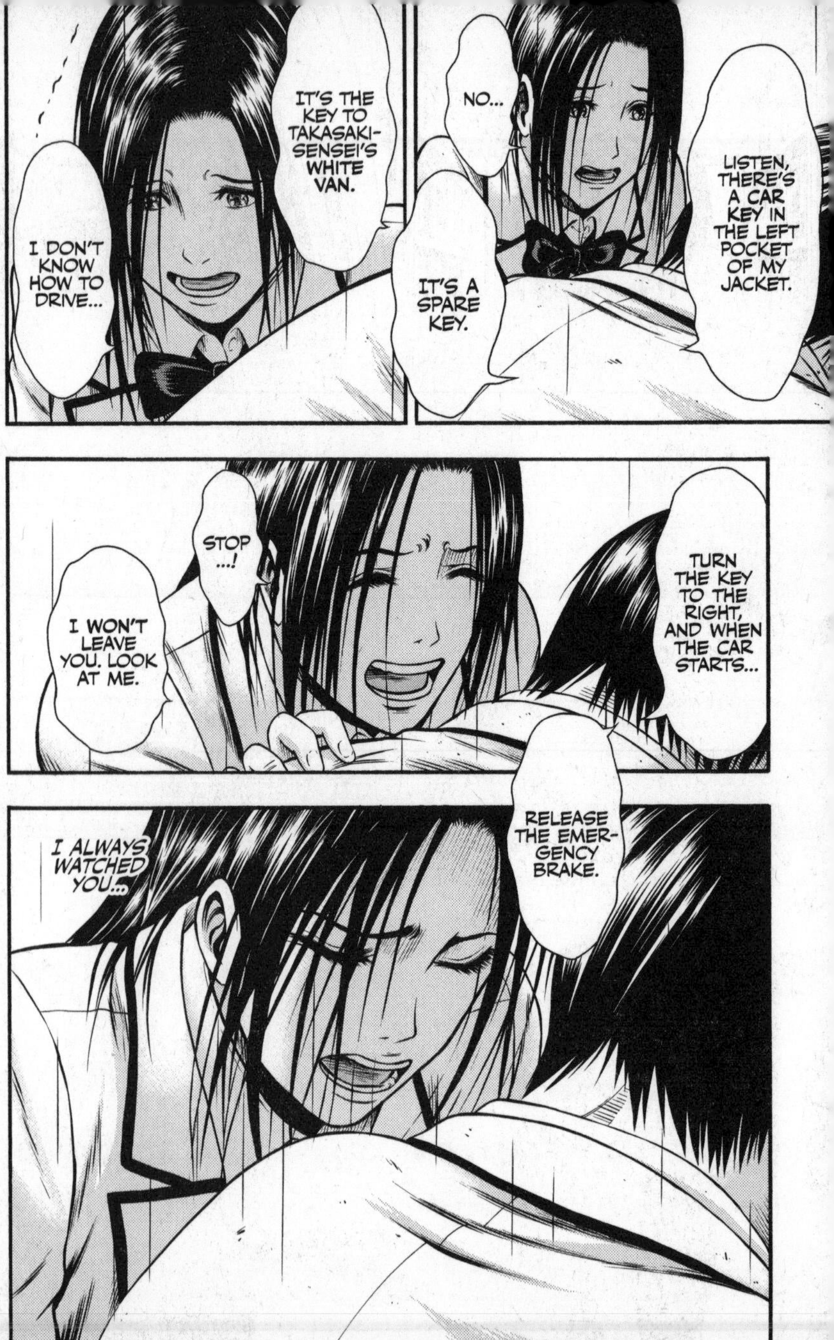
LISTEN, THERE'S A CAR KEY IN THE LEFT POCKET OF MY JACKET.
NO...
IT'S A SPARE KEY.
IT'S THE KEY TO TAKASAKI-SENSEI'S WHITE VAN.
I DON'T KNOW HOW TO DRIVE...
TURN THE KEY TO THE RIGHT, AND WHEN THE CAR STARTS...
STOP ...!
I WON'T LEAVE YOU. LOOK AT ME.
RELEASE THE EMER-GENCY BRAKE.
I ALWAYS WATCHED YOU...

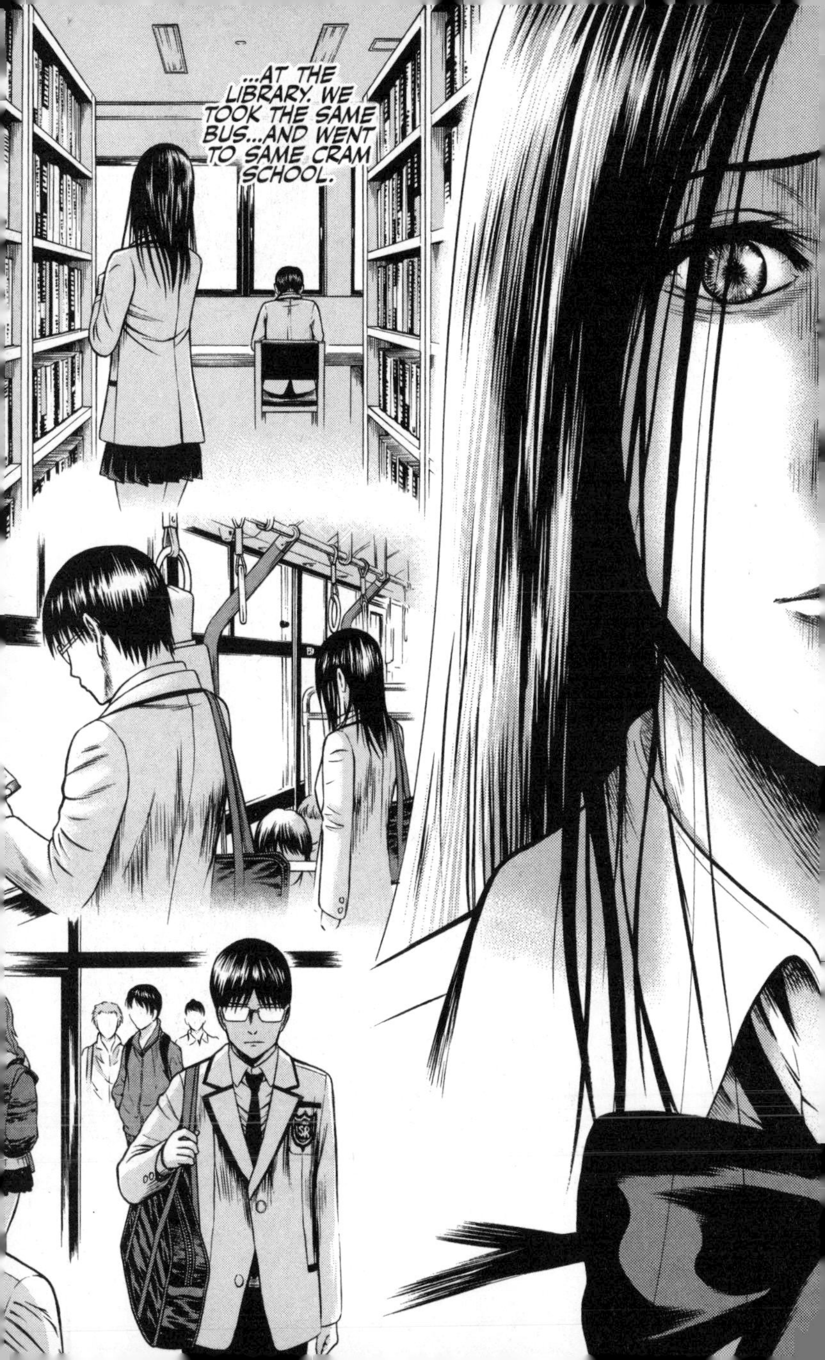
...AT THE LIBRARY. WE TOOK THE SAME BUS...AND WENT TO SAME CRAM SCHOOL.

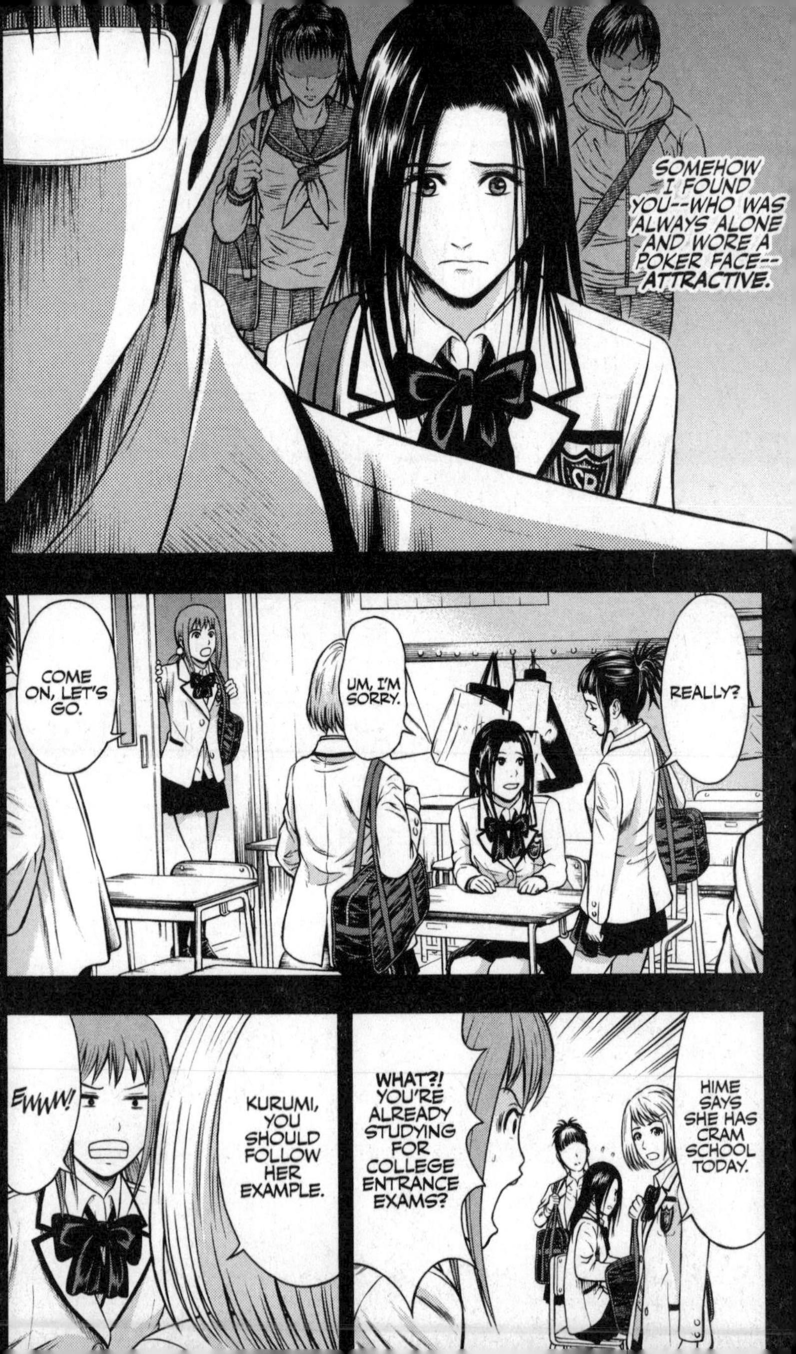
SOMEHOW I FOUND YOU--WHO WAS ALWAYS ALONE AND WORE A POKER FACE--ATTRACTIVE.
REALLY?
UM, I'M SORRY.
COME ON, LET'S GO.
HIME SAYS SHE HAS CRAM SCHOOL TODAY.
WHAT?! YOU'RE ALREADY STUDYING FOR COLLEGE ENTRANCE EXAMS?
KURUMI, YOU SHOULD FOLLOW HER EXAMPLE.
EWWW!

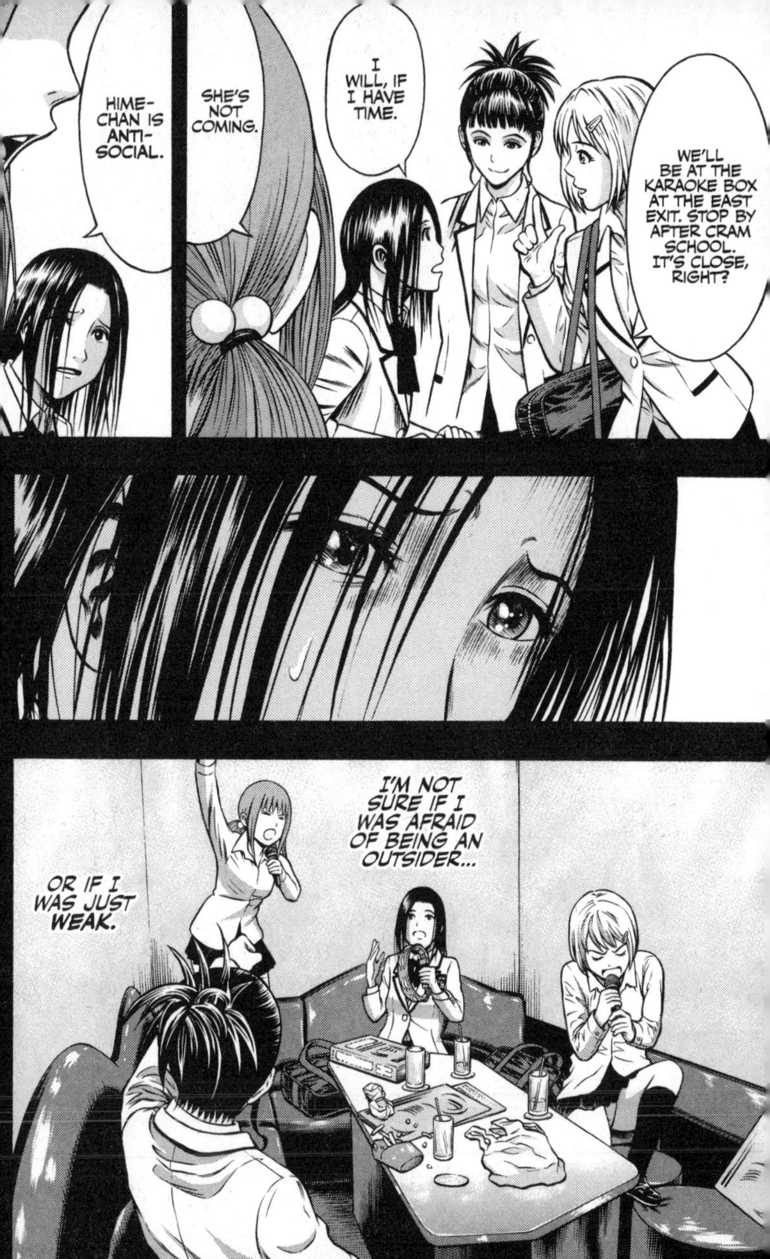
WE'LL BE AT THE KARAOKE BOX AT THE EAST EXIT. STOP BY AFTER CRAM SCHOOL. IT'S CLOSE, RIGHT?
I WILL, IF I HAVE TIME.
SHE'S NOT COMING.
HIME-CHAN IS ANTI-SOCIAL.
I'M NOT SURE IF I WAS AFRAID OF BEING AN OUTSIDER...
OR IF I WAS JUST WEAK.

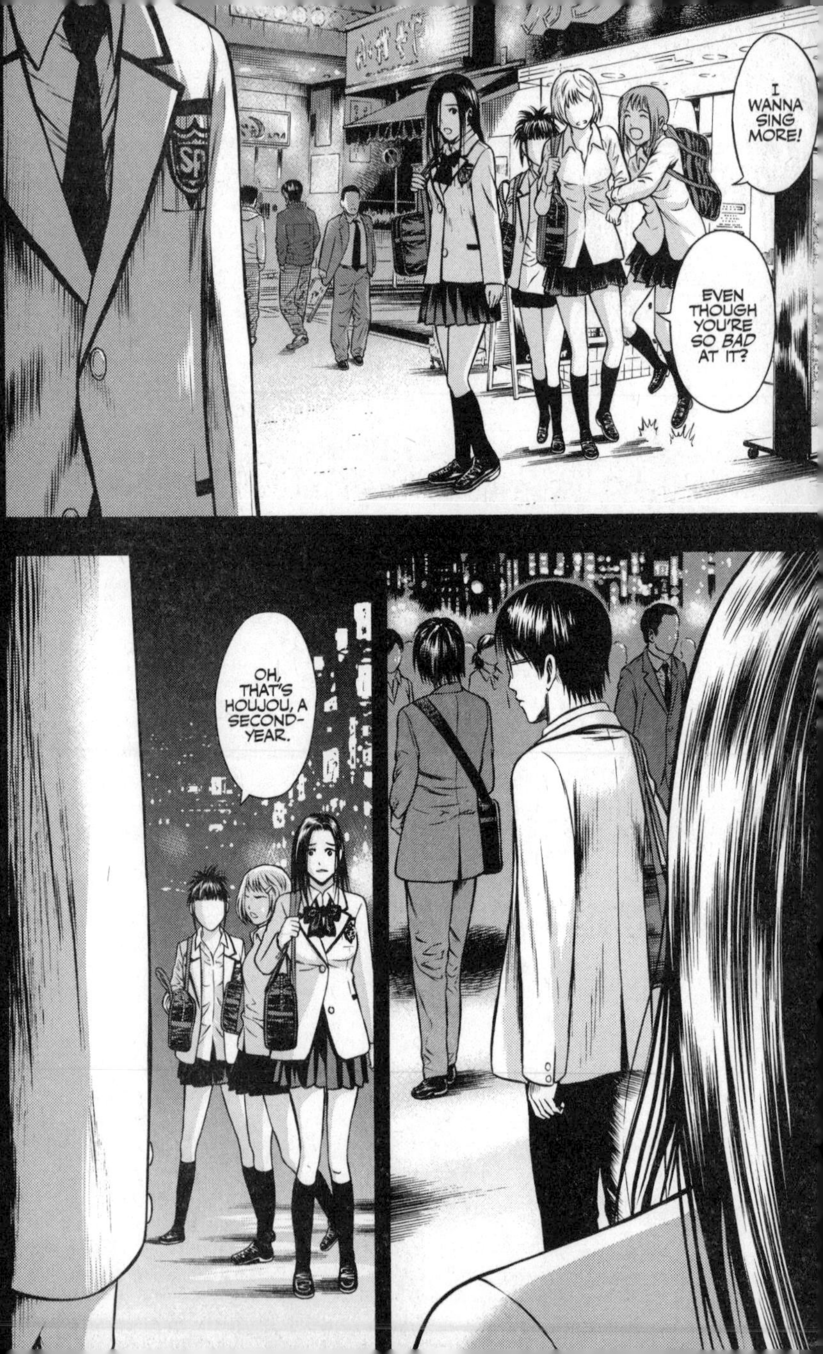
I WANNA SING MORE!
EVEN THOUGH YOU'RE SO *BAD* AT IT?
OH, THAT'S HOUJOU, A SECOND-YEAR.

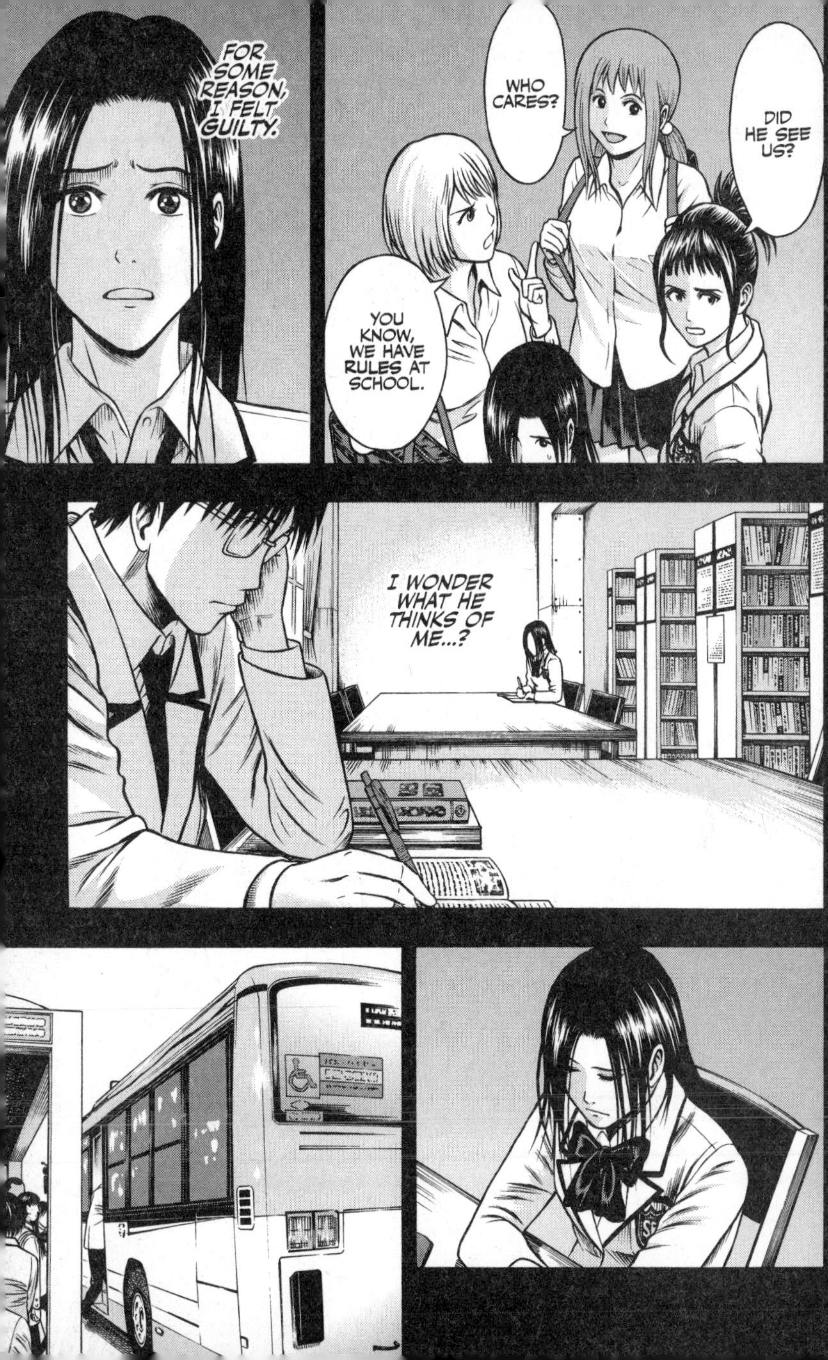
DID HE SEE US?
WHO CARES?
YOU KNOW, WE HAVE RULES AT SCHOOL.
FOR SOME REASON, I FELT GUILTY.
I WONDER WHAT HE THINKS OF ME...?

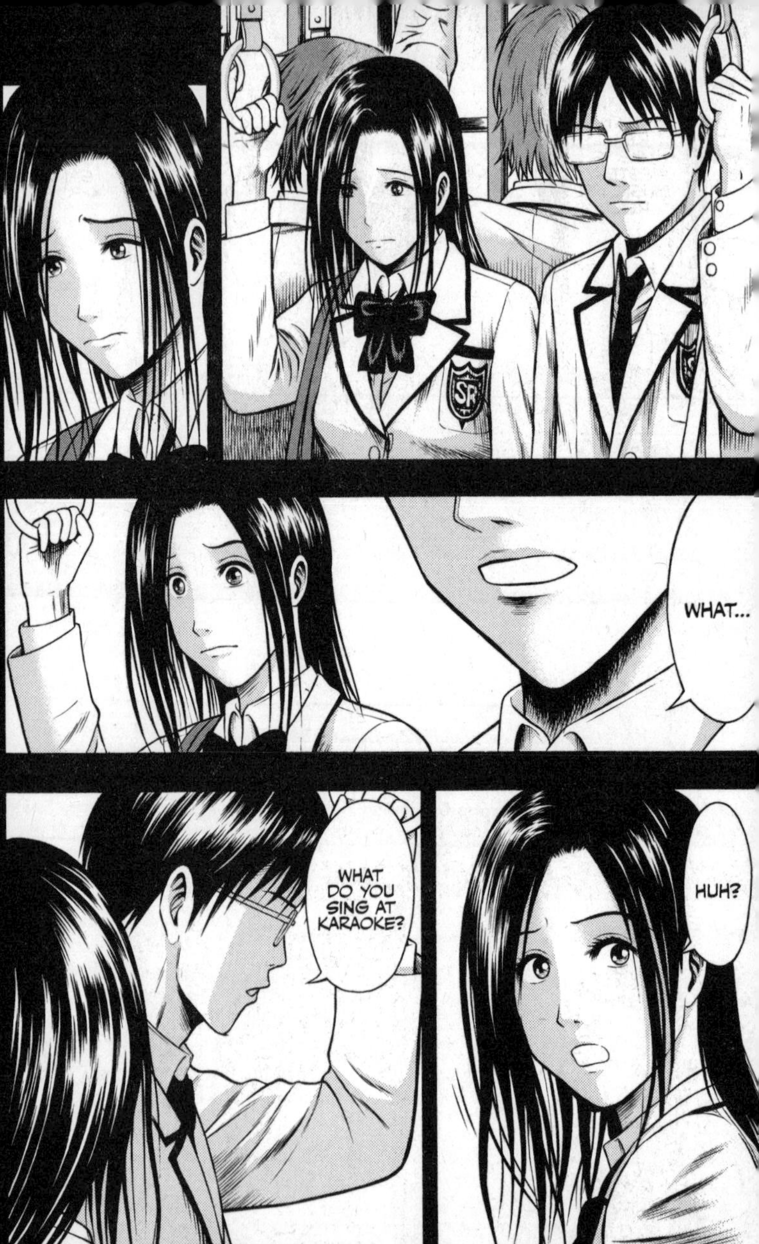
WHAT...
HUH?
WHAT DO YOU SING AT KARAOKE?

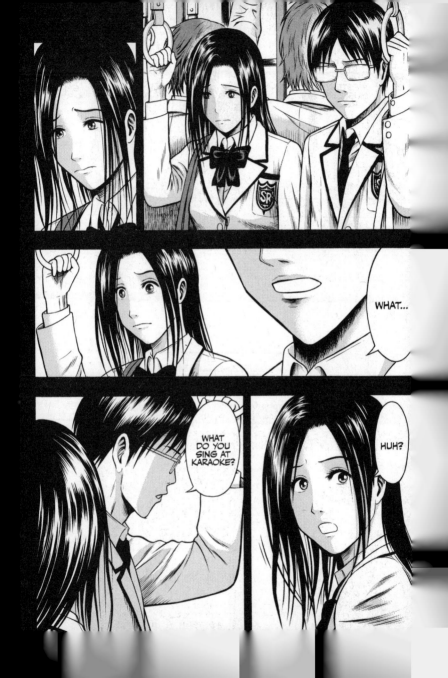

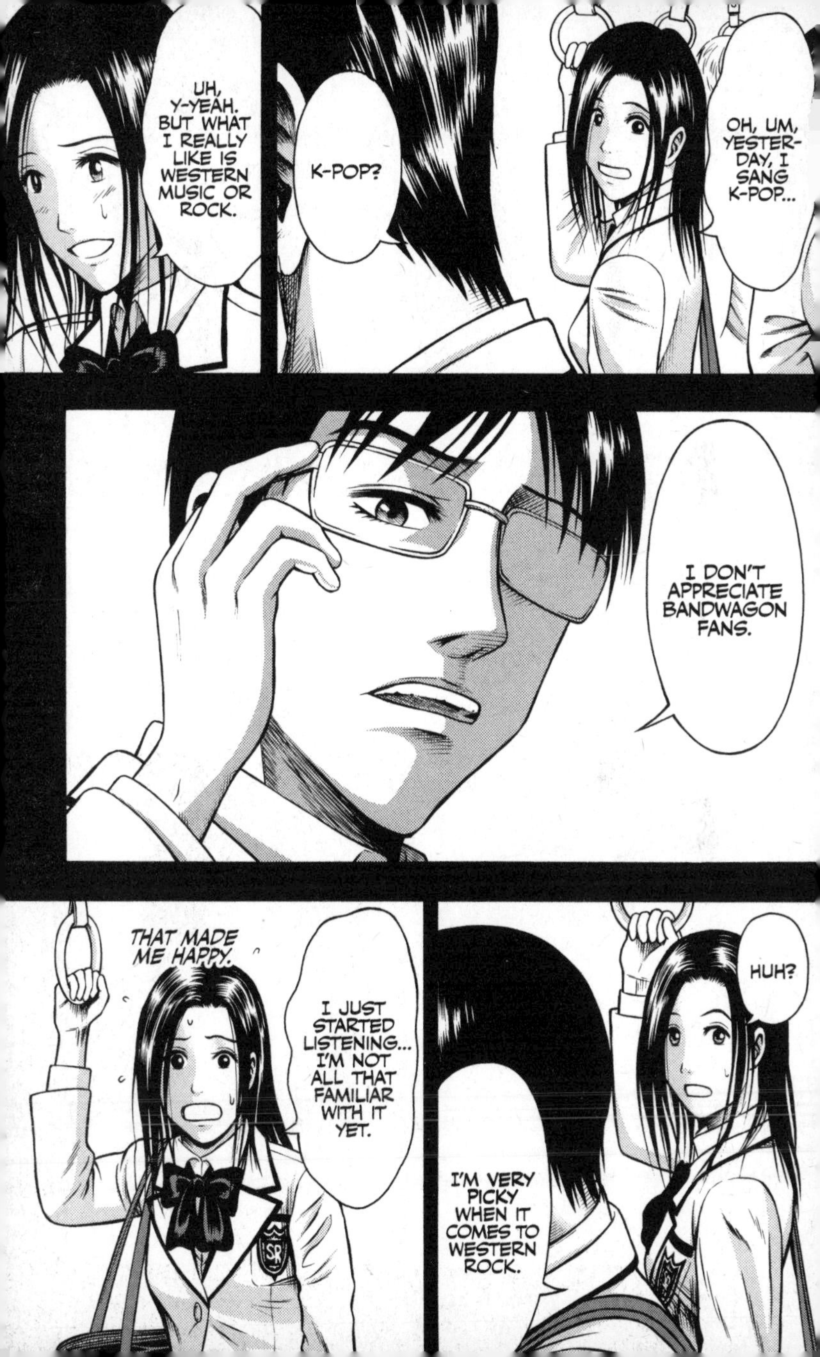
OH, UM, YESTER-DAY, I SANG K-POP...
K-POP?
UH, Y-YEAH. BUT WHAT I REALLY LIKE IS WESTERN MUSIC OR ROCK.
I DON'T APPRECIATE BANDWAGON FANS.
HUH?
I'M VERY PICKY WHEN IT COMES TO WESTERN ROCK.
I JUST STARTED LISTENING... I'M NOT ALL THAT FAMILIAR WITH IT YET.
THAT MADE ME HAPPY.

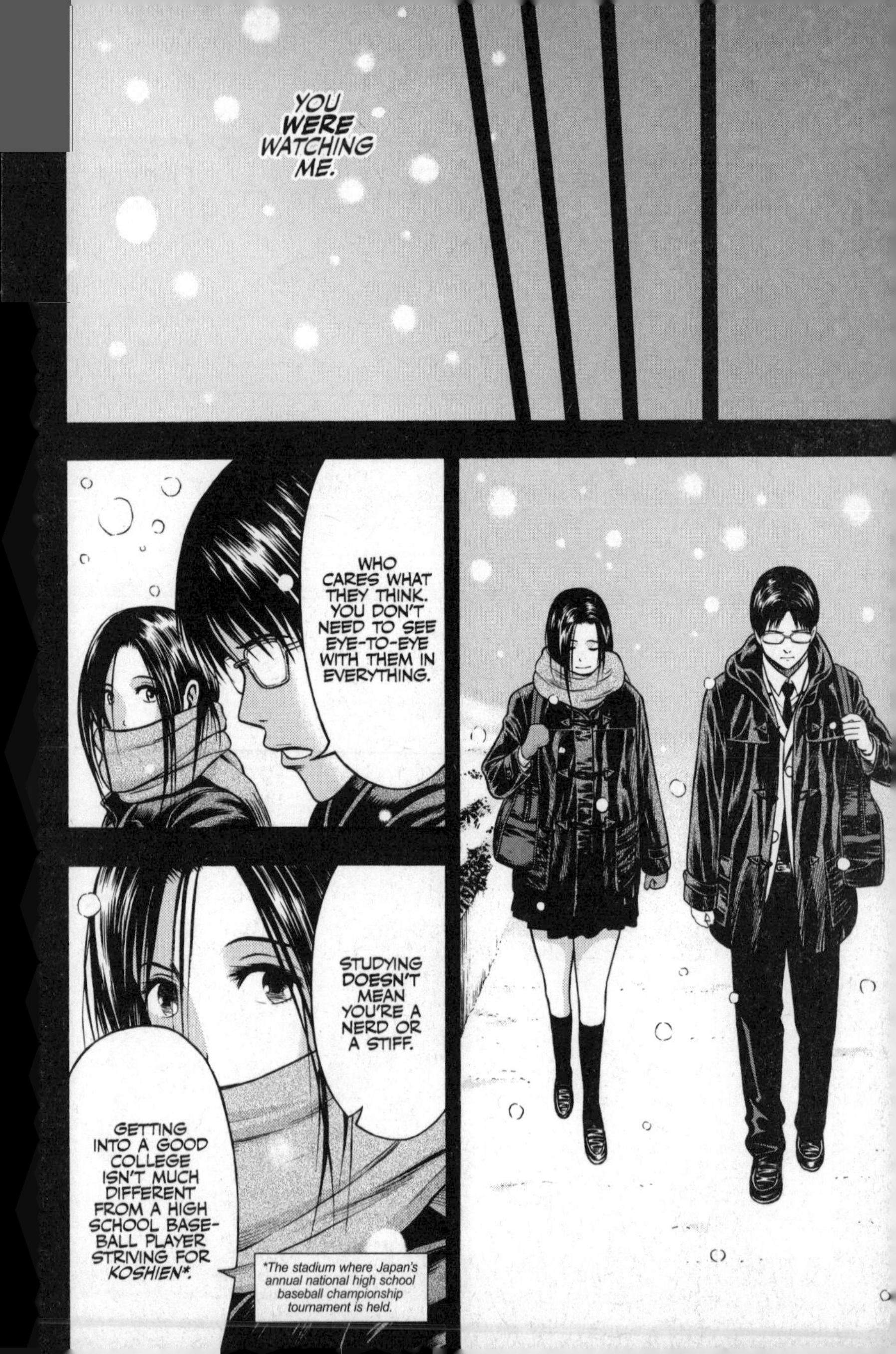
YOU WERE WATCHING ME.
WHO CARES WHAT THEY THINK. YOU DON'T NEED TO SEE EYE-TO-EYE WITH THEM IN EVERYTHING.
STUDYING DOESN'T MEAN YOU'RE A NERD OR A STIFF.
GETTING INTO A GOOD COLLEGE ISN'T MUCH DIFFERENT FROM A HIGH SCHOOL BASE-BALL PLAYER STRIVING FOR *KOSHIEN**.
*The stadium where Japan's annual national high school baseball championship tournament is held.

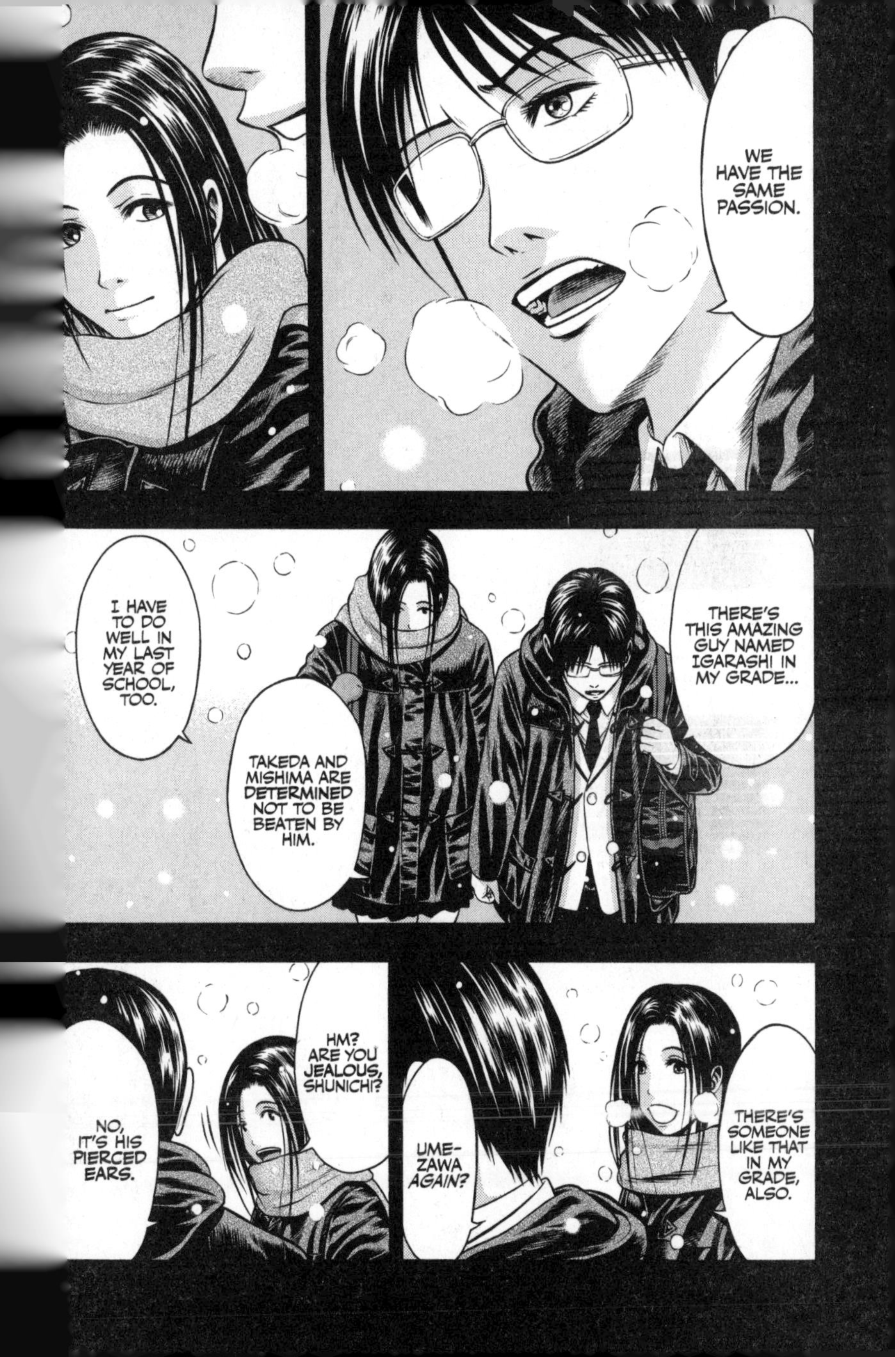
WE HAVE THE SAME PASSION.
THERE'S THIS AMAZING GUY NAMED IGARASHI IN MY GRADE...
TAKEDA AND MISHIMA ARE DETERMINED NOT TO BE BEATEN BY HIM.
I HAVE TO DO WELL IN MY LAST YEAR OF SCHOOL, TOO.
THERE'S SOMEONE LIKE THAT IN MY GRADE, ALSO.
UME-ZAWA AGAIN?
HM? ARE YOU JEALOUS, SHUNICHI?
NO, IT'S HIS PIERCED EARS.

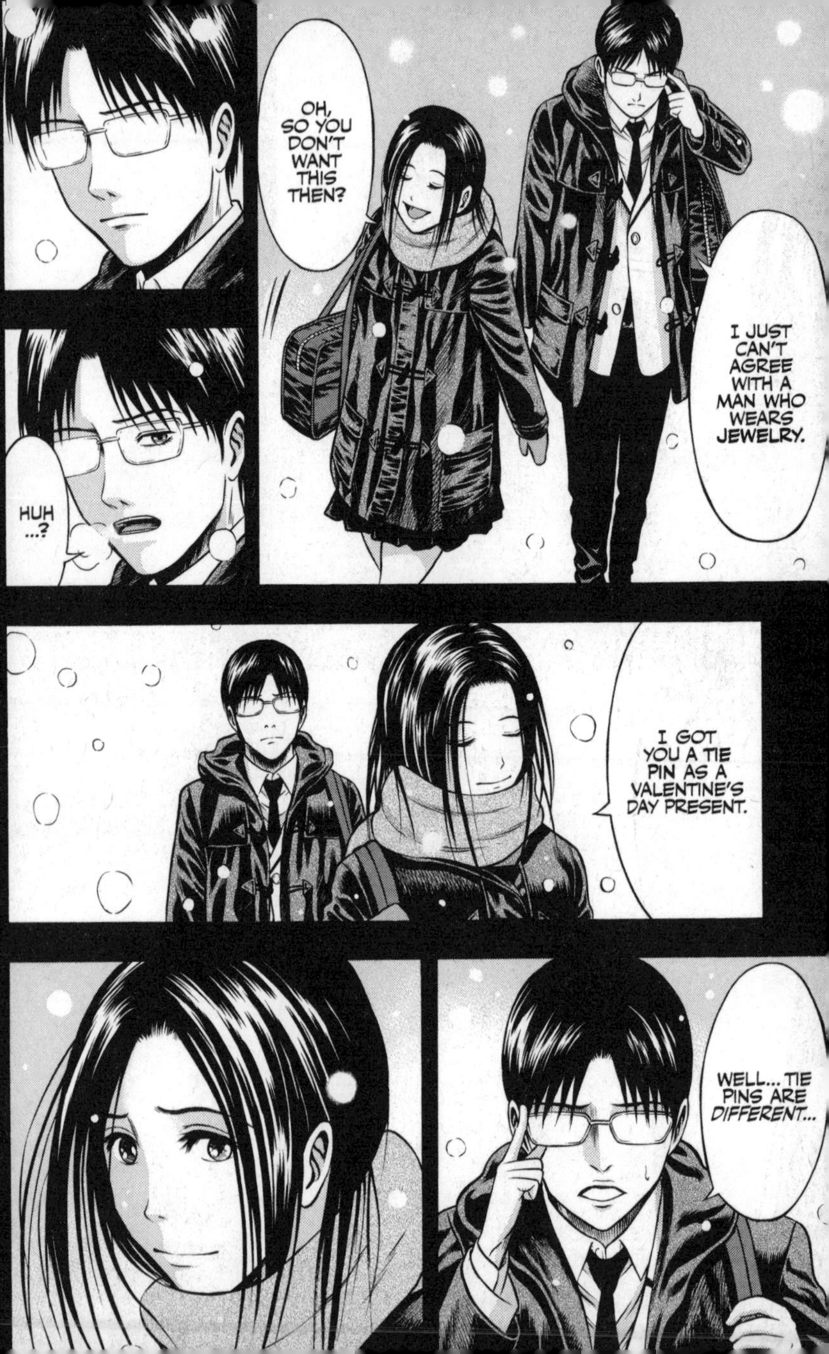
I JUST CAN'T AGREE WITH A MAN WHO WEARS JEWELRY.
OH, SO YOU DON'T WANT THIS THEN?
HUH ...?
I GOT YOU A TIE PIN AS A VALENTINE'S DAY PRESENT.
WELL... TIE PINS ARE *DIFFERENT*...

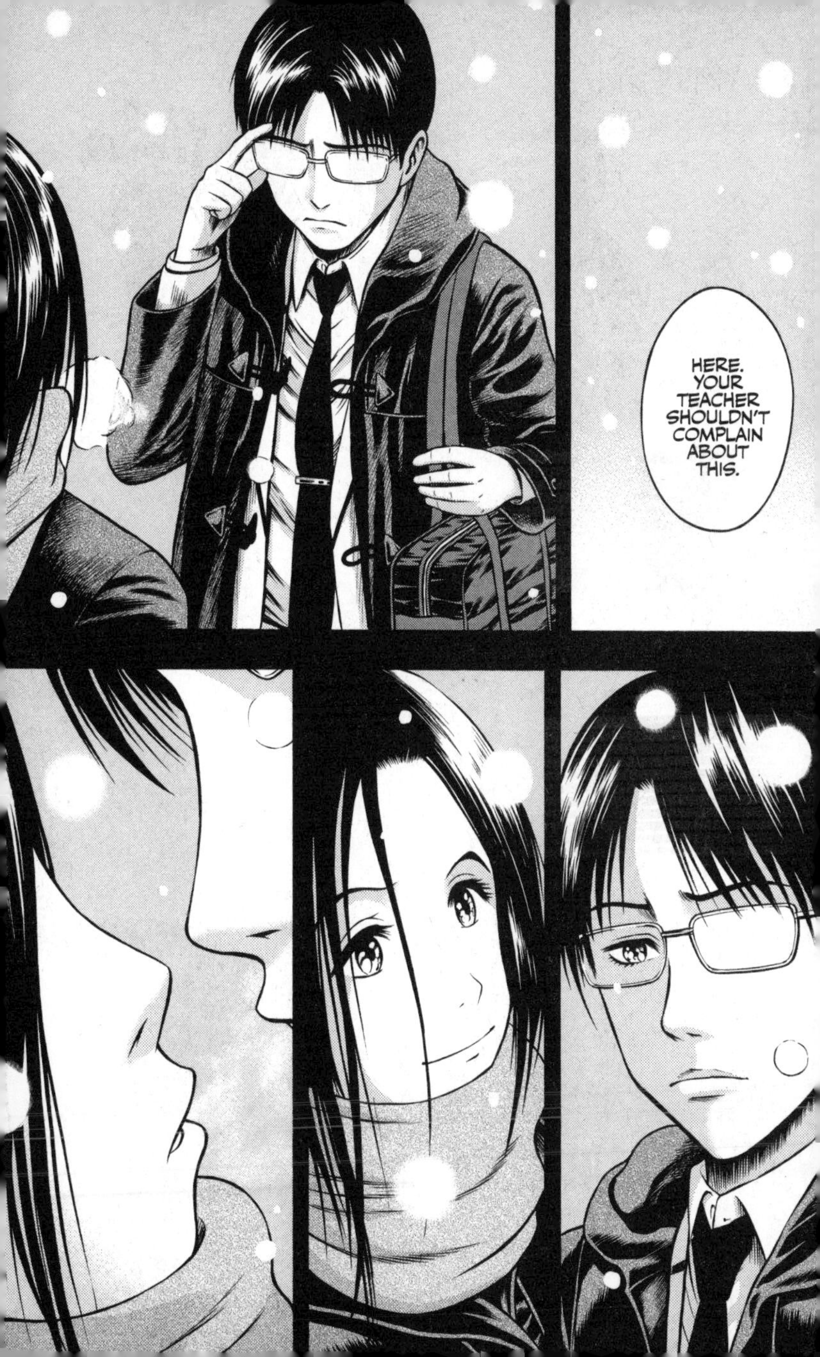
HERE. YOUR TEACHER SHOULDN'T COMPLAIN ABOUT THIS.

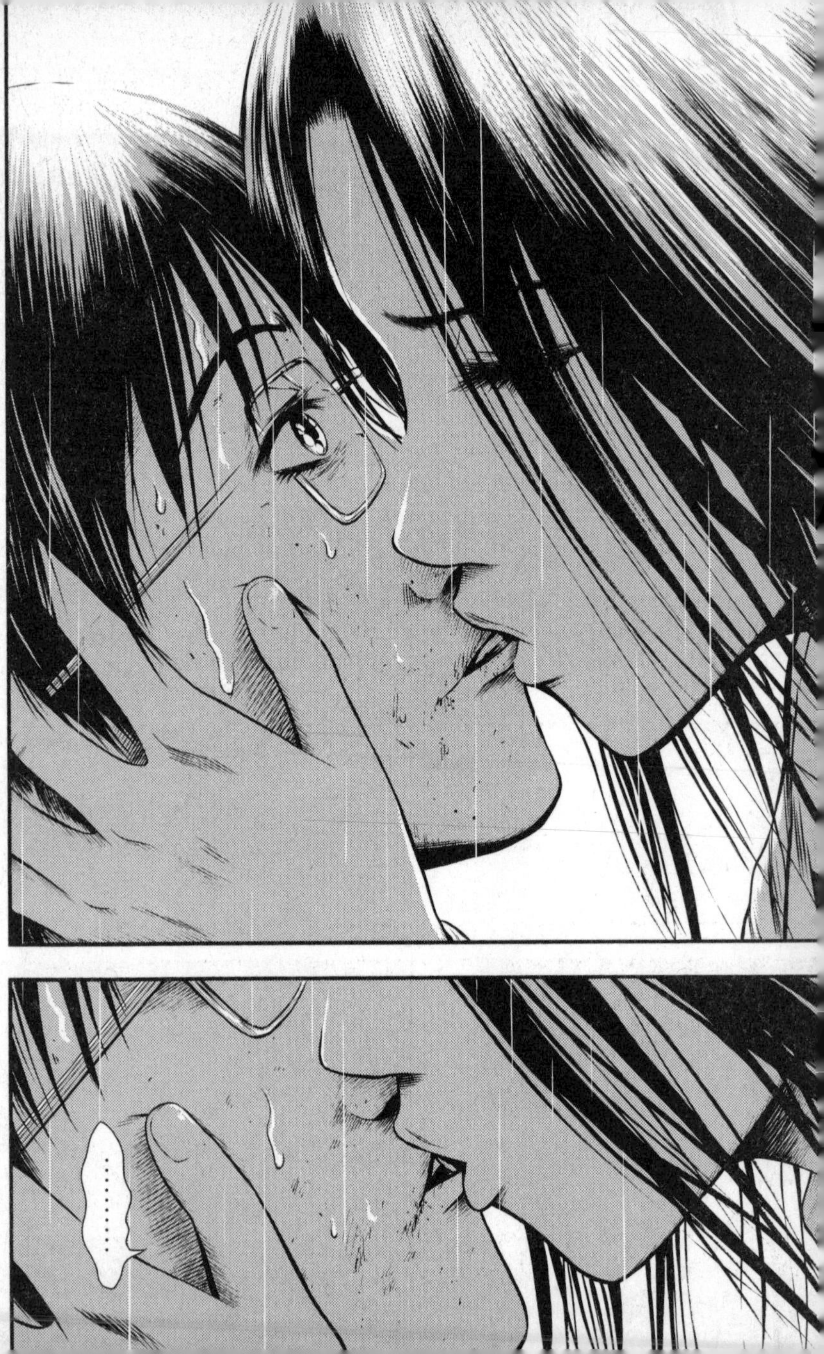

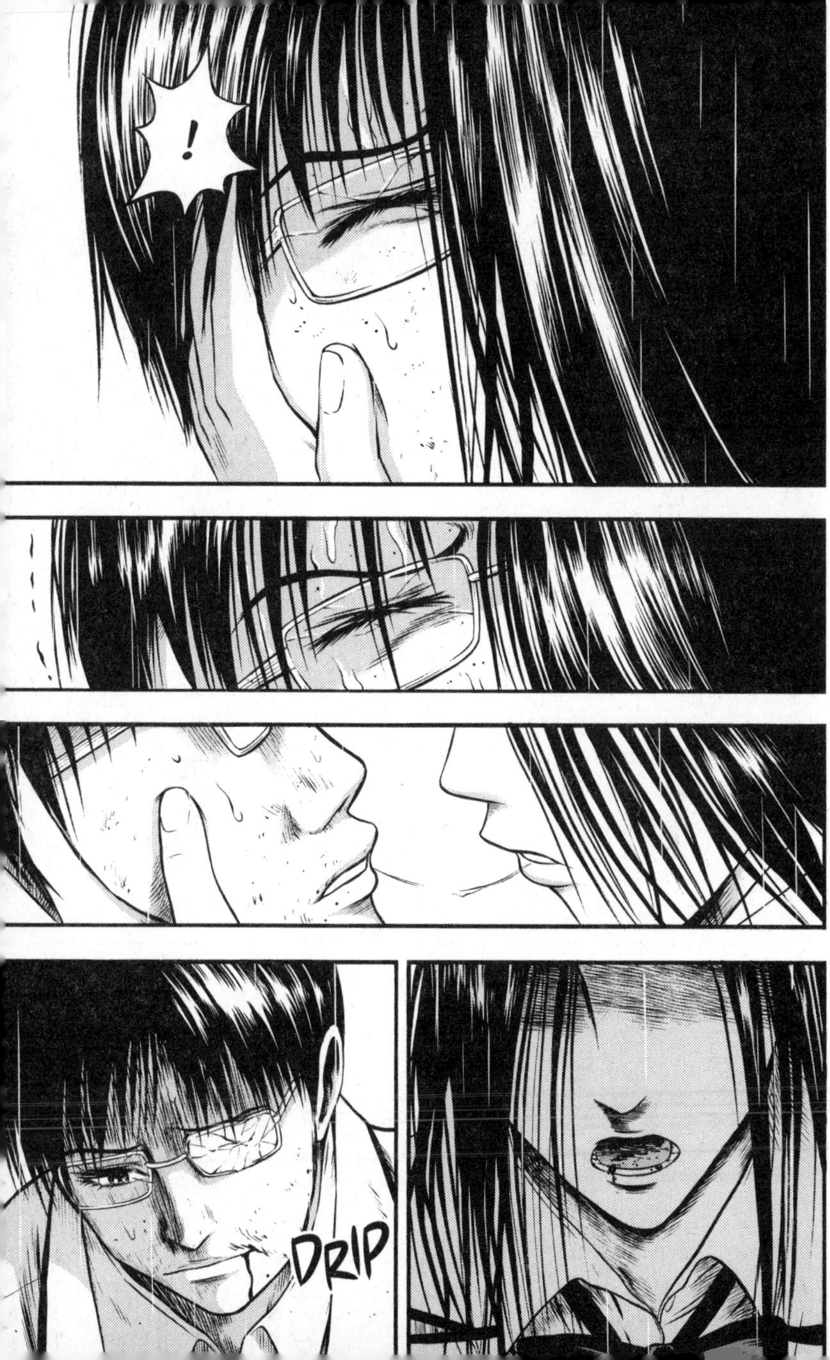
!
......
DRIP

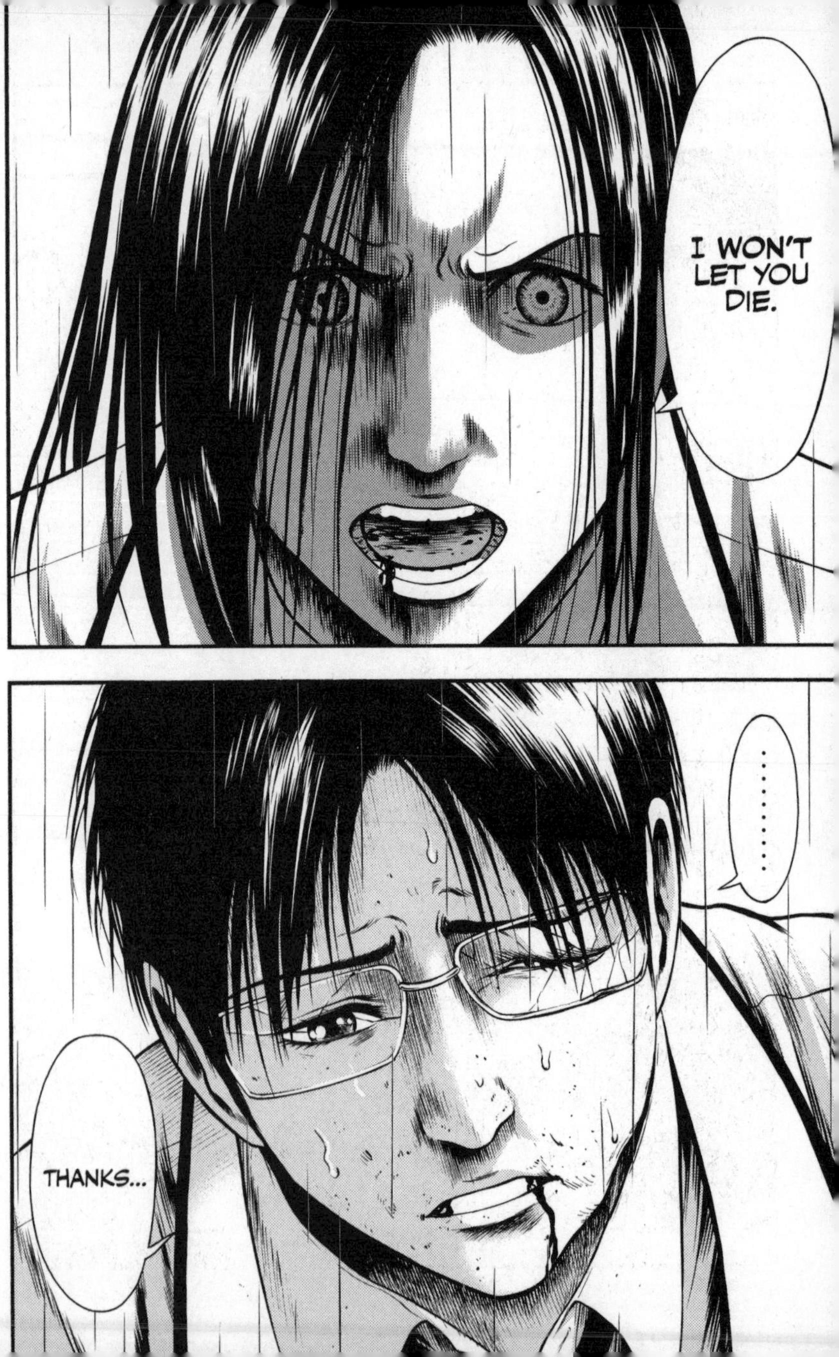
I WON'T LET YOU DIE.
......
THANKS...

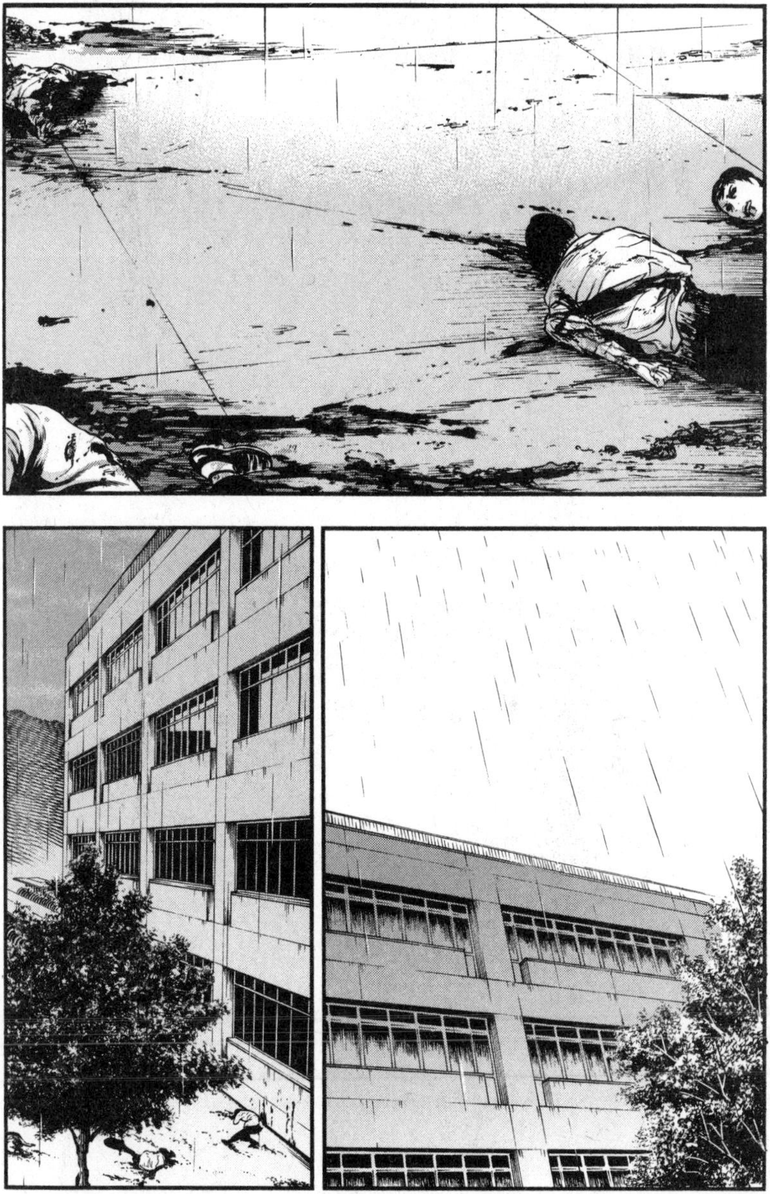

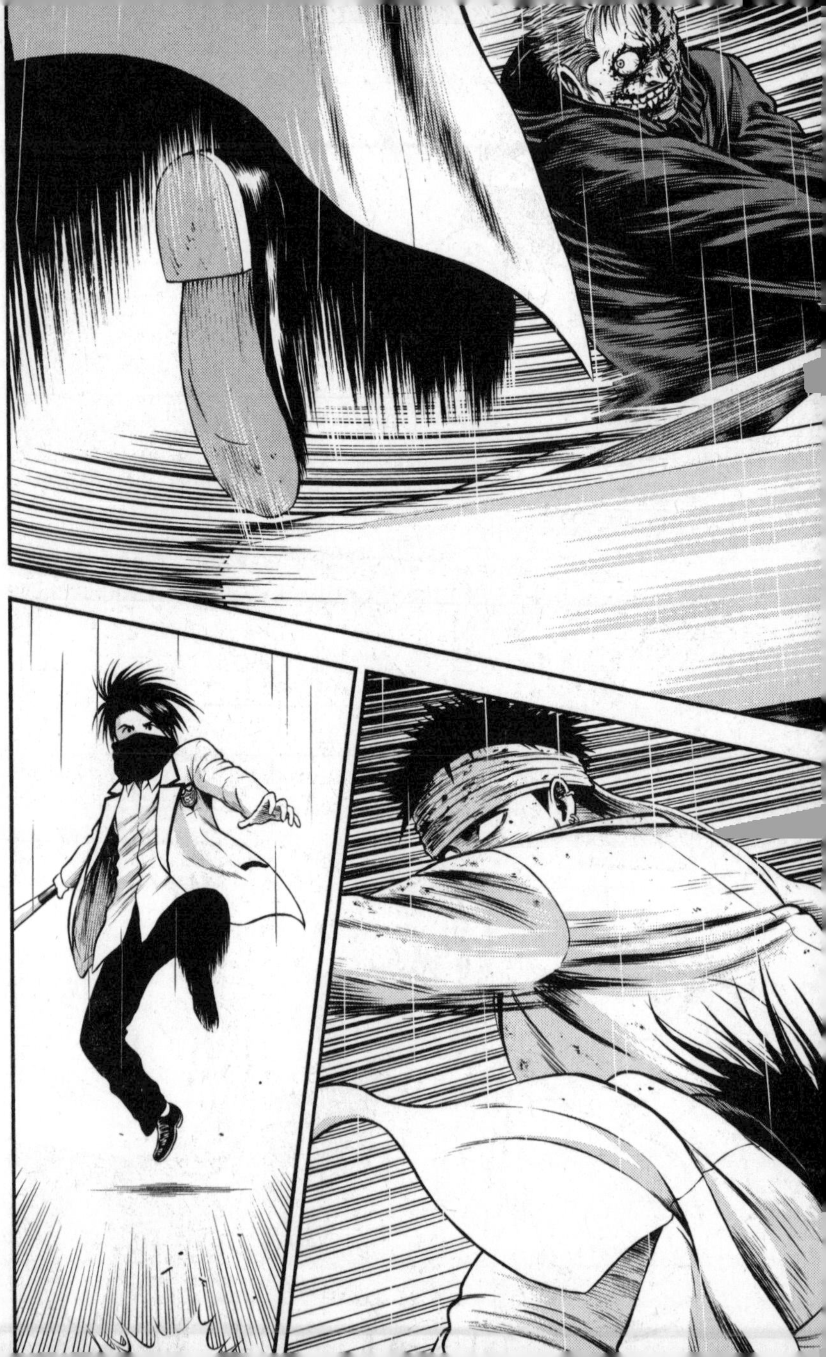

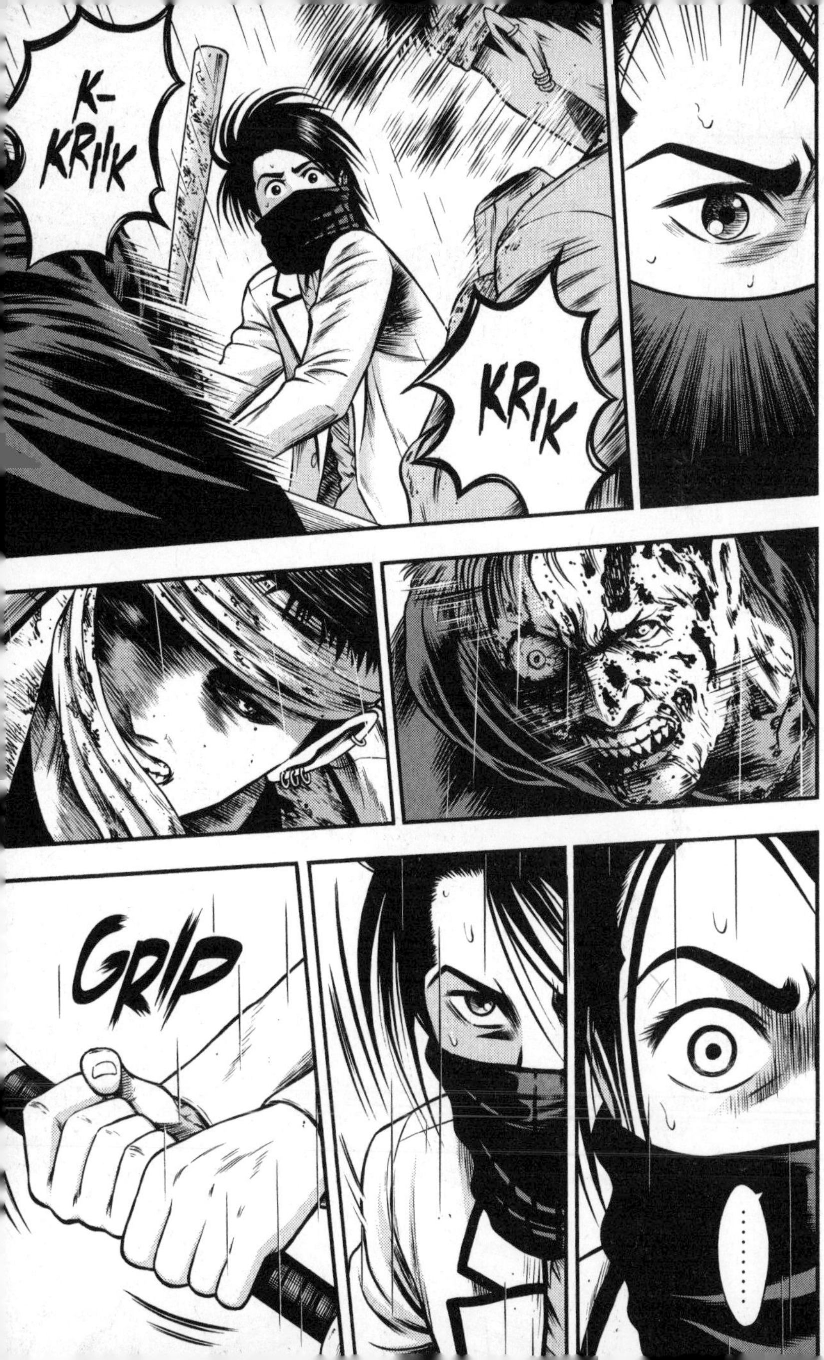
K-
KRIIK
KRIK
......
GRIP

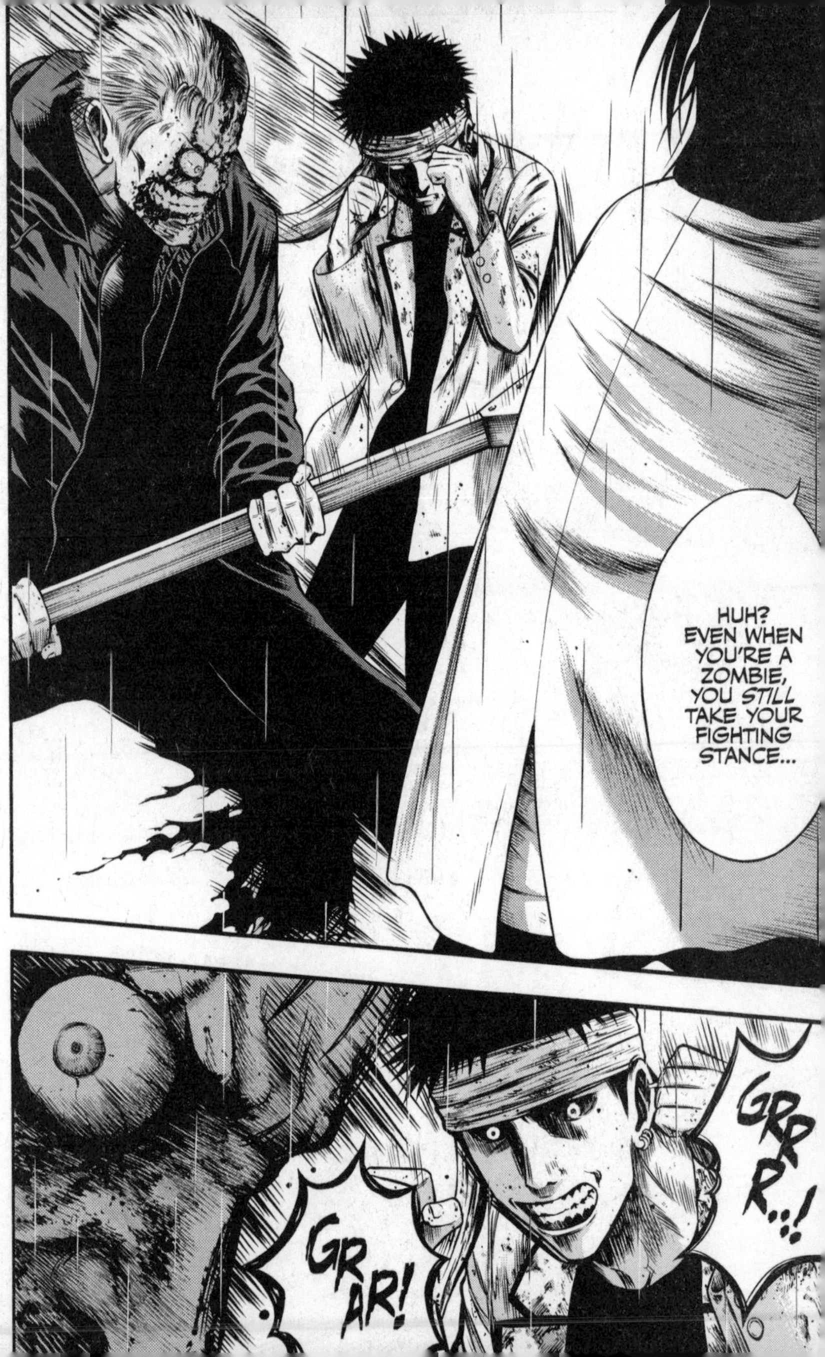
HUH? EVEN WHEN YOU'RE A ZOMBIE, YOU STILL TAKE YOUR FIGHTING STANCE...
GRRR...!
GRAR!

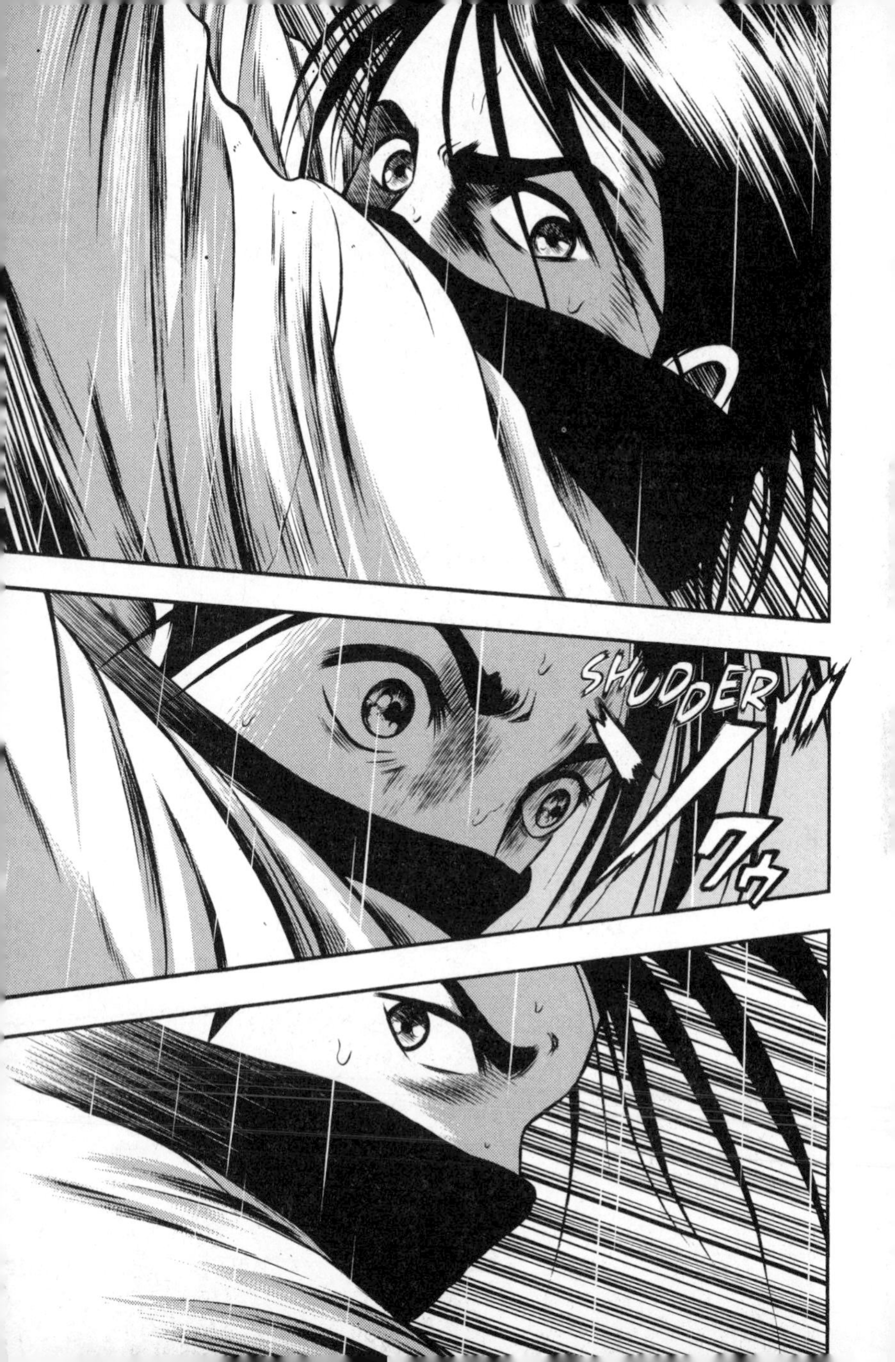
SHUDDER
クゥ

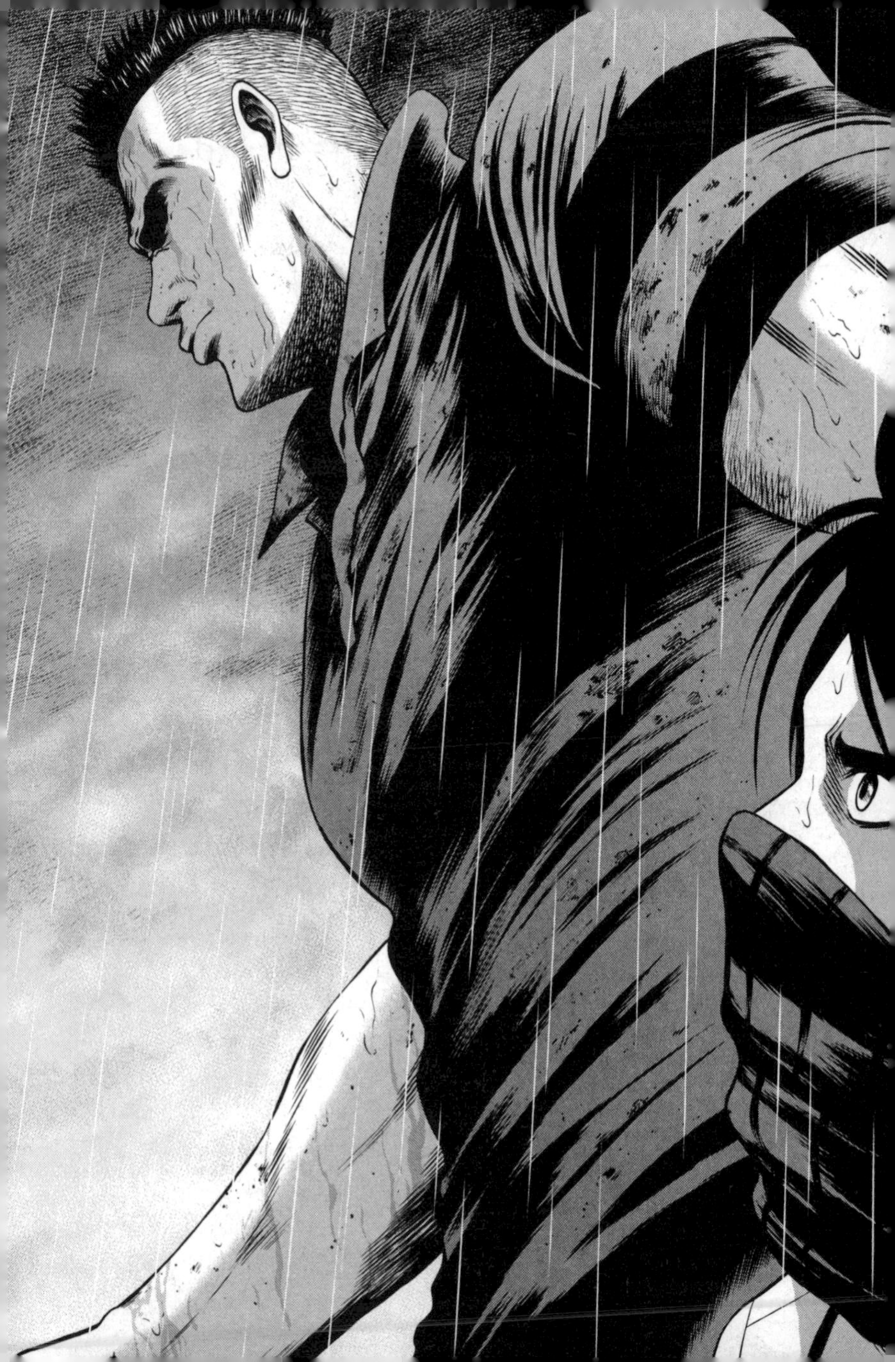

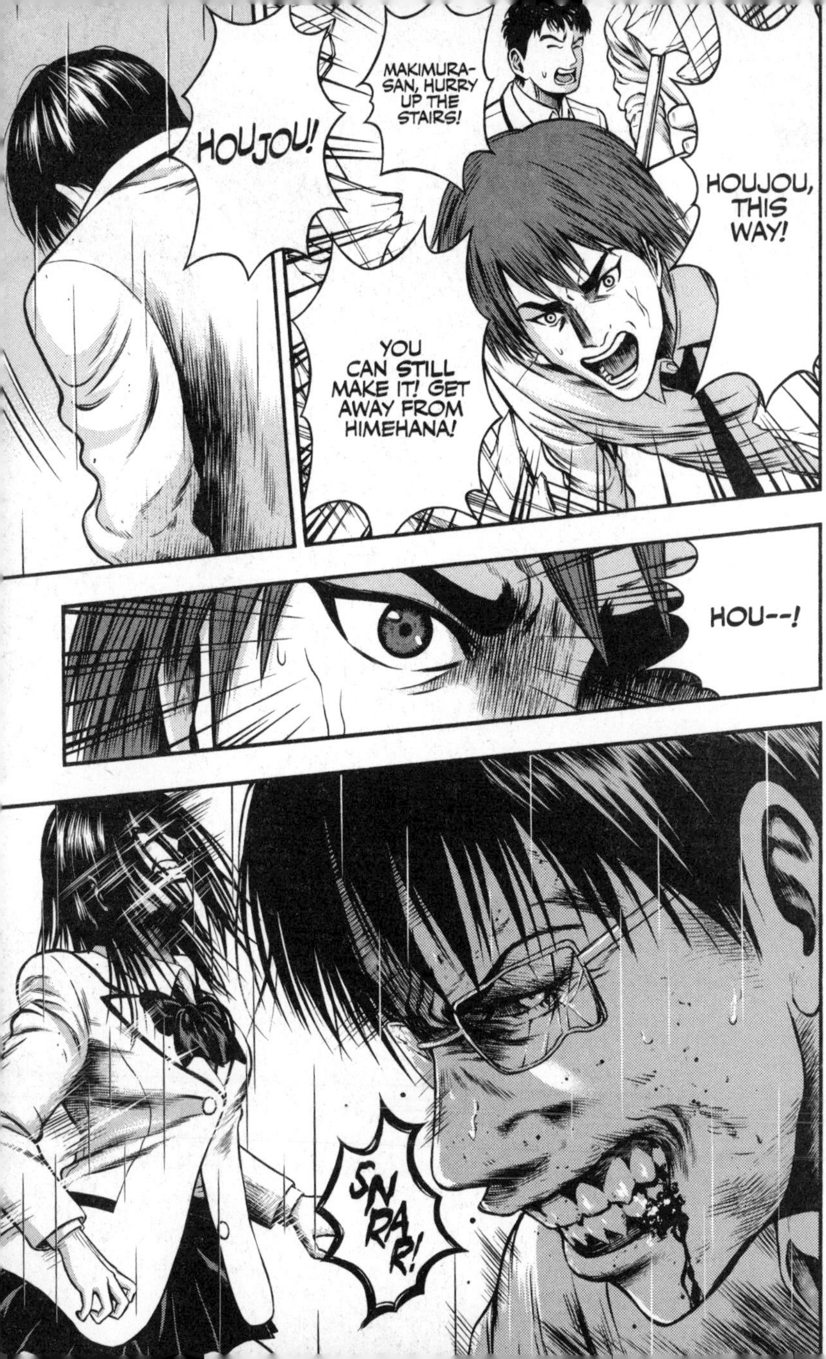
MAKIMURA-SAN, HURRY UP THE STAIRS!
HOUJOU, THIS WAY!
YOU CAN STILL MAKE IT! GET AWAY FROM HIMEHANA!
HOUJOU!
HOU--!
SNRAR!

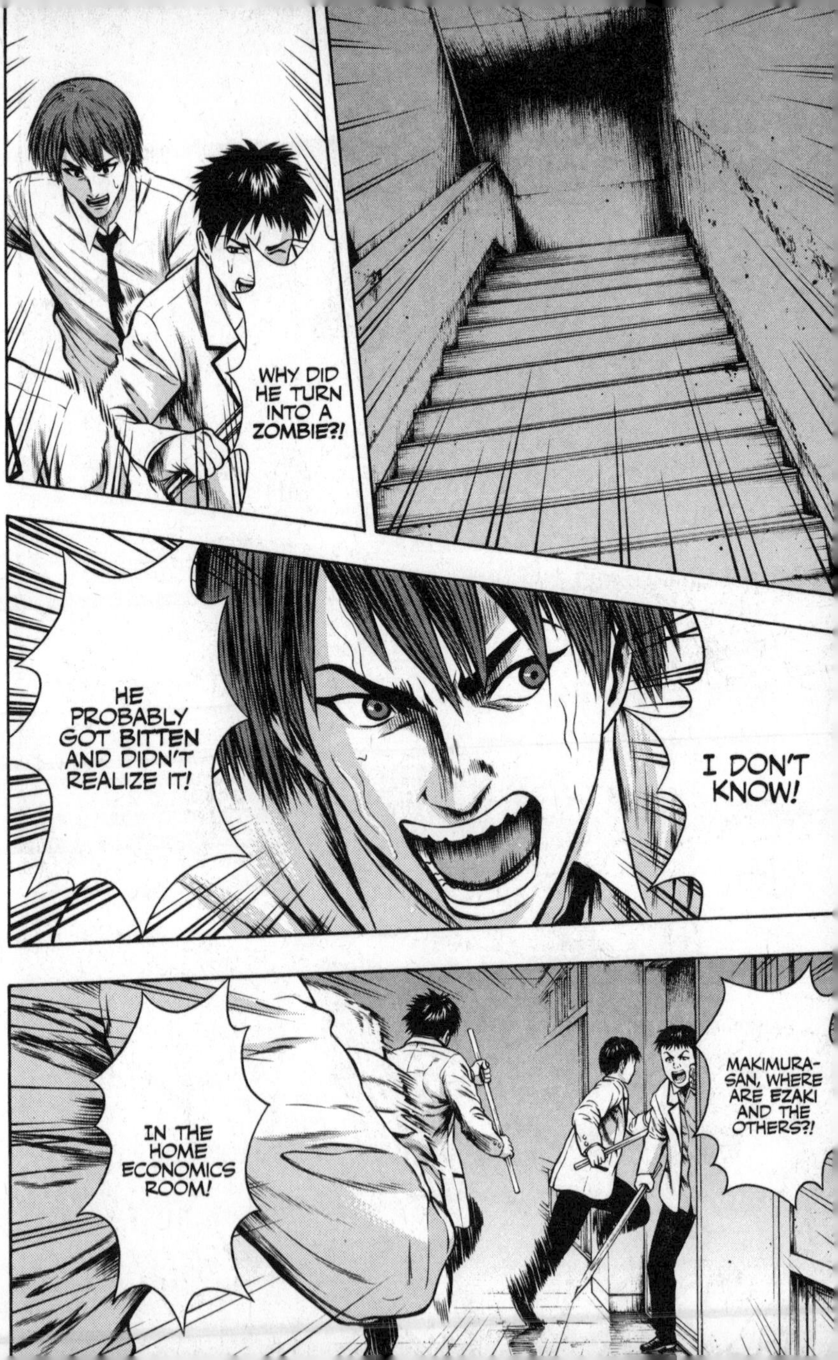
WHY DID HE TURN INTO A ZOMBIE?!
I DON'T KNOW!
HE PROBABLY GOT BITTEN AND DIDN'T REALIZE IT!
MAKIMURA-SAN, WHERE ARE EZAKI AND THE OTHERS?!
IN THE HOME ECONOMICS ROOM!

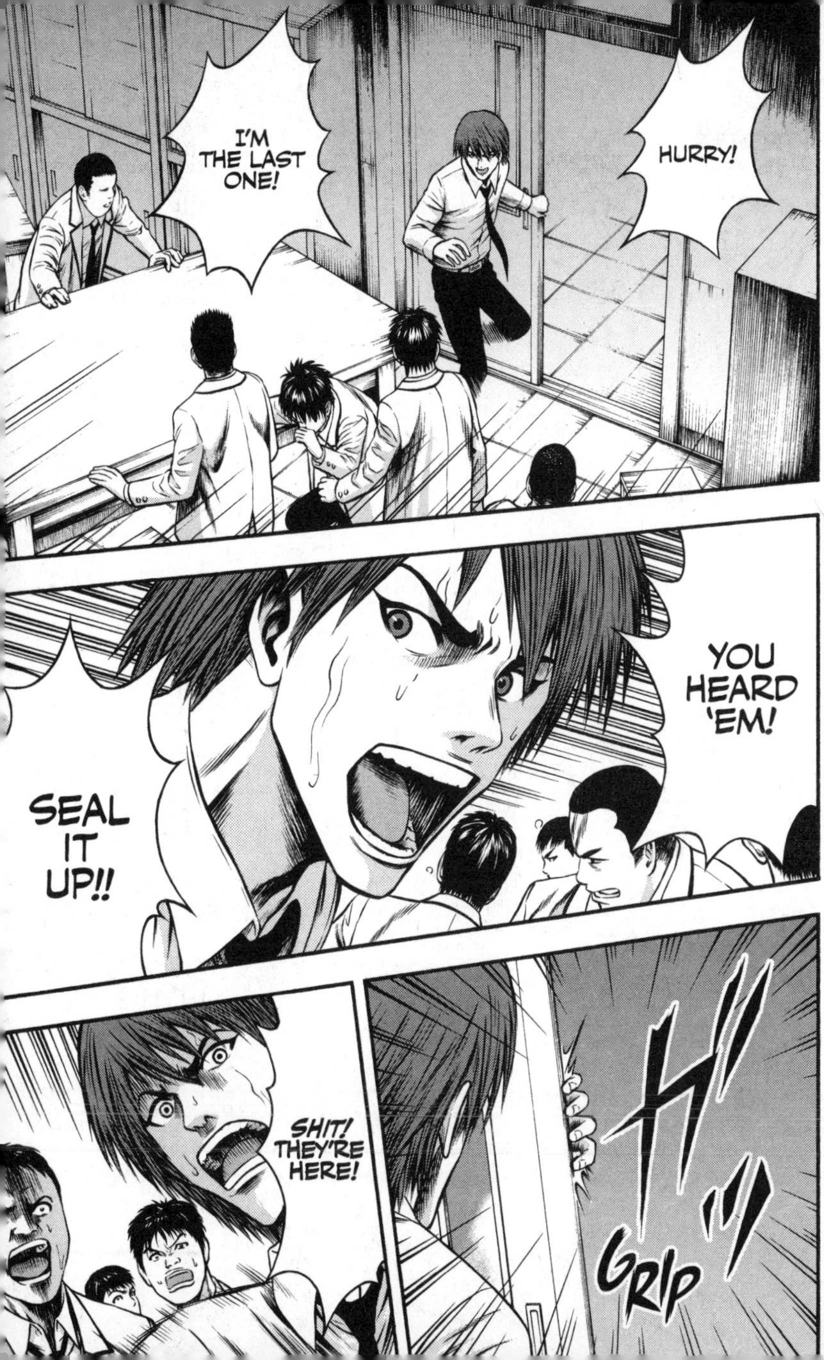
HURRY!
I'M THE LAST ONE!
YOU HEARD 'EM!
SEAL IT UP!!
GRIP
SHIT! THEY'RE HERE!

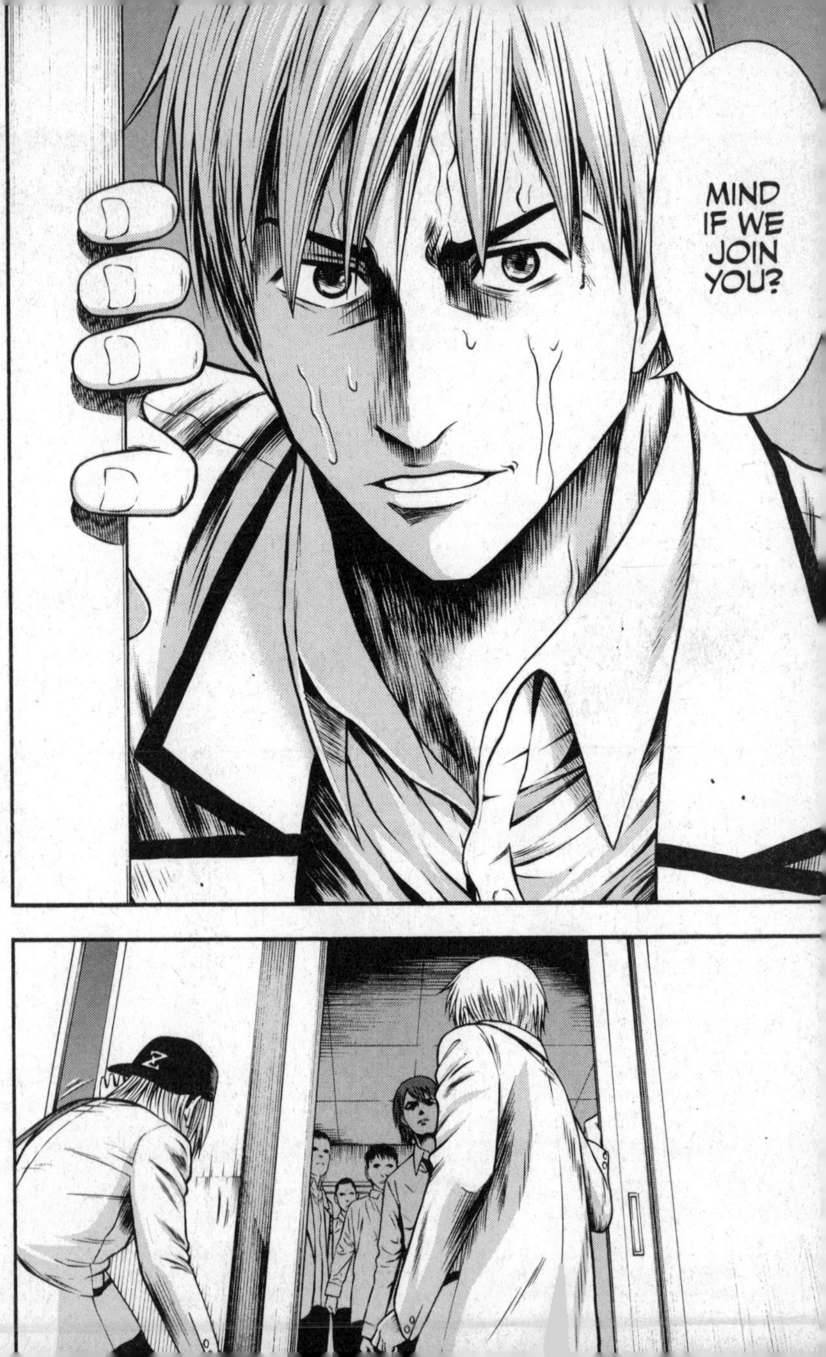
MIND IF WE JOIN YOU?

TO BE CONTINUED...

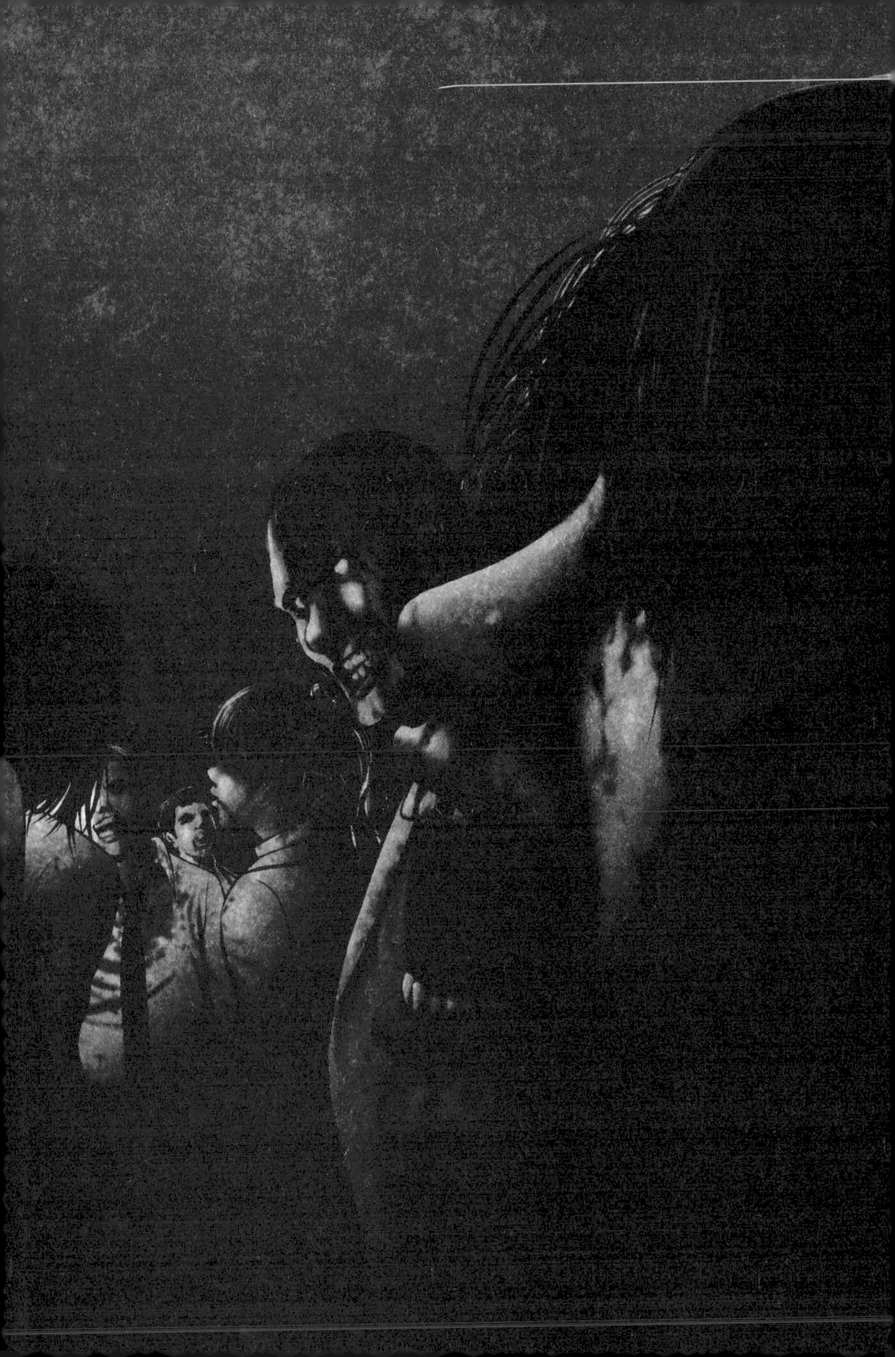

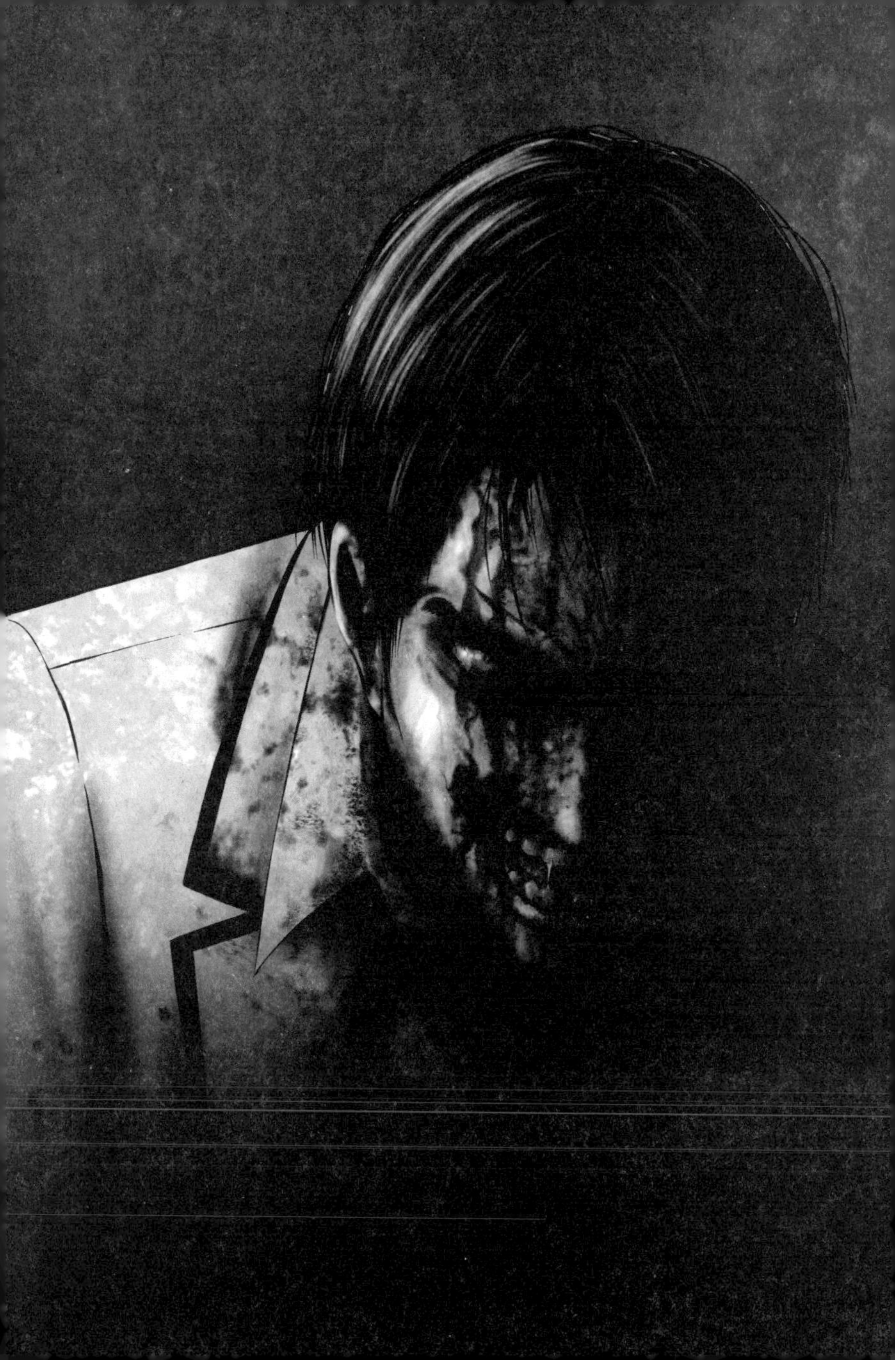

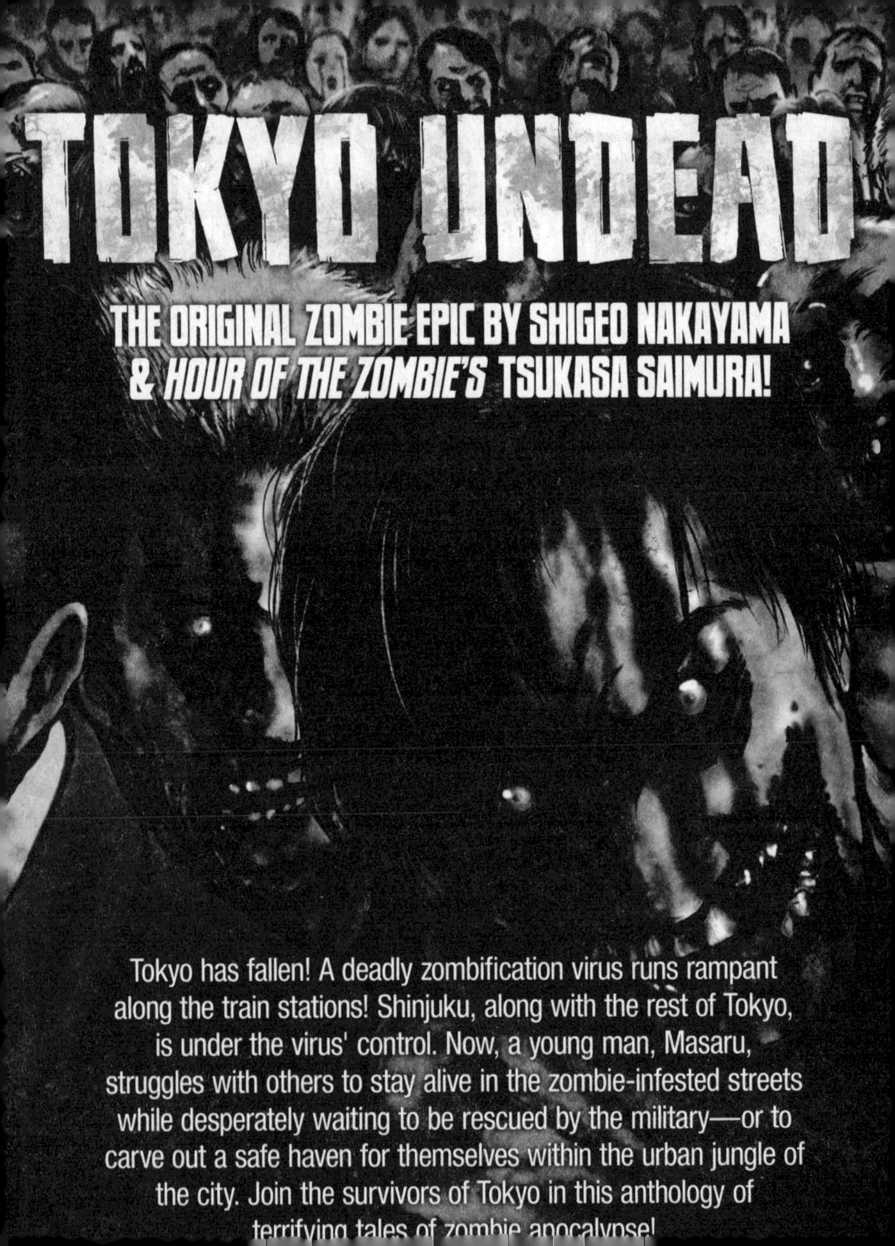
TOKYO UNDEAD
THE ORIGINAL ZOMBIE EPIC BY SHIGEO NAKAYAMA
& *HOUR OF THE ZOMBIE'S* TSUKASA SAIMURA!
Tokyo has fallen! A deadly zombification virus runs rampant along the train stations! Shinjuku, along with the rest of Tokyo, is under the virus' control. Now, a young man, Masaru, struggles with others to stay alive in the zombie-infested streets while desperately waiting to be rescued by the military—or to carve out a safe haven for themselves within the urban jungle of the city. Join the survivors of Tokyo in this anthology of terrifying tales of zombie apocalypse!

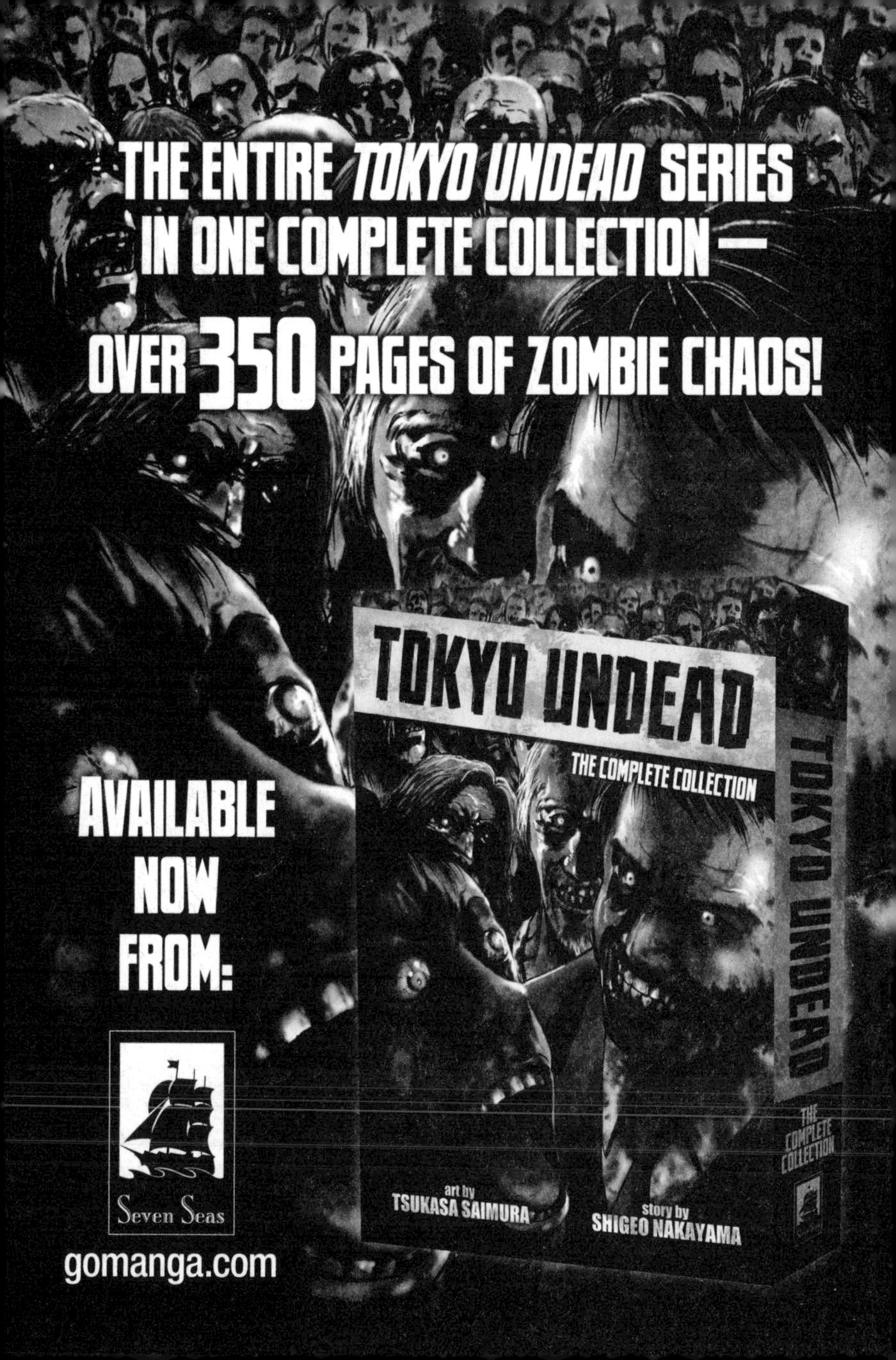
THE ENTIRE TOKYO UNDEAD SERIES IN ONE COMPLETE COLLECTION—
OVER 350 PAGES OF ZOMBIE CHAOS!
TOKYO UNDEAD
THE COMPLETE COLLECTION
art by TSUKASA SAIMURA
story by SHIGEO NAKAYAMA
AVAILABLE NOW FROM:
Seven Seas
gomanga.com

HOUR OF THE ZOMBIE

SEVEN SEAS ENTERTAINMENT PRESENTS

HOUR OF THE ZOMBIE

story and art by **Tsukasa Saimura**   **VOLUME 3**

TRANSLATION
Elina Ishikawa

ADAPTATION
Janet Houck

LETTERING AND COVER
Nicky Lim

LOGO DESIGN
Karis Page

PROOFREADER
Shanti Whitesides

PRODUCTION MANAGER
Lissa Pattillo

EDITOR-IN-CHIEF
Adam Arnold

PUBLISHER
Jason DeAngelis

IGAI -THE PLAY DEAD/ALIVE- VOLUME 3
© TSUKASA SAIMURA 2015
Originally published in Japan in 2015 by TOKUMA SHOTEN PUBLISHING
CO., LTD., Tokyo. English translation rights arranged with TOKUMA SHOTEN
PUBLISHING CO., LTD., Tokyo, through TOHAN CORPORATION, Tokyo.

Seven Seas books may be purchased in bulk for promotional, educational, or
business use. Please contact your local bookseller or the Macmillan Corporate
and Premium Sales Department at 1-800-221-7945, extension 5442, or by
e-mail at MacmillanSpecialMarkets@macmillan.com.

Seven Seas and the Seven Seas logo are trademarks of
Seven Seas Entertainment, LLC. All rights reserved.

ISBN: 978-1-626923-54-6

Printed in Canada

First Printing: November 2016

10 9 8 7 6 5 4 3 2 1

FOLLOW US ONLINE: *www.gomanga.com*

READING DIRECTIONS

This book reads from *right to left*, Japanese style. If
this is your first time reading manga, you start
reading from the top right panel on each page and
take it from there. If you get lost, just follow the
numbered diagram here. It may seem backwards at
first, but you'll get the hang of it! Have fun!!

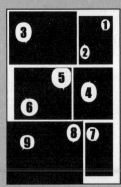